Network Printing

Todd Radermacher & Matthew Gast

O'REILLY®

Beijing · Cambridge · Farnham · Köln · Paris · Sebastopol · Taipei · Tokyo

Network Printing
by Todd Radermacher and Matthew Gast

Published by O'Reilly & Associates, Inc., 101 Morris Street, Sebastopol, CA 95472.

Editor: Mike Loukides

Production Editor: Colleen Gorman

Cover Designer: Edie Freedman

Printing History:

October 2000:   First Edition.

CIP data can be found at *http://www.oreilly.com/catalog/netprint/*.

ISBN: 0-596-00038-3

[M]

Table of Contents

Preface

Microcomputer proliferation and the networks that stitch them together are the Full Employment Act for our profession. Jobs are easy to find because modern computer networks are complex and challenging to run.

Even if a network runs only TCP/IP, each vendor adds its own specific layers on top of TCP/IP. Modern networks have Windows protocols, such as SMB, Unix-centric protocols, such as NFS and NIS, and standard Internet protocols, such as SMTP and HTTP. Keeping a modern network running places a huge demand on staff. An organization must have an expert in every protocol suite used.

Success is based on efficent use of resources and information. For years, that resource was computing power. It no longer is.

Computing power, driven by Moore's Law, is now coming out our ears. Scarcity is now most evident in the problems any technology organization observes when trying to hire staff (especially technical staff). Finding the best and brightest people to run networks is now the hardest task for IT departments. Talent is the component of modern networking that is in the shortest supply. With limited staff and increasing demands, what is a company to do? Simply put, they must find a way to make the technical management side of networks scalable.

Enabling network administrators to be more efficient is the key to modern networking.

Overture for Book in Black and White, Opus 1

This is a book about an ancient idea—printing. Being able to commit words to paper changed history, allowing it to exist outside the oral tradition. In more recent years, an electronic counterpart to the oral tradition has arisen: the theory that electronic communication would enable people to share more information more quickly than ever before, and do so without using any paper. The reality is that the "paperless" bit is bogus; important documents, even if distributed electronically, are always printed. Computers and the information sharing they enable have actually led to more paper. And still, nothing can replace the pen—paper and pen were used extensively in the preparation of this book.

Printing is a critical service on today's networks because of the importance of physical documents. Printing documents quickly by using expensive shared printers was a major motivation in building office local area networks (LANs). With print and file sharing well established, connecting users to a network is assumed to also connect them to print services. In many fast-growing enterprises, though, adding users is difficult enough; making services work for all of them seems impossible. In today's economic climate, it is nearly impossible to hire skilled network administration staff quickly enough to keep up with the growing user population in a rapidly growing company. Even the most skilled network administration staff can easily be swamped if constrained by solutions with poor scalability. This book helps network administrators build scalable print servers.

If you are a network administrator, you are undoubtedly responsible for print service in some form or another, or know somebody who is. If you have multiple client platforms, you may offer print services in several forms. That gives you several software and hardware platforms to be familiar with, several protocol stacks to be familiar with, and several sets of interactions that have the potential to cause problems. What is the harried network administrator to do?

If we had a magic solution to that problem, we would seek venture funding, sell our solution, and retire early. This book is not about magic. Instead, we have a few simple, time-tested formulas for you.

1. Standardize your print server platform on a scalable, robust operating system. For many years, organizations have used standards to reduce desktop support burdens. Standardization can be applied to servers as well.

2. Centralize print services on that operating system, so that all clients print through dedicated print servers. Centralized solutions are, by definition, maintained in one logical place.

3. Allow your clients to print using their native protocol. This simplifies client administration.

Organization of the Book

This book is divided into three sections, each of which elaborate on a core theme.

Part I is about Unix print services, the cornerstone of our architecture. The theme of the first section is standardization.

Part II shows how to adapt the print server to different client platforms. Each chapter first introduces a client protocol stack and then demonstrates how to offer Unix-backed print services to that platform. In broad terms, the second section is about the flexibility of Unix.

Part III builds on the first two sections by concentrating on the dark side of network services: management. Effectively managing services after deployment and providing enough service to meet demand is as important as providing the service itself. Applying the first two sections of the book is a good start, but without top-notch management systems, any system will fail. In broad terms, the third section is about helping people rise to the challenge of providing large scale services.

Part IV contains reference appendices that would be far too boring to read as standalone chapters, but contain valuable reference material.

Part I, *The Basics: Unix Queuing*

Chapter 1, *Introduction, Architecture, and History,* is about the mess we are in now, how to get out of it, and how we fell into the pit in the first place. After presenting the problem at hand in more detail and sketching an architecture to solve it, Chapter 1 closes with a history of printing from classical antiquity to the modern day.

Chapter 2, *Printer Languages,* is an introduction to page-description languages, which underpin desktop publishing. Printer languages are the final form a print job takes and must be a prime consideration when selecting printer hardware.

Chapter 3, *Exploring the Spooler,* introduces the BSD printing system and the System V printing system and describes how to configure both.

Chapter 4, *Extending the Berkeley Spooler with Print Filters,* shows how to use print filters with the Berkeley spooler to process jobs based on their contents.

Chapter 5, *The Next Generation Berkeley Spooler: LPRng,* introduces LPRng, a replacement for both classic BSD printing and System V printing.

Part II, *Front-End Interfaces to Unix Queues*

Chapter 6, *Connecting Windows to Unix Servers: Let's Samba,* describes the Windows networking protocols and how the Samba package implements them.

Chapter 7, *Connecting Macintosh Networks to Unix Servers*, describes AppleTalk networking and how to use the *netatalk* package to interact with Macintosh clients.

Chapter 8, *Connecting NetWare Networks to Linux Servers*, will talk about IPX and NetWare protocols and how the *ncpfs* package for Linux can connect your Linux server to a NetWare network.

Part III, *Administration*

Chapter 9, *Using SNMP to Manage Networked Printers*, shows you how to use SNMP to manage a large number of printers more effectively by taking advantage of SNMP support in modern printers.

Chapter 10, *Using Boot Servers for Basic Printer Configuration*, shows you how to boot a printer from the network with BOOTP or DHCP to eliminate the need to do front-panel configuration.

Chapter 11, *Centralized Configuration with LDAP*, has a short introduction to the Lightweight Directory Access Protocol (LDAP), and shows you how to use LDAP to be a central store of information about your print system so that you don't need to distribute lots of configuration files to various servers.

Chapter 12, *Accounting, Security, and Performance*, explains how to use filter scripts to do accounting and talks about the basics of print server tuning.

The last chapter, *Epilogue*, adds an important message for the reader.

Part IV, *Appendixes*

Appendix A, *printcap Reference*, has a complete list of the options used in the *printcap* file for both the stock Berkeley spooler and LPRng.

Appendix B, *SNMP MIB Objects for Managing Printers*, is a list of the most useful SNMP objects used in printer management.

Documentation Conventions

Italic
> Used for Unix pathnames, filenames, and program names, Internet addresses such as domain names and URLs, and new terms when first defined.

Bold
> Used for names of GUI items: window names, buttons, menu choices, etc.

`Constant width`
> Used for command lines and options that should be typed verbatim, including method names, variable names, and class names.

How to Contact Us

We have tested and verified all of the information in this book to the best of our ability, but you may find that features have changed (or even that we have made mistakes!). Please let us know about any errors you find, as well as your suggestions for future editions, by writing:

O'Reilly & Associates, Inc.
101 Morris Street
Sebastopol, CA 95472
(800) 998-9938 (in the U.S. or Canada)
(707) 829-0515 (international/local)
(707) 829-0104 (FAX)

You can also send us messages electronically. To be put on the mailing list or request a catalog, send email to:

info@oreilly.com

To ask technical questions or comment on the book, send email to:

bookquestions@oreilly.com

We have a web site for the book, where we'll list examples, errata, and any plans for future editions. You can access this page at:

http://www.oreilly.com/catalog/netprint/

For more information about this book and others, see the O'Reilly web site:

http://www.oreilly.com

Acknowledgments

First and foremost, we owe this book especially to Ali Burek and Angie Radermacher, who have put up with more than we dare mention during the time we spent writing this book. You hold this book right now because they accepted living with authors for far longer than we would prefer to admit. Now that the book is finished, we can go back to being married to them.

Our editor, Mike Loukides, is everything a high tech editor should be. Throughout the process, he offered valuable feedback, both technical and stylistic, and faithfully represented your interest. He offered numerous suggestions, one of which grew into a chapter in its own right. Above all, Mike remained committed to producing a quality book.

Several of our colleagues have helped make this book far better than it would have been had it just been printed as it came off our word processors, and as it was first proposed. Ben Woodard, now at VA Linux Systems, aided us in understanding some of the challenges in running a large printer network based on work he did while at Cisco. The book is better for his bits of wisdom and experience.

More improvements than we can list are due to the comments we received from the technical review team. Wayne Fiori (Nokia) read the book as he would a scientific paper. His comments were on point, accurate, and very encouraging. John Forrest (UC Berkeley) wrote a meticulous review that led to extensive revisions in the text as well as some minor changes to the overall structure. We asked Brian McMahon (Nokia) to review this book because of his expertise with a few of the technologies that are less familiar to us, and we were very pleased to learn that he didn't find any major problems. John Stone (Grinnell College) submitted an extremely throrough review that addressed everything from small details to large components of the text. It is our hope that we were able to adequately incorporate most of his comments into our final draft. In spite of the efforts of all who reviewed the text, any errors that remain are, of course, our responsibility as authors.

Finally, this book is much more interesting than it would have been five years ago, due to contributions made by far too many people to list here. Many of the software packages used by our architecture have grown into production-quality systems in those years. For that, we owe a debt of gratitude to the volunteer developers.

Todd Radermacher

The idea for this book came while I was working on a consulting engagement with a close friend and colleague of mine, Hyle Campbell. We were working on an assignment for a large semiconductor manufacturer in Silicon Valley, and to our amazement (of all the possible things they could have paid us to work on), they asked us to "fix their printers." During this assignment, we came to the conclusion that there is a serious lack of printed material on printing.

The rest, as they say, is history. While attending the Java One conference in 1998, I met Mike Loukides at the O'Reilly booth in the Moscone Center. We spoke for a while and eventually the topic turned to printing. I told Mike about our book idea, and here we are.

There are several people I would like to thank. First, Matthew—for putting up with me for the entire time we have been working on this project and for doing most of the work. Dr. Peter Kocks provided a perpetual ear to bend and didn't laugh too hard at the idea to begin with. Abe Raher of Silicon Graphics provided early feedback on several chapters (and arranged for a loaner O2 for our lab).

Matthew Gast

If the parts of the book I wrote are at all readable, it is due largely to the influence of two exceptional English teachers. The first, Carolyn Rebholz, pushed me to discover my love of public speaking and presentation; she also critically read everything I wrote for her, and even encouraged a submission to a poetry journal. (It was not accepted.)

The second, Randall Hendee, constantly challenged me with offbeat assignments that required me to discover creativity I denied having. The ideal teacher is supposed to remain open-minded, foster debate, and teach critical thinking without the slightest hint of ridicule. Teachers everywhere could learn a great deal from Mr. Hendee. It was Mr. Hendee who helped me hone my satirical voice in written work; I expect he would easily recognize that voice in many of the footnotes throughout this book.

It was in college that I first became acquainted with Unix. My growing relationship with Unix made it inevitable that I would learn from John Stone. To this day, I have not encountered a network as well run as his (and that includes my own!). Dr. Stone supported my fascination with computing and networking, and helped me construct the foundation for my career.

I

The Basics: Unix Queuing

1

Introduction, Architecture, and History

Architecture is frozen music.
—Goethe

Architecture is the learned game, correct and magnificent, of forms assembled in the light.
—Le Courbusier

Although many modern commentators talk about the rapid flow of information caused by the Internet and electronic communication, the Internet is nothing compared to the invention of the printing press. The printing press was unique—a discontinuous innovation, to borrow the language of economics. Suddenly, authors could distribute information on a scale previously believed impossible. In terms of publishing, the Internet is not as abrupt a change. The Internet has sped information transfer and made it easy for anybody to publish to a worldwide audience.[*] Unlike books, however, the Internet is not printed material. If you want a "hard" copy of information on the Internet, you need to be able to put the web page on paper.

And people do. Networks carry millions of print jobs each day. Some networks carry so many print jobs that print service is overwhelmed and threatens to crash and burn on a regular basis. There is a better way: standardize on Unix or Linux print servers.

For reasons described in detail later, we build print servers on readily available open source technology. Rapid evolution of open source packages is a double-edged sword when building services. To write a book, we must take a snapshot of the world and present it to you.

---

[*] Indeed, the very ease of publication causes its own problem: how do you sort through the results? That question has yet to be answered. It is likely that gatekeepers will continue to be important; traditional publishers fill that role in the paper world.

Today's Networking Swamp

Computers were supposed to create the paperless office, remember? Networked documents on central servers were supposed to eliminate the need to print out most documents. We now know that is not true. The Internet has made more documents easily available to computer users than ever before, resulting in more printouts than ever before.

Efficient information sharing resulted from the adoption of local area networks (LANs) in offices or business departments. Part of sharing information required putting documents on paper, especially documents meant to be legally binding. Large, fast printers capable of printing tens of pages per minute have never been cheap, but LANs allowed groups of users to take advantage of shared facilities.

Unfortunately, no common method for accessing printers developed. Instead, multiple printer access methods were deployed in parallel. Unix workstations accessed printers with *lpd*, Windows with SMB networking, and Macintoshes with AppleTalk.* Complexity grew, and productivity fell, especially in the staff charged with maintaining these systems.

Readers of this book are likely one of those staff members, or certainly know somebody who is one of those staff members. Complexity is the bane of efficient network administration. Networks of today are very complex, though, which drags down the efficiency of the staff charged with making it run. Many a system administrator has slogged through a day of problem reports, user email, and meetings, only to fall farther behind because there simply is too much to do and too few people to do it.

The high technology industry has always made a great deal of noise about productivity. High tech products have the power to enable productivity by making work more efficient. Technologies make people rich because those technologies make efficient use of some key resource in tight supply, such as CPU power, memory, or network bandwidth. In the past, those limiting factors (lack of adequate CPU power, memory, or network bandwidth) have constrained the underlying technology, but that is no longer the case. Skilled administrators are now the limiting factor for every modern network; lack of administrative talent is what holds networks back now.

However, that is not to say network administrators are unproductive or ineffective. They are only capable of working 80 hours a week, at most. (And 80 hours is hardly a sustainable pace!) When the network presents 90 hours of work per week, simple arithmetic shows the folly of trying to keep up. In many cases,

---

* The Internet Engineering Task Force's (IETF) Printer Working Group is currently developing the Internet Printing Protocol (IPP) to fill the void, but the IPP is probably years from widespread deployment.

administrators are as productive as they can be, given the management tools most of them work with. As an industry, the technology field has provided lousy management tools. Take the problem of sharing printers on a network. What is so inherently hard about it? Nothing! In practice, the problem is complexity: each client operating system needs to have its own print server, multiple servers are deployed in parallel for different OS platforms, and each server may even have a separate administrator. Similar situations exist for many network applications, and this is ridiculous.

Information is the lifeblood of modern businesses, whether they are hip dot-coms or more traditional businesses. If information is the lifeblood, then networks are the arteries. Keeping the network running is a task of paramount importance. Cut off the blood supply, and cells die. If network administrators are effective, everybody will be more productive.

The Book in a Nutshell

The network administration skills gap is not likely to shrink soon. Technological development continues to grant many wishes and appears ready to continue to do so into the future. What does not grow nearly as fast is the number of people skilled enough to harness and direct this ever-growing technology. When too many mages dabble in the affairs of wizards, well, you know what happens.*

Printing is a key service on modern networks. For some groups, such as legal and marketing departments, the loss of printing service can deal a crippling blow until service is restored.

This book is about building scalable, reliable print servers. It is about one small facet of creating a scalable network and taking best advantage of scarce administrator resources.

Scaling network administrators is not new. We do not have any new secret formulas for doing it. You probably have heard of all of them because they are all absurdly simple:

Standardization
> Pick one thing, and stick with it as long as it works. By choosing a single server operating system, only one set of skills is required. We believe in building print servers on Unix because of its flexibility and remote management capabilities.

Centralization
> If everything is run in one place, only that one place requires maintenance!

---

* Consider this book a spell book for the network administrator.

Your objective is to build a reliable print server infrastructure that supports clients without regard to their operating system or geographic location. Running this service should not take up much of your time, even if you have a rapidly growing number of clients (or client platforms).

Administrative Scalability

Making effective use of network and system administrators' time and energy is our primary goal and, hence, the leitmotif of this book. You can throw more memory, disk, CPU, or even whole new machines at a problem far more easily than you can recruit qualified staff. Extra hardware does not complain about repetitive work, the lack of a corner office with big windows, or the quality of its colleagues. The key to running any network service is the scalability of the administrator's time.

Standardization simplifies your workload by reducing parallel systems. There is only one learning curve for your print server platform, and just one platform to watch for new features and bugs.

Choosing an operating system for offering print services

Desktop operating systems, such as low-end members of the Windows family (Windows for Workgroups, Windows 3.1, Windows 95, and Windows 98) and the Macintosh operating system, implement peer-to-peer network services. Peer-to-peer networking has no central administrative control. Lack of central control means in practice that there is no central troubleshooting focus and lots of time spent running around. Peer-to-peer networking is no way to run a scalable service, unless you like late nights and want to lose all your hair. Windows NT and Windows 2000 are more robust, but still fall short in the area of remote administration.

Our system of choice is Unix. Flexibility and extensibility have always been Unix hallmarks. The Unix print system, although originally designed for text-only line printers, has adapted to the modern world of laser printing, page-description languages, and diverse client platforms. Unix is not a panacea for printing woes. "Steep learning curve" and "Unix" are synonymous, and for good reasons. Unix system administration requires a diverse set of skills. Keeping a Unix system secure and functional is a full-time task even for highly skilled administrators. The architecture described in the rest of the book works with any version of Unix with minor exceptions, so feel free to pick the one you are most comfortable with, or that runs on the hardware platform you are most comfortable with.

Open Source Software

In recent years, open source software has taken the world by storm. Critical pieces of the Internet infrastructure are run primarily by open source software packages. As this book was written, the most widely used DNS implementation (BIND), the leading web server (Apache), and the most powerful scripting language (Perl) are all open source packages. Without BIND, Apache, and Perl, where would the Internet be?

As the scientific world has known for centuries, peer review is the most important component of high quality results. Historically, peer review was made possible by the development of printing presses, which allowed quick distribution of journals and meeting proceedings to subscribers. Now, peer review is made possible by the Internet, which distributes information more quickly to more subscribers. Open source packages are used by millions of technically sophisticated users who have the desire and the capability to fix bugs, a capability that is wasted with closed source software distributions. Electronic communication channels such as the Internet also enable users to form a community so that bug reports and patches can quickly be shared. It is not uncommon for a patch to be released within hours or days of an initial bug report. BSD-derived systems and Linux are routinely patched within hours of the release of security vulnerabilities.

Several open source implementations of Unix-like operating systems are available. Three main teams now maintain 4.4BSD-inspired systems. NetBSD focuses on continuing the portability of the BSD code base to as many architectures as possible. FreeBSD runs only on the Intel PC platform, but has solid performance and reliability; it is used to run some major Internet sites, including Yahoo!'s web site. The OpenBSD team takes security extremely seriously and performs regular source code audits and often fixes security holes before they are exploited on other platforms. In recent years, much attention has also been given to the Linux operating system, written by Linus Torvalds and a team of volunteers. Since its release in the early 1990s, the number of Linux users has grown rapidly and now stands around 10 million. Shortly after we started work on this book, Oracle and Informix ported their database systems to Linux, and Corel ported the WordPerfect suite to Linux. Even IBM, the standard bearer of corporate conservatism, felt the need to develop a "Linux strategy."

Any of these systems would make a fine print server. Several commercial Unix flavors also make fine choices for a print server. Unix is only the base of our architecture. No matter what flavor, we apply the same software to front-end the Unix queues to other platforms. The architecture of this book does not require any particular software or hardware platform.

Free Software: the Antidote to Bloatware?

One recent trend in software that concerns us is feature bloat. New releases of most commercial packages demand at least 128 MB RAM and ultra-fast processors, to say nothing of disk space. While this tends to be very good for hardware vendors, it is not so good for your budget when you are stuck having to upgrade the hardware in order to run new software. (Perhaps the only good point is it lets us recall the Bad Old Days when RAM cost $40/MB.) Much of this bloat is due to new features that are not widely used.

We are glad to see free software bucking this trend. Plain Pentium processors, three generations behind the current hardware produced by Intel, will run any of the free Unices admirably. Even better, performance often increases between major revisions. Even if the source code expands, you still can choose what to link in and what to leave out, so you only "pay" (in runtime performance) for features you want.

To be fair, modern distributions are getting bigger, and new window managers like KDE and Gnome have large footprints. On print servers, though, sophisticated windowing desktops are not necessary because most administration work is conducted remotely.

Many network and system administrators "recycle" old hardware by putting FreeBSD or Linux on it. Replacing the operating system can have profound effects—hardware that would have been considered "obsolete" is now capable of running interesting services, perhaps even better than the original operating system could!

Building the Ideal Print System

To build something, start with the requirements. Ask the question: what is the ideal print system? Answering the question then suggests the architecture for the printing system.

- No matter what protocol the client uses, it should be understood by the print system. The client should also be free to send the job to the print system and then disconnect and move on to other tasks.

- Management should be centralized. Client management should be moved to the print server wherever possible. Print service administrators should only need one set of permissions to work with queues, not permissions on each client machine.

- Robustness should be a part of the system, rather than an afterthought. When a print server fails, its jobs should be requeued to a functional server, and new jobs should be routed to a back up server.

- Servers should be standardized. All print jobs should be funneled through a print server so that jobs are queued and given fair access to printers. If servers are the only devices that talk to printers, only servers need to be updated when printer changes occur.

- Flexibility and scalability are important to many institutions, especially hyper-growth small businesses.

Supplying the ideal print system

If you consider the qualities of the ideal print system, our architecture naturally suggests itself. Use the flexibility of Unix as the back-end of the print system to queue jobs and talk to printers. For the front-end, use software to present those Unix queues to clients using their native protocols. Using this architecture, you also gain the benefit of a modularity. Any one front-end system can be replaced and upgraded without disturbing the others. A conceptual block diagram is shown in Figure 1-1.

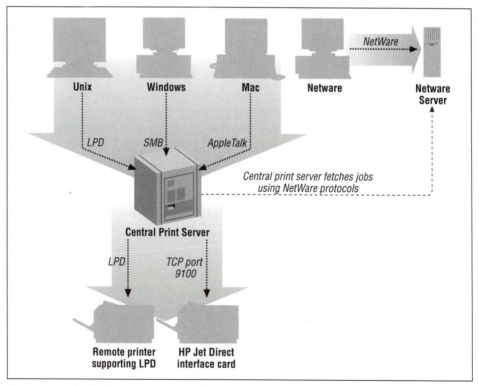

Figure 1-1. This book's print service architecture

That is it. There are no complex ideas. You reap the benefit of standardizing on a single server platform for maintenance and administration. Troubleshooting gets simpler because there is only one path from the client to the printer for jobs to travel. The path of the job does not depend on the client operating system.

Our printing architecture allows you to divorce the selection of a server operating system from the client operating system you already use. It also frees you to use platforms not widely supported by commercial server systems. For example, many academic institutions have Macintosh desktops, but commercial server systems that support both Macintosh clients and Windows clients well do not exist.

Cisco's print system: a case study

Consulting work has made both of us well aware of the problems faced by the first institution to adopt anything. (This applies to much more than technology, of course.) Do not worry that you are on the bleeding edge of technology. If you follow the suggestions we present in this book, you will be in the company of industry leaders like Cisco Systems. Cisco uses PCs running Linux to run their printqueues and uses Samba to share those queues with Windows clients. The print servers range from 120 MHz Pentiums with 32 MB RAM to 266 MHz Pentiums with 80 MB RAM—hardly budget-busting hardware.

The result is impressive scalability: Cisco's San Jose headquarters has approximately 10,000 print clients supported by just 17 print servers—almost 600 clients per server. For cost and reliability reasons, print servers are placed in some remote offices. The worldwide network has approximately 90 print servers for 20,000 clients and serves more than two thousand printers.* Cisco does this with a much smaller staff than you might expect: two. Extra administrative tools were developed to enable such impressive efficiency. These tools, called CEPS (Cisco Enterprise Printing System), are now available online. It's worth investigating, even if your printing needs are modest; see *http://ceps.sourceforge.net.*

File Service: the Other Half
of the LAN Server

When setting up a LAN server, print service is only half the story. Providing reliable file sharing service is also a must.

This book is about printing, so file service is beyond the scope of this book. That said, all of the server software packages that we discuss in this book include file sharing capability as well as print sharing capability. Adventurous, do-it-yourself readers can use this book as a starting point for providing file service using Unix servers. For each of the client platforms we present, you can use the introduction

---

* Remote offices have print servers placed in them for reliability reasons. Printing should survive the failure of a wide area network (WAN) link.

to its networking technology and protocols to understand the basic issues involved in providing service to that platform, and then you can use the software packages in that chapter to provide file service.

Before taking this road, you should probably obtain copies of *Using Samba* by Robert Eckstein, David Collier-Brown, and Peter Kelly, and *Managing NFS and NIS* by Hal Stern; both are published by O'Reilly & Associates, Inc.

A Brief History of Printing and Publishing

For most of history, knowledge was sacred and books were closely guarded. Now, torrents of written material threaten to overwhelm us. Readers now have incredible choices and variety in bookstores, rather than needing to make special pilgrimages to jealously guarded secrets in monastic libraries. The transition was not an easy one, and involved the interplay between several economic, social, and technological factors.

Before the printing press, life was locally focused, and the idea of communicating with the entire world would have been considered impossible. Impossible, that is, until Johann Gutenberg catapulted into world history because he did the impossible. Shortly afterward, Martin Luther put the press to service in creating the world's first propaganda. Luther created medieval multimedia for the masses by combining words for the literate with pictures for the masses on posters denouncing the Roman Church. However, to begin our history with the invention of the printing press is inappropriate, and would leave off the more interesting half of the story.

Printing in Classical Antiquity

Classical antiquity is the logical place to start the story of printing. We do not intend to minimize the contributions of other advanced ancient societies, but classical antiquity left us a relative abundance of written material that survives to this day.

Greece

In the ancient Greco-Roman world, bound books did not exist. Written work was laboriously copied by hand on to scrolls of parchment or vellum. Due to the high value of writing media, many ancient scrolls are written continuously with no breaks. Occasionally, Greek scrolls exhibit a break between thoughts with white space, or with a small horizontal line called a *paragraphos*. Continuous writing, without even the basic modern feature of paragraph breaks, persisted in various forms until the eleventh century. Believing the ancient Greeks did not understand white space would be a mistake—the works of Homer appear with very generous white space. For most documents, generous white space would be an unthinkable extravagance; the white space appearing in Homeric scrolls shows the reverence in which he was held by Greek society. Many writers in addition to Homer were popular: Athens supported a vibrant scroll market in the fifth century B.C.

At the beginning of the third century B.C., the Ptolemies of Egypt founded the Great Library at Alexandria. At its peak, the Great Library held over a million scrolls and attracted scholars from across the world. One million books is quite a good-sized library today; in classical antiquity before the mass production of books and wide-spread literacy, it was truly enormous. The Egyptian government funded the library, including its large staff. About 235 B.C., a second branch of the library was founded, in part to store the greatest works of Greek literature and to translate them into all the other major world languages (or at least all languages known at the time!).* Some of the groundbreaking work conducted at the library included the mainte-nance of a bibliography and standardization of punctuation. Scribes also divided lengthy works into *books*, which correspond to the amount of text that could fit on a single papyrus scroll. Sadly, a Roman civil war in the third century A.D. partially destroyed the library, and Christians burned the surviving parts in A.D. 391.

In the second century B.C., the king of Pergamum began building a library which he hoped would rival, or even surpass, the Great Library of Alexandria. Defensive Egyptian rulers banned the export of papyrus to Pergamum to inhibit the growth of the library at Pergamum and preserve the Alexandrian library as a leading research center. Undeterred, the king of Pergamum funded trailblazing research into the use of animal hides as a writing material. The research was successful, and the city of Pergamum became a hub in the worldwide parchment trade. Per-gamum's trade position was so strong that the word parchment derives from the name Pergamum.† Parchment is superior to papyrus. In an interesting twist, the Egyptian embargo triggered a revolutionary technological advance. In 133 B.C., Pergamum became part of the Roman Empire, and Mark Antony may have given the contents of the library to Cleopatra, merging the two rival libraries.

Rome

With books, as with so much else, the Roman contribution was not so much to build on the Greeks, but to distribute Greek ideas and methods widely through-out the Roman Empire. No major changes are evident from the Greek tradition, except for the use of Latin instead of Greek.

---

* It was at Alexandria that the Septuagint, the translation of ancient Hebrew scriptures into Greek, was completed.

† Both the Latin and Greek words for "parchment" mean "stuff that is from Pergamum."

Roman society valued books, although part of this value may have been that libraries became trendy possessions, much like high-definition television sets today. The Roman general Lucullus, one of the richest men in the world at the time, opened his library for public use. Despite such generous actions, some Roman historians complained that libraries were becoming as common as bathrooms and wrote bitterly about "book clowns."

Modern publishing also began in Rome. Slave laborers, working from dictation, made up to 30 copies of a scroll at a time. Roman publishers decided what to duplicate, purchased rights to those manuscripts, and sold the resulting merchandise to the public. Records indicate that books were affordable to many, in large part because the use of slave labor kept costs down.

Printing in the Middle Ages

After the fall of Rome, it fell to the Church to protect the surviving books. Monasteries safeguarded and duplicated the manuscripts they possessed, although the monks did not always understand the contents of what they painstakingly copied. As a measure of the stagnation of publishing, a monastery with a library of 600 volumes was considered large. In 1424, the Cambridge University library had only 122 volumes; it now has over six and a half million. Medieval scribes would often place a short note or prayer at the end of a manuscript, a practice which eventually became the colophon.

After being crowned emperor, Charlemagne sought to restore civilized life, in part by founding schools and monasteries throughout his empire. His appointed scholar, Alcuin, developed a standard script of lower case letters. Later, Alcuin's minor characters, combined with formal Roman capitals, would form the basis for the modern typefaces.

Charlemagne's actions encouraged the formation of schools, some of which would eventually grow into universities. The University of Paris was founded in the middle of the twelfth century, and many institutions emulated it. After English students were barred from attending, English scholars established Oxford University. Referring to a university post as a "chair" dates from the medieval times, when the lecture would be delivered by a seated professor to students at his feet. Well-respected scholars would attract other scholars and their "chairs" to growing universities. By the time that the next actor in the story, Johann Gutenberg, took the stage, there were only 44 universities in the entire world, which must have made distributing research money and financial aid considerably simpler. Oh, wait, financial aid had not been invented yet.

The codex

Written work began to resemble its modern form with the introduction of the codex, which was a set of parchment bound like a book, rather than in a single continuous roll. Because the text was bound like a book, written works now had properties we take for granted at the dawn of the twenty-first century. It became practical to write on both sides of the parchments, and finding a particular point in the text was much easier because cumbersome rolling and unrolling was eliminated.

The oldest codices that survive are from the second century A.D., but historical records suggest the existence of the codex from the first century B.C. After the fourth century A.D., parchment and the codex became the standard means of written communication.

Johann Gutenberg and the Early Publishing Industry

Before the printing press, publishing was a labor-intensive process. Three obstacles stood in the way of the printed word as a mass medium: adequate supplies of durable movable type, printing presses to handle the volume, and a suitable ink to use in printing. Gutenberg's contribution was not seminal work in any one of these areas, but rather the combination of all of them.* His ink was capable for the task at hand, but not as innovative as either his new typecasting methods or printing press.

Gutenberg was born in Mainz, although he was exiled and did much of his work in nearby Strassburg in Alsace (now Strasbourg, France). From surviving legal records, we can tell that Johann Fust loaned Gutenberg a substantial sum of money to fund development of his printing methods. Equity financing is a modern business construction, but Fust's high risk loan was the medieval equivalent of venture funding. In 1455, for reasons that are unclear, Fust foreclosed on his loan to Gutenberg and used much of Gutenberg's equipment to found the world's first commercially successful printing firm. Two motives have been proposed for Fust's lawsuit. One is that Fust grew impatient with Gutenberg's slow progress and wished to see some return on his investment. The other more commonly held explanation is that Fust was well aware of the value of Gutenberg's new printing system and he waited until Gutenberg proved the viability of his new technology before using legal proceedings to take over the business.

---

* Much of what we know about Gutenberg is unclear. Part of this may be due to international relations in Renaissance Europe. Gutenberg's work was done in the cities of Mainz, in modern day Germany, and Strassburg in Alsace, now Strasbourg, France. Franco-German rivalry would lead to dubious scholarship from both sides as they both attempted to claim Gutenberg as one of their own.

Movable type

Gutenberg's contribution to movable type was not its invention, but its perfection. Long before Gutenberg, Pi Sheng, a Chinese court official and alchemist in the eleventh century, developed movable type by baking clay characters that could be re-ordered as necessary. Almost three centuries later, another magistrate named Wang Chen commissioned more than 60,000 characters on movable wooden blocks; he is also credited with inventing a system to organize all those characters. Wood and clay, however, could not stand up to the repeated punishment of producing large numbers of copies, leading to investigations in casting type. Metal type was first cast in Korea in the late fourteenth century.

Roman-style alphabets had an important advantage over Asian written languages. Creating type for alphabets requires far fewer symbols. On the other hand, those symbols must have an extremely consistent appearance. Early movable type pieces were individually crafted, leading to variation in the appearance among the resulting printed characters, and even in the spacing between them. Gutenberg's major contribution was his method for casting type. He handcrafted a punch in the shape of the desired letter in relatively hard metal, and used the punch in softer metal to create a matrix, which would then have a recessed copy of the letter on the punch. By using the resulting matrix in a variable-width cast, a type caster could then produce large numbers of identical letters. Innovations this ingenious are usually patented today. Don't worry, though, intellectual property law will make an appearance later in this story.

Creating uniform characters was not Gutenberg's only contribution to type casting. Previous attempts at casting usable metal type failed because the metal used for casting did not have all the desired properties. Type metal must melt at a low enough temperature to be easily cast, but be hard enough to withstand the rigors of use in a press. Type pieces must also resist damage from ink and cleaning solutions for used type. Brass and bronze meet all the criteria for casting metal, but suffer one flaw. Like most metals, brass and bronze shrink when cooled, and thus fail to fill in minute details in the casting matrix. Gutenberg's innovation drew on the knowledge of a rare metal that did not fit in with this general pattern. Antimony, and alloys containing antimony, expand when cooled. Expansion forces the cooling alloy to fill very fine lines and detail in the typecasting matrix. Through a presumably prolonged trial and error process, Gutenberg settled on a formulation of 80% lead, 15% antimony, and 5% tin. His alloy, later dubbed *type metal*, proved to be ideal and did not change substantially in the subsequent five centuries.

Pieces of type were stored in cases when not in use by the printer. Type cases were hinged like briefcases, with half the type in the upper half and the remainder in the lower half. Capital letters and numbers, which were used less frequently, were kept in the upper case, while the more commonly used small letters were kept in the lower case so that they were more accessible. Medieval type organization gives us the terms *upper case* and *lower case* letters.

Printing press

Gutenberg probably adapted an existing agricultural press for the work of printing. Several different press types were used in agriculture at the time, although they all used a vertical screw to move a horizontal plate to apply pressure. His exact design is lost from historical records, although the basic design is clear. Type was laid in the printing bed, which was moved to waist level, and the sliding bed allowed pages of type to be easily positioned under the press. The printing press changed little over the next four centuries. It was not until the rotary press in 1848 that Gutenberg's design became obsolete.

From Gutenberg to the Industrial Revolution

Following Gutenberg's death, little innovative work was done until the application of steam power to the printing process at the start of the Industrial Revolution. Printing presses became more efficient, metal replaced wood as the material of construction, and new fonts were introduced, but the basic techniques would have been accessible to Gutenberg or his contemporaries.

Early industrial printing supported the university system as an outgrowth of the cultural changes of the Renaissance. Initially, printed books were viewed as cheap commodities without the artistic value of handwritten books. Selling books in the face of artistic disdain required clever marketing. Early typefaces, today called *Gothic* or *black letter*, were based on the formal script of the time. By using typefaces similar to formal script, publishers made early printed books appear similar to handwritten books of the day.

In the fifty years after the introduction of the printing press, Venice was a hotbed of innovation, due in part to Italian leadership of the humanist revival. In 1470, Nicholas Jensen perfected the Roman typeface, and in 1490, Aldus Manutius introduced italic type for his wildly popular pocket editions of the classics. Success for Manutius came with a price. He was the first publisher to fall victim to widespread piracy. By 1500, nearly 150 presses competed for business in Venice. Widespread demand for books, coupled with the power of the press to turn out large numbers, increased the number of books in Europe from thousands before the introduction of the printing press to nine million!

Due in part to governmental restrictions, the first book published in English was not printed in England. William Caxton, an Englishman living in Bruges, Belgium, set up a press in 1474. The instrument of royal restriction was the Stationers'

Company, a former guild given a royal monopoly. Elizabeth I's restrictions on the press allowed printing only in London (plus one press each for Oxford and Cambridge, in deference to the academic tradition) and gave the Stationers' Company the right to search out and destroy offending material. The Stationers' Company enthusiastically carried out its new mission, motivated in large part to preserve its monopoly. In 1577, John Wolfe led a revolt against the Stationers' Company, claiming the right to publish anything he wanted. Wolfe was twice imprisoned before being bribed into submission with a membership in the Stationers' Company.

In the latter part of the seventeenth century, licensing for the Stationers' Company was a political football due to the domestic turmoil in England; Parliament opted not to renew the license of the Stationers' Company in 1694. Parliament modernized copyright restrictions with the Copyright Act of 1709, which set a 14-year copyright on all new work. The late seventeenth century also saw a welcome development for authors everywhere (and in the future): the right of authors to share in the profits from their work. Alexander Pope, perhaps the greatest English poetic satirist, was the first author to support himself entirely by writing for publication.

Across the ocean, the nascent American publishing industry suffered from a shortage of type. Printing presses and type were imported from England. In a subtle slap at the English, Benjamin Franklin suggested that the first authenticated versions of the Declaration of Independence be printed in Caslon type, named after William Caslon, an Englishman who had developed the first font in England.

Printing Becomes an Industrial Process

Early printing was almost a cottage industry. Small printers with low volume presses cranked out as much as humanly possible. The Industrial Revolution was about to make printing even more widespread and more of a democratizing force.

Duplicate originals

Soaring demand for printed material forced publishers to print greater volumes faster than ever. Most of the cost in printing was for the skilled typesetters who laboriously laid out the type into sheets. When text was justified with the right margin, as it is in most modern publications, inter-word spacing needed to be adjusted by hand on a line-by-line basis with spacing markers between words. As demand for printed material soared, a single page of type could be dulled to the point of unsuitability by repeated pressure from the press. After wearing a page of type down, a typesetter would need to replace the old type with fresh type.

Time-critical information, such as in newspapers, was set several times to enable parallel press runs. Whether copies were printed sequentially or in parallel, the typesetting cost was identical. Publishers turned to duplicate originals, a method of taking a page of type and creating a full page duplicate of it. The first and cheapest method was called the stereotype, while later methods involved electroplating and were called electrotypes.

Steam power

Until the early nineteenth century, printing presses were completely human powered. Refinements had increased the size of machines and automated many tasks, but printing still depended entirely on muscle power. With the dawn of the Industrial Revolution and the invention of the steam engine, many entrepreneurs were drawn to the challenge of powering a printing press by steam. Newspaper publishers offered lucrative rewards for the successful application of steam power because of the potential cost reductions from eliminating labor to hand crank the presses.

Friedrich Koenig, a German engineer, developed semi-functional prototypes of steam-powered presses on the Continent, but moved to London to seek his fortune. He was drawn there by the large number of daily newspapers and the opportunity they represented. Legal protections for inventors were stronger in England than on the Continent as well, potentially allowing Koenig to reap greater rewards from his work. We told you intellectual property rights would come into the story again! John Walter, publisher of *The Times*, funded Koenig's work because he saw the competitive advantage of a mechanically driven press. After enduring death threats from unions concerned about the jobs that would be lost to the new machine, Koenig installed the first steam-powered press at *The Times* of London in 1814.

Mechanical typecasting

Automating the process of pressing words onto the page proved to be a valuable labor-saving innovation. Koenig's early machines could print 1,000 pages per hour, several times that of the fastest hand cranked machines. Typesetting, however, still remained a laborious and expensive task, and a major cost that publishers wished to reduce.

Ottomar Mergenthaler turned movable type on its head with his Linotype machine, which he patented in 1884 and installed at the *New York Tribune* in 1886. Various prior attempts to mechanically set type had failed, but Mergenthaler stepped into the void with a unique solution: he cast the type as needed. The movable type is actually the matrix from which the type is cast. Based on operator input, the Linotype assembled matrices used for type casting. Machine-adjustable spacing bars filled in spaces between words.

When a line of type was completed, the Linotype would adjust the spacing to automatically justify the text with the right margin and cast an entire line of type. Metal with a relatively low melting point would be injected into the line of matrices, and the Linotype would produce an entire justified line of type and return the matrices to be used again. When the typecast line had been used for printing (or, more likely, producing stereotypes), it was melted down and recycled by the Linotype.

One problem with the Linotype is that error correction is a relatively expensive process because an entire line must be melted down and recast. In 1897, Tolbert Lanston introduced the Monotype machine to address these faults. The Monotype cast one letter at a time into a galley, making errors relatively easy to correct.

Phototypesetting (photocomposition) and computerized typesetting

Monotype machines remained in common use until the early 70s. But as computers started to become less exotic, it became clear that they could advance the printing process to the next level. Rather than casting each line individually and then using the cast lines to create duplicate plates of each page, computerized phototypesetters can create full page metal plates directly from the text input. Furthermore, computerization offers a significant speed advantage. Casting machines such as the Linotype can produce five characters per second and depend on the operator to hypenate words, while a computerized typesetting system can be more than an order of magnitude faster and relieve the operator of the laborious task of hyphenation.

Electronic Document Preparation

Electronic methods ushered in *planographic* printing, in which the printing plate is no longer necessary. Both the image and the negative share the same plane; chemical reactions and electrostatic forces have both been used to apply the ink to the image areas. Lithography was the first planographic method to be widely used, but it has been largely superseded by computerized desktop publishing methods.

The Computerization of Printing

Computers initially promised the paperless office. We now know that's not true—computers enable us to waste more paper than anybody ever dreamed of. But the widespread use of computers has enabled individuals to take part in publishing. And that brings us to the present day, when desktop computers and desktop printers are commonplace.

Enter Unix

The origins of Unix are probably well known to the readers of this book. What may not be as well known is that the proposal made by Ken Thompson and Dennis Ritchie for Bell Labs to purchase a PDP-11 was justified by a promise to write software for text processing. Their text processing package was delivered to the Bell Labs patent department in the summer of 1971 and was a success, which secured official support for Unix development from that point onward.

Interestingly enough, Unix was used instead of a commercial software package available at the time. Unix was chosen because of its support of a particular terminal model that allowed the patent writers to use a wide variety of math symbols, a feature not available on the commercial package. Although flexible terminal support is not such a large deal now, the flexibility of the Unix programming environment and customizability of software continue to this day and in fact make the printing architecture in this book possible.

Unix was also instrumental in the development and deployment of networks, which have proven to be a flexible and effective way for computers to send documents to printers. A modern computing environment that isn't networked is scarcely imaginable.

Exit Unix: the microcomputer and desktop publishing

Preparing patent applications in the Unix text editing environment would have been tedious, even with typesetting languages. The Macintosh and Adobe's PostScript language changed that. Work previously done by the typesetter and page layout artist is now done by page-description languages (PDLs), such as PostScript. PDLs, the subject of the next chapter, made it possible to produce professional quality output without needing to know anything about printing technology. No knowledge of typesetting, stereotyping, or lithography was needed. You simply designed a document on your screen and printed it out. To serve users grouped in a common area, people built LANs to hook several desktops to one print server.

Getting the ink from computer to paper

Most printers today use either ink jet or xerographic methods. Ink jet printers use heat or electrical charge to spray tiny ink droplets on to the paper. Laser printers also use electrical charge to transfer the image to paper. After bombarding a photoconductive surface, usually a rotating drum, with laser light, exposed areas will acquire an electric charge. Charged areas correspond to the dark areas of the image to be printed. When fine toner particles are given a slight electrical charge and sprayed against the surface, they stick to the charged areas of the drum. The drum is heated to fuse the toner to the paper and produce the image. LED printers work identically, but use LEDs rather than lasers as the source of light.

A DIFFERENT KIND
of Animal

O'REILLY®
sysadmin.oreilly.com

Expect Something Different! The O'Reilly Sys Admin & Networking Series

Our readers expect a lot! They won't settle for run-of-the-mill answers to their tough questions. And when they need reliable information, they don't have time to waste. That's why they turn to O'Reilly's Animal Guides for dependable, no-nonsense solutions to their challenging technical problems.

Our readers know we never publish ten-pound door-stops that have been rushed into print. They count on us to deliver meticulously researched, unbiased, authoritative books written by experts. Demanding technical professionals come back to O'Reilly again and again. Why? Because they know O'Reilly is different. And they trust us.

Part # 8674 © 2000 O'Reilly & Associates, Inc. O'Reilly is a registered trademark of O'Reilly & Associates, Inc.

That's how we got to the present situation: even a small organization can have hundreds of computers communicating over a network to dozens of printers. And commercial printing uses the same model. Typesetting for this book was done on a desktop computer, and the results shipped over the Internet to a commerical printer in PDF format. (The details are given in the Colophon.) But as we said earlier, the biggest problem facing us now isn't the printing technology; it's managing the communications between the computers and printers. That's what we'll discuss for the rest of this book.

2

Printer Languages

Sending plain text* to a printer generally results in plain output. The page will be printed in a plain font, possibly without line wrapping, and in portrait mode. More complicated output is desirable, but requires more complicated input.

Early attempts at formatting output were based on *escape codes*. Applications or print drivers would place control codes in the stream of data sent to the printer, and these control codes would direct the printer to do something more interesting with the data following the control code. Most control codes began with the escape character, hence the name escape code.†

Each vendor developed a proprietary set of escape codes. Large vendors with several different independent product lines sometimes developed escape codes for each product line without any coordination between any product lines. Chaos ensued for driver developers. Escape codes proved to be too inflexible.

Page-description languages (PDLs) differ from escape codes because they describe the contents of a printed page. Modern printers commonly implement either Adobe's PostScript language or HP's Printer Control Language (PCL).‡ Both Post-Script and modern versions of PCL describe a page in terms of geometrical objects such as lines, arcs, and circles. Before printing a PDL document, a raster image processor (RIP) converts the PDL description to a bitmap to be printed, a process called *rasterization*.

---

* By plain text we mean textual data with no formatting code.

† There's a strong analogy here with HTML and web browsers. If you send plain text to a browser, you will see plain text. However, when you add HTML tags to the text, the browser can make specifc text more interesting with boldface, italics, and so on.

‡ PCL is a hybrid: it started off as simple escape codes, but evolved into a PDL.

This chapter only discusses printer languages as commands for the print engine. It does not, for example, tell you how to use a PCL printer when you want to print PostScript files, but we will get to that in due course.

PostScript

In 1985, Adobe announced PostScript and ushered in the desktop publishing revolution. PostScript was inspired by the Forth programming language.* From the beginning, PostScript was intended to be independent of any output technology. At the output device, the PostScript description is rasterized at the best resolution possible for that output device. Typical monitors are capable of 75 dots per inch (dpi), laser printers 300–1200 dpi, and image-setters up to 2400 dpi.

Publishers rapidly adopted PostScript. Images printed on a 300 dpi laser were laid out identically to those printed on a 2400 dpi image setter. Any platform could generate PostScript instructions if it had software drivers to translate a platform-specific representation into PostScript, which made PostScript output devices extremely popular.

PostScript Level 2 was released in 1990, and added device-independent color, data compression, and other enhancements for graphics. To address complaints about performance, memory and resource management were improved. PostScript Level 3, released in 1999, offered further enhancements to graphics processing and improved shading, color control, and performance.

The power of PostScript is that it provides a convenient, widely available language that describes images in a device independent manner.† Device independence means that the image is described without reference to any specific device features, such as output device resolution. The same PostScript file can be used on any PostScript output device without modification. A detailed exploration of PostScript is certainly outside the scope of this book, but you can get detailed information on the language from the Adobe web site. Specifically, you can download the PostScript Language Reference Manual in PDF format from *http://www.adobe.com/print/postscript/pdfs/PLRM.pdf*.

---

* Charles Moore created Forth in the 1960s to give computers real-time control over astronomical equipment. A number of Forth's features, such as its interactive style, make it a useful language for AI programming. Devoted adherents have developed Forth-based expert systems and neural networks. Functions in Forth are called *words*. The programmer uses Forth's built-in words to create new ones and store them in Forth's *dictionary*. In a Forth program, words pass information to one another by using a last-in, first-out *stack*. Forth's unique contribution to the world of programming languages was this method of stack usage.

† Think of it this way: PostScript is to printers as Java is to microprocessors.

PostScript Language Overview

PostScript is stack-based, and functions like a fancy scientific calculator that uses Reverse Polish Notation. A program pushes arguments onto a stack and then invokes an operator. Typically, the operator will have some result, which is returned to the top of the stack. As a trivial example, to multiply 2 by 3, use the following PostScript code:

```
2 3 mul
```

The first two words *2* and *3* push the numbers 2 and 3 onto the stack. *mul* invokes the multiply operator, which pops two values off the stack, multiplies them, and then pushes the result back onto the stack. The resulting value, 6, is then on top of the stack. The general syntax is:

```
arg1 arg2 argN ...operator
```

The operator will return a result and place it on top of the stack. Some operators may not return a result.

PostScript Data Types

The PostScript language is fairly simple. Before working with the syntax, it helps to know the basic elements of the language:

Comment

> The % symbol is used for comments in a PostScript program (comments begin with the % and continue to the end of the line). The special combination %! is used as the first two characters of a PostScript program. The %! tag marks the file as PostScript code on many systems. Magic print filters, a topic we'll cover later in Chapter 4, *Extending the Berkeley Spooler with Print Filters*, use this tag to process PostScript jobs correctly.

String

> A string is exactly what you would expect: it is a sequence of characters. In PostScript Level 1, you can express strings either by enclosing them in parentheses, or as hexadecimal code in angle brackets.
>
> The string `Hello, World!` is expressed in the first form as *(Hello, World!)*, and the string `ABC` is expressed in the latter form as *<414243>*, using the ASCII ordinal values for A (41), B (42), and C (43).

Number

> PostScript can use both integers and real numbers. Numbers can be expressed either in radix form, or in scientific notation. Radix form is written like

radix#value, where radix is the base for value. Scientific notation is the standard *mantissaEexponent* used in many other languages.

— Radix example: 101#8 = 65

— Scientific example: 1E7 = 10⁷

Name

Any character sequence that is not a number is a name. The space character, as well as (,), [,], <, >, {, }, /, and %, are not legal components of a name. Names may start with digits, but exercise caution—*1Z4* is a name, but *3E4* is a number in scientific notation. A name is a reference to a value in a dictionary.

Dictionary

A dictionary is a collection of names and values associated with those names, much like an associative array in Perl. All named variables and operators are stored in dictionaries. PostScript maintains a *dictionary stack* of all open dictionaries.

Array

PostScript arrays are like arrays in most other languages, except that they can contain objects of different types. An array is written as a list of objects enclosed in brackets. For instance, *[1 2 3]* is a three element array containing the number 1, the number 2, and the number 3.

Procedure

New operators are defined using procedures. In fact, a procedure is simply an executable array, written with braces instead of brackets. A procedure to square the top element in the stack would be written as { fdup mulg }. To define this procedure as the *square* operator, use the *def* operator: /square { fdup mulg } def.

A Few Simple PostScript Programs

Following in the time-honored tradition of all programming books that have come before us, we will start with the *Hello, World!* program. In PostScript, you need to set up a font, and then display it on the output device with the *show* operator, as in Example 2-1.

Example 2-1. "Hello, World!" in PostScript

```
1 %!
2 /Times-Roman findfont    % Get the basic font
3 14 scalefont             % Set the font size to 14 points
4 setfont                  % Make it the current font
5 newpath                  % Start a new path
6 72 72 moveto             % Set the point to start from
7 (Hello, World!) show     % Print it
```

Line 1 marks the program as PostScript code. Lines 2, 3, and 4 set the font to 14 point Times Roman. Line 5 starts a *path*, which is essentially a drawing element, as if you are going to move a pen along the path. In this case, the path is quite simple: move to a location (Line 6), and print the string `Hello, World!` New paths must always start off with the *moveto* operator.

PostScript also allows you to compose graphic objects. Example 2-2 draws a box in the lower left corner of the page.

Example 2-2. PostScript Box Drawing Program

```
 1 %!
 2 %% Draw a one-inch square box
 3 /inch {72 mul} def       % Define an inch as 72 points for simplicity
 4 newpath                  % Start a new path
 5 1 inch 1 inch moveto     % Start one inch in from the lower left
 6 2 inch 1 inch lineto     % The bottom edge
 7 2 inch 2 inch lineto     % The right edge
 8 1 inch 2 inch lineto     % The top edge
 9 closepath                % Automatically completes the left edge
10 stroke                   % Draw the box
11 showpage                 % Eject the page
```

Line 3 defines a function called *inch*, which multiplies its argument by 72. Defining an inch operator makes later operations simpler because the PostScript interpreter operates in *points*, where 72 points is equivalent to 1 inch. By using the inch function, the human readable string *1 inch* will be evaluated as 72 points. Lines 6 to 8 draw three sides of the box. Line 9, the *closepath* operator, notifies the interpreter that the path has been completed and connects the end of the path to its starting point. The *stroke* operator in line 10 will take the defined path and paint a line on it, which is what draws the box. Finally, line 11 invokes the *showpage* operator, which instructs the interpreter to put the painted box onto the output medium.

Talking directly to the PostScript interpreter

Remember when you first spoke directly with a mail transport agent by connecting to port 25? Many PostScript printers allow you to connect directly to the interpreter, usually on port 9100. Once you connect to port 9100, type `executive` to get a `PS>` prompt, which tells you that you're connected to the interpreter. When you're finished, press Ctrl-] to quit; most interpreters will also gracefully exit when they encounter Ctrl-C or Ctrl-D. Example 2-3 shows interactive input directly to the PostScript engine.

Example 2-3. Hello, World! Entered Directly into the PostScript Interpreter

```
unix% telnet hp5 9100
Trying 10.10.1.124...
```

Example 2-3. Hello, World! Entered Directly into the PostScript Interpreter (continued)

```
Connected to hp5.
Escape character is '^]'.
executive
PostScript(r) Version 2014.108
(c) Copyright 1984-1995 Adobe Systems Incorporated.
Typefaces (c) Copyright 1981 Linotype-Hell AG and/or its subsidiaries.
All Rights Reserved.
PS>/Times-Roman findfont
/Times-Roman findfont
PS>14 scalefont
14 scalefont
PS>setfont
setfont
PS>newpath
newpath
PS>72 72 moveto
72 72 moveto
PS>(Hello, World!) show
(Hello, World!) show
PS>showpage
showpage
PS>quit
quit
```

If you entered everything correctly, you should see a printout containing the string *Hello, World!* in the lower left corner of the page.

PCL

Hewlett Packard initially developed the Printer Control Language (PCL) for use with dot matrix printers. PCL began life as a simple escape code control language, but later versions added more complex functionality; PCL has now grown into a complete PDL.

PCL History

Because PCL originally consisted of a series of escape codes, PCL commands are also called *escape sequences*. Like PostScript, PCL revisions are called levels, and PCL levels are backwards compatible. PCL level 5 printers, for example, can print PCL level 5, as well as PCL levels 4, 3, 2, and 1.

PCL levels 1 and 2 were introduced in the 1980s with early Hewlett Packard printers. Both were escape code languages capable of printing only text, making them irrelevant today. It was not until the release of PCL 3, with its support of basic graphics, that PCL became a useful printer language. Table 2-1 shows the evolution of PCL since PCL 3, along with the printer hardware supported by each version of PCL.

Table 2-1. PCL Evolution

Level	Hardware	Advances
PCL 3	LaserJet, LaserJet Plus	First PCL level to support simple graphics. Work-alike versions implemented by many other manufacturers; often called *LaserJet Plus Emulation*.
PCL 4	LaserJet	Wider typeface selection than PCL 3.
PCL 4e	LaserJet II Series	Added support for bitmapped fonts.
PCL 5	LaserJet III Series	Targeted at complex desktop publishing market; includes more advanced typeface handling and HP-GL/2 graphics.
PCL 5e	LaserJet 4, 5, and 6 series	First PCL version to support 600 dpi. Allowed bidirectional communication, so printer could return status information to the host driver software.
PCL 5c	Color LaserJet, DeskJet 1200C, and other DeskJet *C* models	Added support for color.
PCL 6	LaserJet 4000 LaserJet 2100	A complete rewrite aimed at reducing complexity of print jobs by making the language more efficient and incorporating several improvements to graphics processing.

PCL Job Flow on Windows

The following shows you how a Windows print job arrives at the output tray of a PCL printer:

1. Documents are displayed in Windows using the Windows Graphics Device Interface (GDI). Applications use GDI to display documents on the screen. PCL printer drivers take GDI commands and translate the commands into PCL.

2. The PCL document is sent to the printer, either over the network or a cable. The processor in the printer takes the PCL commands and produces a bitmap image from the PCL input.

3. The printer puts those dots on paper.

HP's Printer Job Language

HP developed the Printer Job Language (PJL)* to provide control over whole print jobs, not just individual files in a print job. Each print job sent to a PJL-compatible printer is wrapped in PJL, and each PJL job may contain several files to be printed.

PJL provides an interface to the printer at a higher level than pages or documents. With PJL, each job may contain instructions on how the paper should be handled, such as stapling or sorting the output into bins.

---

* PJL should not be confused with PCL; they are different languages with different purposes.

PJL job structure

PJL uses the command sequence `Ec%-12345X` extensively, which we call the Super Escape Code. (As you might guess, the Super Escape Code has a far more boring name in other documentation.) The Super Escape Code interrupts the current language interpreter and hands control back to PJL.

HP documentation uses `Ec` to refer to the escape character used by HP printers. It is not an exotic escape code—just the character with an ASCII value of 27. To avoid confusion, we will use `Ec` here, although other documentation will refer to the escape character as *Esc*.

Part of creating PJL files is entering the escape character into the file. To generate the escape character in *vi*, type `Ctrl-V` and press the escape key. On the screen, you'll see `^]`. In the DOS/Windows *EDIT* program, type `Ctrl-P` followed by Esc. On the screen, you will see an arrow pointing to the left.

Each PJL job begins with the Super Escape Code, followed immediately by *@PJL*, which labels the job as a PJL job. Several PJL commands are allowed for each component of the job, provided each PJL command is on a separate line and begins with the magic *@PJL* prefix. Jobs must end with the Super Escape Code, and may also end with the *@PJL EOJ* identifier.

PJL examples

PJL can be used to instruct the printer to provide information. For example, modern HP LaserJet printers have several typefaces. To get the typeface list, send the file in Example 2-4 to the printer.

Example 2-4. PJL Command File to Get Typeface List

```
Ec%-12345X@PJL SET TESTPAGE = PCLTYPELIST
Ec%-12345X
```

One major benefit of PJL is that you can submit multiple print files in a single job, and use PJL to switch languages. Example 2-5 shows a PJL job with multiple languages in it. (PCL jobs must begin and end with the code *EcE*.)[*]

Example 2-5. PJL Language Switching

```
Ec%-12345X@PJL ENTER LANGUAGE = PCL
EcE. . . . . . pcl data. . . . . . EcE
@PJL ENTER LANGUAGE = POSTSCRIPT
```

---

[*] PJL commands have been known to confuse Unix print filters that look for certain prefix characters, resulting in the entire job being printed as an ASCII file.

Example 2-5. PJL Language Switching (continued)

```
%! PS-ADOBE
. . . . postscript job data. . . .
^D
Ec%-12345X
```

GDI

One problem with PDLs like PostScript or PCL is that the rendering engines that translate page-descriptions into dots on the page are CPU intensive and can be slow for complex graphics. Including a rendering engine in a printer also increases its cost. For these reasons, vendors developed low cost devices called *GDI printers*. You may also hear Graphics Device Interface (GDI) printers referred to as *WinPrinters* for reasons that will become clear shortly.

GDI printers use the host PC CPU to perform the page rendering task. When an application prints, the printer driver takes the GDI output and performs the rendering directly on the PC. The result of the rendering process is a device-dependent bitmap that is sent to the printer. Because GDI printers don't have to perform their own rasterization, there is no need for expensive processors or large amounts of on-board RAM on the printer. The downside is that the computationally expensive rendering process is done on the host CPU.

GDI printers are not suitable for demanding environments. Translation of the GDI output to a device-dependent bitmap requires a driver that understands both GDI and the low-level details of the print engine. Such drivers are typically only released for Microsoft Windows environments.

3

Exploring the Spooler

This and the following chapter are the linchpins of the whole book. Creating robust print services begins with a solid understanding of how print jobs are processed. The Unix printing system is the heart of our architecture, keeping jobs flowing smoothly from client to server to printer. Flexibility makes the Unix spooler ideal for this role. It can deal with nearly every type of printer, ranging from small printers directly connected to I/O ports on the server to large, powerful, networked laser printers capable of tens of pages per minute and digesting small forests in a single job.

Before constructing a skyscraper, first lay a strong foundation. This chapter helps you build the foundation by guiding you through setting up print service on your Unix system and using the associated administrative programs.

Like many other members of the Unix family, the print spooler has split into a BSD line and an SVR4 line. We discuss both. For completeness, we also discuss Microsoft TCP/IP printing in the final section of this chapter.

If possible, standardize on one spooler. Entrenched systems already in place may prevent standardization. Depending on circumstances at your office, you may find that volunteering to run print services gives you a freer hand to design and implement the system. No matter what your decision, this chapter is your reference.

The Berkeley Spooler: lpr and lpd

To appreciate the age and flexibility of the Berkeley spooler, consider the purpose for which it was designed and how much it has adapted to changing computing environments. The *lp* in the Berkeley commands stands for *line printer* because the BSD spooler was originally written when printers were only capable of printing a single line of text at a time. Most Unix print servers today use BSD-derived printing code, including some commercial Unix versions.

Line Printer Request (lpr)

Users submit jobs to the print system with *lpr*. If no specific printer is specified, jobs are submitted to the queue named *lp*, although you can change the default queue in two ways. First, the default queue name can be changed with the PRINTER environment variable. Alternatively, you can always specify the queue on the command line with the *–P* option.

The normal syntax for *lpr* is quite simple:

```
$ lpr filename
```

If you don't supply the filename, *lpr* will assume standard input, which is handy for printing the output of other programs. A simple example would be to have *lpr* print out the output of the *ls* command:

```
$ ls | lpr
```

Components of a Job in the BSD Spooler

Figure 3-1 illustrates the path a job takes through the BSD spooler. *lpr* submits a job by putting the data file and control information in the spool directory and passing the buck to *lpd* to deal with it further. *lpd* saves job-control information, such as the name of the user submitting the job, in a *control file* in the spool directory.

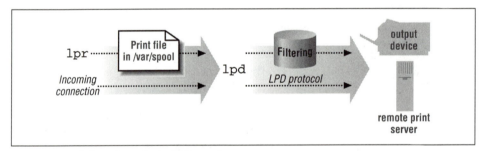

Figure 3-1. Job flow through the BSD spooler

As an example, say that we print the file *words.txt* on the printer *lp* attached to *bastet.fofz.com*. As you will see later, print requests are often stored in */var/spool/ lpd/printername*. Spool directories are not readable by normal users:

```
[gast@bastet]$ lpr words.txt
[gast@bastet]$ su -
[root@bastet]# cd /var/spool/lpd
[root@bastet lpd]# ls
lp/  lpd.lock
```

```
[root@bastet lpd]# cd lp
[root@bastet lp]# ls
cfA000bastet.fofz.com  dfA000bastet.fofz.com  lock*  status
```

When a file is printed, it is assigned a job number, which ranges from 000 to 999.* The control and data files for the job will have the job number in the filename, and will generally take the form cfA(job number)(hostname) for control files and dfA(job number)(hostname) for the associated data file. The control file for job 0, *cfA000bastet.fofz.com*, is shown in Example 3-1.

Example 3-1. Anatomy of a Print Job

```
[root@bastet lp]# cat cfA000bastet.fofz.com
Hbastet.fofz.com
Pgast
Jwords.txt
Cbastet.fofz.com
Lgast
fdfA000bastet.fofz.com
UdfA000bastet.fofz.com
Nwords.txt
[root@bastet lp]# cat dfA000bastet.fofz.com
This is a file of words.
```

The data file is simply a copy of the data to be printed. The control file is composed of several lines, each of which begins with a single letter. Table 3-1 lists the meaning of each control character.

Table 3-1. Control File Characters and Associated Meanings

Character	Meaning
H	Name of host that submitted the job.
P	Name of user who submitted the job.
J	Name of the job to be printed on the banner page.
C	Name of the print *class* on the banner page, which is usually set to the name of the host the request originated on.
L	Indicates name of user on banner page, when banner page is printed.
f	Name of the ASCII data file to be printed. When a file is specified with the *f* option, most ASCII control characters are stripped out of the data stream. Only tab, carriage return, line feed, form feed, and backspace are preserved.
l	Name of the data file to be printed, but no control character stripping is performed.
U	Indicates that the data file may be deleted.
N	Name of the source file used in the print job; blank indicates the file came from standard input to *lpr*. This line is used for the filename display in the output of *lpq*.

---

* The next job number to be used is stored in the *.seq* file in the spool directory for the queue.

The Line Printer Daemon (lpd)

lpd is the heart of the BSD spooler. When *lpd* starts up, it checks its configuration file, */etc/printcap*, to discover printers and make them available to print clients. *lpd* will print to both locally attached printers and to remote printers over the network.

A master *lpd* process runs on the print server, checking to see when complete jobs are deposited in spool directories. When jobs arrive, *lpd* forks a child copy of *lpd* to print jobs on that queue. *lpd* children exist only to service jobs in the queue, so if there are no jobs in a particular queue, no child *lpd* process will be running to serve it. If a job should be printed locally, *lpd* sends a copy to the local I/O port. If a job is destined for a remote print server, *lpd* will open a network socket to the remote print server and send the control and data file to the remote host. When *lpd* sends a job over the network, it uses the Line Printer Daemon Protocol. The LPD protocol specification in RFC 1179 was written after widespread deployment.

Checking the Contents of a Queue (lpq)

Checking on the contents of a print queue is simple with the BSD spooler. Just run the *lpq* command, and it will tell you what is in the spool directory by reading control files:

```
printhost:/# lpq
Rank    Owner      Job  Files                      Total Size
1st     root       65   /etc/hosts                 843 bytes
2nd     root       66   ...                        1363 bytes
3rd     root       67   /etc/services              3643 bytes
4th     root       68   /etc/passwd                118 bytes
```

Deleting a Job (lprm)

Users must use *lprm* to remove a job from a queue because the spool directory is inaccessible to normal users. The syntax of *lprm* is simple. It takes one argument: the job ID to delete, which you can obtain by using *lpq*. If the user executing *lprm* submitted the job, the control and data files will be deleted from the spool directory and the job will be removed (*root*, of course, may remove any job):

```
printhost:/# lpr /etc/hosts
printhost:/# lpq

Rank    Owner     Job  Files                       Total Size
active  root      61   hosts                       843 bytes
printhost:/# lprm 61
pserver: dfA61printhost dequeued
pserver: cfA61printhost dequeued
printhost:/#
```

Line Printer Control (lpc)

BSD print-queue administration is done with the *lpc* command. With *lpc*, the system administrator may enable and disable printers, rearrange the order of jobs in the queue, and check the status of printers and their associated queues and service daemons. Most *lpc* actions are only possible as *root*, although normal users are allowed to use *lpc* to display the status of print queues.

lpc can be used on the command line, or it can be used interactively by typing *lpc* with no arguments. Arguments to *lpc* are shown in Table 3-2, and will be explained in more detail later in this section.

Table 3-2. Arguments to lpc

Argument	Purpose
status	Display status of a printer or of the entire print system.
topq	Change the order of jobs in the queue. See the section "Rearranging the order of jobs with topq" for details.
restart	Kill and restart the copy of *lpd* serving the queue.
start	Begin sending jobs to the printer.
stop	Stop sending jobs to the printer and kill the *lpd* daemon associated with the queue.
enable	Begin accepting new jobs.
disable	Stop accepting new jobs.
up	Start printing and enable spooling.
down	Stop printing and disable spooling.
abort	Terminate the *lpd* process associated with the queue and disable printing.
clean	Clean out the spool directory.
help/?	Show available commands, or get a brief summary of a particular command.
exit/quit	Exit *lpc*.

Status reporting with lpc status

The most basic printer-administration task is to check on the status of a queue, which is done with *lpc status*.

> Usage: `lpc status { printer | all }`

If no argument is supplied, the argument *all* is assumed, and status for every printer on the system is displayed. You may choose to display status for only one printer by including its name. Here is a basic example:

```
[root@printhost /root]# lpc status lp
lp:
        queuing is enabled
        printing is disabled
```

```
2 entries in spool area
no daemon present
```

lpc reports status for printing and queuing. When a queue is enabled, the server accepts jobs and spools them. Jobs are not sent to the printer, however, unless printing is enabled. Table 3-3 shows the effects of different combinations of printing and queuing settings.

Table 3-3. Interpreting Printing and Queuing Status

	Queuing Enabled	Queuing Disabled
Printing Enabled	Jobs are spooled and sent to the printer.	No new jobs are accepted, but existing jobs are sent to the printer.
Printing Disabled	Jobs are spooled and held in the spool directory. No jobs are sent to the printer.	No new jobs are accepted, and no spooled jobs are processed.

lpc can be used interactively as well, although the syntax is oddly familiar:

```
[root@printhost /root]# lpc
lpc> status lp
lp:
        queuing is enabled
        printing is disabled
        2 entries in spool area
        no daemon present
lpc>
```

Do not be alarmed by the *no daemon present* report from *lpc*. The daemon referred to in the message is the child copy of *lpd* that services the printer's spool directory. When the child *lpd* provides this service, it removes jobs from the spool directory and sends them to the printer.

A child *lpd* process is active only when jobs need to be handled. That means that when printing is disabled or no jobs are present in the queue, no child *lpd* will be running, and *lpc* will report that no daemon is present.

When a queue is actively being serviced by a child *lpd* process, *lpc* reports that the printer is *ready and printing*:

```
[root@printhost /root]# lpc status lp
lp:
        queuing is enabled
        printing is enabled
        11 entries in spool area
        lp is ready and printing
```

Changing the status of print queues with enable, disable, start, and stop

Table 3-3 shows you how the printing and queue status determine what actions
are taken by the spooler. When printing is enabled, jobs are sent to the printer.
When queuing is enabled, jobs are accepted into the spool directory. You may
wish to change these states separately. For example, before taking a printer down
for routine maintenance, such as adding toner, you will want to prevent jobs from
being sent to the output device so that you can turn it off:

```
[root@printhost /root]# lpc enable lp
lp:
        queuing enabled
[root@printhost /root]# lpc stop lp
lp:
        printing disabled
[root@printhost /root]# lpc status lp
lp:
        queuing is enabled
        printing is disabled
        5 entries in spool area
        no daemon present
```

But if you were going to move a printer, you would want to prevent new jobs
from entering the queue and allow all existing jobs to be printed. In that case,
you'd want to disable queuing but leave printing enabled until the queue is empty:

```
[root@krypton /root]# lpc disable lp
lp:
        queuing disabled
[root@krypton /root]# lpc start lp
lp:
        printing enabled
        daemon started
[root@krypton /root]# lpq
Warning: lp queue is turned off
no entries
[root@krypton /root]# lpc status lp
lp:
        queuing is disabled
        printing is enabled
        3 entries in spool area
        lp is ready and printing
```

 If you need to be sure a queue is disabled, make sure to test it as a
normal user, not as *root. lpr* submits jobs by copying them to the
spool directory. *root* is always able to write to any directory because
root is allowed to do anything in the Unix security model. However,
normal users will be unable to submit jobs when the queue is disabled because they lack sufficient permission to write to the spool
directory.

Normal users are notified the queue is disabled when they try to enter jobs into it:

```
[gast@bastet gast]$ lpr words.txt
lpr: Printer queue is disabled
```

When you disable a queue for long periods of time, you may wish to take advantage of the notification mechanism built into the spooler. *lpc down* allows you to enter a message that will be displayed when users run *lpq*.

```
[root@krypton /root]# lpc down lp "Printer is on fire"
lp:
        printer and queuing disabled
[root@krypton /root]# lpq
Warning: lp is down: Printer is on fire
Warning: lp queue is turned off
no entries
```

Rearranging the order of jobs with topq

There comes a time in every system administrator's life (or day!) when users ask for preferential treatment for print jobs. Whether or not you choose to honor such requests is up to you. Regardless of your feelings on the matter, you need to know how to move jobs around, if for no other reason than to put your jobs at the top of the queue when you think nobody is looking. With the BSD spooler, *lpc topq* enables you to reorder jobs.

Usage: `lpc topq` *printer* `[`*job numbers*`]`
       `lpc topq` *printer* `[`*user name*`]`

lpc topq has two arguments. The first is the queue to manipulate, and the second is either the job(s) to move to the top of the queue, or the user whose jobs should be moved to the top of the queue. Consider the following list of four jobs:

```
[root@krypton /root]# lpq
Rank    Owner      Job  Files                              Total Size
1st     gast       47   more-words.txt                     2 bytes
2nd     todd       48   /etc/hosts                         678 bytes
3rd     gast       49   words.txt                          25 bytes
4th     todd       50   /etc/inetd.conf                    3076 bytes
```

The system administrator may move a single job, by job number, to the top of the queue. When the job is moved successfully, *lpc* prints out a confirmation message:

```
[root@krypton /root]# lpc
lpc> topq lp 50
lp:
        moved cfA050krypton
```

topq lp 50 simply moves job 50 to the top of the queue:

```
[gast@krypton gast]$ lpq
Rank    Owner     Job   Files                          Total Size
1st     todd      50    /etc/inetd.conf                3076 bytes
2nd     gast      47    more-words.txt                 2 bytes
3rd     todd      48    /etc/hosts                     678 bytes
4th     gast      49    words.txt                      2 bytes
```

The second form of *lpc topq* moves all the jobs belonging to a user to the top of the queue:

```
lpc> topq lp gast
lp:
        moved cfA049krypton
        moved cfA047krypton
```

All jobs belonging to *gast* are moved to the top of the queue:

```
[gast@krypton gast]$ lpq
Warning: no daemon present
Rank    Owner     Job   Files                          Total Size
1st     gast      47    more-words.txt                 2 bytes
2nd     gast      49    words.txt                      2 bytes
3rd     todd      50    /etc/inetd.conf                3076 bytes
4th     todd      48    /etc/hosts                     678 bytes
```

Finally, *lpc topq* can be given the job numbers of several jobs to be placed at the top of the queue. The chosen jobs are placed at the top of the queue in the order specified, and all other jobs retain their relative order below the chosen:

```
lpc> topq lp 50 47 49 48
lp:
        moved cfA047krypton
        moved cfA049krypton
        moved cfA048krypton
        moved cfA050krypton
```

The effect is that all four jobs are repositioned in the specified order:

```
[gast@krypton gast]$ lpq
Rank    Owner     Job   Files                          Total Size
1st     todd      50    /etc/inetd.conf                3076 bytes
2nd     gast      47    more-words.txt                 2 bytes
3rd     gast      49    words.txt                      2 bytes
4th     todd      48    /etc/hosts                     678 bytes
```

Miscellaneous administrative actions with lpc

lpc abort terminates an active child *lpd* for a local queue and then disables printing. If an extremely large print job is in progess, you might be able to prevent some portion of the job from being sent to the printer. *lpc abort* also disables printing to prevent new copies of *lpd* from being started.

Usage: `lpc abort { printer | all }`

lpc clean removes garbage from the spool directory. For various reasons, incomplete print jobs (a data or control file without a companion) collect in the spool directory. *lpc clean* removes everything except the necessary control files and complete jobs yet to print.

Usage: `lpc clean{ printer | all }`

The Printer Capability Database (/etc/printcap)

The Berkeley spooler stores its configuration information in */etc/printcap*. *lpd* and its friends consult */etc/printcap* each time a job is submitted, which allows system administrators to add and delete printers dynamically.

Like many other Unix configuration files, *printcap* has a precise syntax. *printcap* uses the same format as the *termcap* and *terminfo* files.[*] The basics needed for creating *printcap* entries are quite simple—you can get a decent feel for them by looking at a skeleton *printcap* file included with a BSD spooler distribution. Vendor web sites may also have *printcap* examples that you can build on. To learn some basic syntax, consider Example 3-2, the skeleton *printcap* file distributed with OpenBSD.

Example 3-2. Skeleton printcap File from OpenBSD

```
#       $OpenBSD: printcap,v 1.2 1996/05/26 10:25:26 deraadt Exp $

#lp|local line printer:\
#       :lp=/dev/lp:sd=/var/spool/lpd:lf=/var/log/lpd-errs:
```

printcap gets its name because it describes the capabilities of each printer. Printer names are defined at the beginning, separated by the pipe character (|). The preceding *printcap* defines a single printer, which may either be referred to as *lp* or as *local line printer*. Each capability is named with a two-letter code, such as **sd**. Interpreting *printcap* depends on knowing what a particular two-letter capability means. Common *printcap* entries are shown in Table 3-4; for a complete listing of *printcap* capabilities, see Appendix A, *printcap Reference*, or the *printcap* manual page on your system.

---

[*] The format of *termcap* and *terminfo* is documented in detail in *termcap & terminfo* by John Strang, Linda Mui, and Tim O'Reilly (O'Reilly, 1988).

Table 3-4. Common printcap Capabilities

Capability	Type	Default Value	Description
lp	String	*/dev/lp*	Name of device file to open for output when sending job to print device; should be set to */dev/null* for remote printers and when filters are used.
sd	String	*/var/spool/lpd*	Directory to place spool files in.
lf	String	*/dev/console*	Name of log file.
af	String	Null	Name of accounting file.
mx	Number	Implementation dependent; usually 1000	Number of *BUFSIZ*[a] blocks that will be printed from each file; 0 allows an unlimited length.
sh	Boolean	False	If true, the header page will be suppressed.
of	String	Null	Location of the output filter (see Chapter 4, *Extending the Berkeley Spooler with Print Filters*, for more information).
if	String	Null	Location of the input filter (see Chapter 4 for more information).
rm	String	Null	Remote machine name that *lpd* should send jobs to. It may be an IP address or hostname.
rp	String	*lp*	When the rm capability is defined, jobs will be sent to the queue named by the rp capability.

[a] *BUFSIZ* is a system-defined block size. On most systems, it is either 512 bytes or 1024 bytes. Check *stdio.h* on your system if you're really curious.

With Table 3-4 in hand, you can easily decipher the printer entry in Example 3-2. The *lp* printer should be connected to the device represented by */dev/lp*. *lpr* will place spool files in */var/spool/lpd*, and *lpd* will log errors in */var/log/lpd-errs*.

Before we proceed, a word of caution: the *printcap* file is sensitive to syntax errors (the following sidebar describes the basic rules for *printcap* syntax). Because of *printcap* syntax constraints, most system administrators write *printcap* files in a way that minimizes frustration. The common practice is to put each variable on its own line, continued with backslashes, and to begin and end each line with a colon. When rewritten in the common format, the *printcap* file of Example 3-2 becomes the more legible Example 3-3. One benefit of the common format is that adding and deleting individual capabilities is much easier.

Example 3-3. Skeleton printcap File Rewritten in the Standard Format

```
lp|local line printer:\
        :lp=/dev/lp:\
        :sd=/var/spool/lpd:\
        :lf=/var/log/lpd-errs:
```

Basic printcap Syntax

- The printer name must begin at the first character on the line. Additional printer names, often called aliases, must be separated by pipe symbols (the vertical bar: |).

- Each capability definition must begin and end with a colon.

- As in many other Unix configuration files, a backslash continues the line to the next. The backslash (\) must be the last character on the line—no spaces or tabs should follow it.

- Capabilities are defined in two different ways, depending on whether they are strings or numbers (where **xx** is the printer capability from Table 3-4). Strings are defined with an equals sign: **xx=string**. Numbers are defined with the number sign: **xx#number**.

- Boolean variables omitted are false by default. Included boolean varibles that are not explicitly defined are given the value *true*.

Local Printer Configuration

Local printer entries have a value for the `lp` capability to tell *lpd* where to send the job by specifying the hardware device name that the printer is connected to. Example 3-4 shows a *printcap* file for a printer connected to a local parallel-port. In this example, the `lp` capability is set to */dev/parallel*. Many system administrators use symbolic links to create a more descriptive name; in this case, */dev/parallel* is a symbolic link to */dev/lpt1*.

Example 3-4. printcap for a Local Printer Connected to the Parellel-Port

```
locallaser|lp|LaserWriter connected to the parallel-port on printhost:\
        :lp=/dev/parallel:\
        :sd=/var/spool/lpd/lw:
```

In the previous example, the printer is given three names: a common name (*locallaser*), an abbreviated name that is easy to type (*lp*), and a descriptive name. Recommended practice is to provide at least those three names for each printer.

 The *lp* alias is a special alias. If no printer is specified on the *lpr* command line or with the **PRINTER** environment variable, jobs will be submitted to the first queue that has *lp* as an alias.

To set up the spooling area, create the spool directory manually. Spool directories should be owned by the user *daemon* in the *daemon* group. Permissions should allow all access to the user and group, but no write access for users. To follow the previous example, here is how to create the spool directory */var/spool/lpd/lw*:

```
[root@krypton ]# cd /var/spool/lpd
[root@krypton lpd]# mkdir lw
[root@krypton lpd]# chown daemon lw
[root@krypton lpd]# chgrp daemon lw
[root@krypton lpd]# chmod u+rwx,g+rwx,o+rx-w lw
[root@krypton lpd]# ls -l
total 3
-rw-r--r--    1 root      root            5 Apr 10 12:36 lpd.lock
drwxrwxr-x    2 daemon    daemon       1024 Apr 10 17:15 lw/
```

Although Example 3-4 is a perfectly good *printcap* entry, in a more realistic setting, printer administrators would probably add a few more options, and the *printcap* would look something like Example 3-5.

Example 3-5. More Realistic printcap for Directly Connected Printer

```
laserwriter|lp|LaserWriter connected to the parallel-port on printhost:\
        :lp=/dev/parallel:\
        :sd=/var/spool/lpd/lw:\
        :sh:\
        :mx#0:\
        :if=/usr/local/print/gen-filter.perl:\
        :lf=/var/log/pa-laser.log:\
        :af=/var/acct/pa-laser.acct:
```

Perhaps the most important addition is the mx#0. mx places a limit on the job size you can submit to the queue, and when the job reaches mx blocks, the job will be stopped. Page-description languages make it impossible to infer the number of pages a job will take from the file size alone. Large files may either be a large number of pages, or it may simply be a full-color graphically rich page. Because of this difficulty, it is best to remove the limit.

The if capability defines an input filter. All Berkeley spooler entries should have an if entry, for reasons that will become clear in Chapter 4.

By including sh in the *printcap* file, the sh variable is set to true. When sh is true, no banner pages will be printed by the spooler. Just because sh is set does not mean a banner page will not be generated—many sites like to generate banner pages in a filter script for more control over their contents.

lf and af specify the locations of the log and accounting files. *syslog* information is kept in the former. For large sites with busy printers, each printer should have its own log file. Large sites may also be interested in printer accounting so that administrators can keep track of who is printing what and how often. Accounting data is stored in the accounting file named by af, but you need print filters to put data in af. If you are interested in accounting, keep reading, because we have devoted Chapter 12, *Accounting, Security, and Performance*, to the topic.

Hardware setup

Of course, configuring software is only half the battle of hooking up a printer. You must also contend with printer hardware. Nearly all printers on the market today support parallel-port interfaces, and those that do not have serial interfaces.

Serial interfaces are common, and cables are easy to construct, but you will need to configure communications options and live with a generally slower data transfer rate (serial connections only transmit one bit at a time). Parallel cables are much faster because they send one byte at a time. If it is at all possible, use a parallel cable.

Parallel printer connection

Parallel cables are also referred to as *Centronics* cables after the manufacturer that popularized the standard. Connecting a printer with a parallel cable is simple because the computer connector and the printer connector are different, so the cable will not fit if you are putting it on the wrong way.

Configuring the operating system kernel to take advantage of a parallel-port is the hard part of using a parallel printer. Refer to the documentation for your operating system for detailed reconfiguration instructions.

On BSD systems, be sure to include the *lpt0* definition in the kernel configuration file, and on Linux systems with modern kernels, be sure to compile in support for the *parport* device driver.

On System V, support for parallel devices is normally configured dynamically. On a Solaris system, for example, touch */reconfigure* or use the *–r* flag and reboot.

Serial printer connections

Serial-port connections may be more complicated because you will need to determine what kind of serial cable to use between the printer and the print server. Refer to the printer documentation for details. Chances are it will be either a *straight-through* or a *null-modem* (also called a *crossover*) cable. Serial communications require you to choose the following communication parameters:

1. The speed, which may be called the baud rate

2. The number of data bits (7 or 8)

3. The number of stop bits (1 or 2)

4. The flow-control method: either hardware (also known as CTS/RTS) or software (also known as *in-band* or XON/XOFF)

Configuration on the printer may be done with DIP switches or some sort of front-panel configuration. If your manuals are not clear, a good first try is 9600 bps, no parity, 8 data bits, 1 stop bit, and software flow-control.

You need to configure your operating system kernel to support serial interfaces. On BSD systems, include the driver for the serial-port you intend to use. The following lines come from the *GENERIC* kernel configuration on OpenBSD, although FreeBSD is identical:

```
pccom0  at isa? port 0x3f8 irq 4        # standard PC serial-ports
pccom1  at isa? port 0x2f8 irq 3
pccom2  at isa? port 0x3e8 irq 5
#pccom3 at isa? port 0x2e8 irq 9        # (conflicts with some video cards)
```

On Linux, be sure to compile the serial drivers into your kernel. A kernel module could be dynamically inserted and passed parameters for the location of the device at runtime.

Remote Printer Configuration

Remote printers are much simpler to configure than local printers. All that you need to do is use the **rm** and **rp** capabilities to point *lpd* at the remote queue. Example 3-5 shows a *printcap* entry for a queue called *laserwriter* on *printhost*. To set up a client machine, you would use a printcap file similar to Example 3-6, which sets **rm** and **rp** to *printhost* and *laserwriter*, respectively.

Example 3-6. printcap File for a Remote Queue

```
remote-laserwriter|lp|LaserWriter on printhost:\
        :rm=printhost:\
        :rp=laserwriter:\
        :sd=/var/spool/lpd/lw:\
        :sh:\
        :mx#0:\
```

The *remote-laserwriter* queue on the client will accept jobs and then pass them off to the *laserwriter* queue on *printhost*.

Printers with Network Interfaces

Modern workstations are capable of generating huge print jobs. Graphics files would take far too long to print if it were necessary to connect each printer to a parallel-port on the server. As a result, many modern printers have high-speed network interfaces.

Frequently, printers with network interfaces support the LPD protocol and can be used as a remote printer in the *printcap* file. The **rm** capability would refer to the hostname or IP address of the printer, and the **rp** would be the *lpd* queue name the printer presents to the world. A common set of remote queue names is *ps* for PostScript jobs, *pcl* for HP PCL jobs, and *auto* for automatic language selection. Different manufacturers may also use names like *raw* for the printer's native language and *ascii* for simple text jobs. Before setting up a LAN printer in *printcap*, you need to consult your documentation for the appropriate remote queue name.

Example 3-7 shows a sample *printcap* file for a print server connecting to a network printer. In the example, the printer is given the hostname *phaser340*, and the remote queue name is *ps*.

Example 3-7. printcap File for LAN Printer

```
phaser|colorprinter|phaser340 in the CAD lab:\
    :lp=:/dev/null\
    :rm=Phaser340:\
    :rp=PS:\
    :mx#0:\
    :lf=/usr/spool/lpd/log:\
    :sd=/usr/spool/lpd/colorprinter:
```

 Although network printers allow you to have individual hosts spool jobs to the printer with the LPD protocol, it is better to have individual hosts all spool to a central print server.

If all clients use a central print server, troubleshooting is much easier for you, and accounting and monitoring are possible.

Permission to Spool from Over There (/etc/hosts.lpd)

By default, *lpd* connection requests from remote hosts are denied. To allow remote *lpd* connections, you need to create */etc/hosts.lpd*, which has the same format as */etc/hosts.equiv. hosts.lpd* is composed of one hostname per line. Each host listed in *hosts.lpd* is allowed to print to any printer on the print server. Blanket permission can be given to all other hosts by using the plus sign (+), although doing so is not a wonderful idea.

System V Release 4 Printing: lp

System V printing is originally derived from the AT&T spooler. Before diving into details, there are a few terms to understand, some of which are used differently from the BSD world. System V printing is far more complex than BSD printing. In this section, we describe the basic System V printing system, as implemented on Solaris 7. We base our discussion on Solaris for two reasons: Sun's commanding market share, and the fact that we own Sun systems.

In the System V world, a printer is not a piece of equipment that puts images on pages. To the System V spooler, a *printer* is a logical name associated with an interface file. The interface file is then associated with the printer.

Printers are organized into *classes* when using the System V spooler. One or more printers can be assigned to a class, although class assignment is not necessary. When printers are organized in a class, the spooler directs jobs to the first available printer in the class.

Print jobs are sent to *destinations*, which may be a specific printer or a class of printers. Requests sent to a specific printer can only be printed by that one printer, but requests to a printer class will be printed by the first available member of that class.

Submitting Jobs with lp

Print jobs in System V are called *requests*. With System V spoolers, requests are given *request IDs* for identification. Request IDs are composed of the printer name and a number, such as *LaserWriter-47*. Requests are numbered on a per-system basis. If a system handles multiple queues, the number component of the request ID will increment for each job, even if jobs are sent to different queues.

Basic job submission with *lp* is simple. Name the file to be printed, and specify the printer with the –*d* option to select the destination:*

```
[gast@systemv ~]$ lp -d LaserWriter words.txt
request id is LaserWriter-47 (1 file(s))
[gast@systemv ~]$ lp -d TekPhaser color-pictures.ps
request id is TekPhaser-48 (1 file(s))
```

Because it is a hassle to specify the destination with every print command, *lp* will use the LPDEST environment variable as the default printer:†

```
[gast@systemv ~]$ LPDEST=LaserWriter; export LPDEST
[gast@systemv ~]$ lp more-words.txt
request id is LaserWriter-49 (1 file(s))
```

Anatomy of a System V Request

A major difference between a BSD print job and a System V request is that by default, the System V spooler does not copy the file to be printed to the spool directory. A side effect of this behavior is that a file can be modified while it is in

---

* When using the System V Release 3 print commands, no spaces can appear between the option and its value (–d *printername*). System V Release 4 allows a space to appear (–d *printername*), which improves readability. We will stick to the Release 4 syntax for two reasons: because we find it easier to read and because System V Release 3 is too antiquated for use on a modern network.

† Print clients use destination information in a very specific manner. See *printers(4)* and *printers.conf(4)* in the standard Unix reference manual for details.

the print queue and the modified version will be printed. The generic job flow through the System V spooler is illustrated in Figure 3-2.

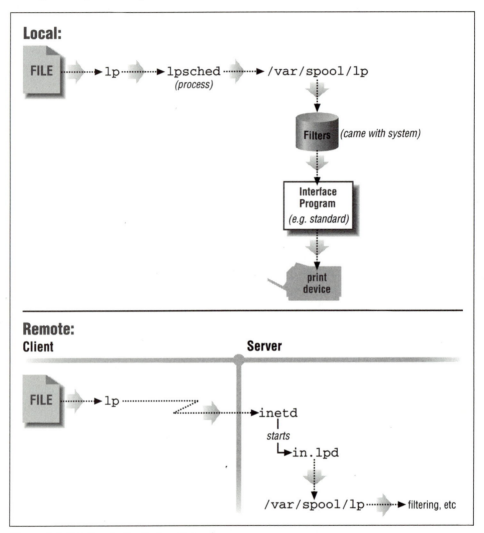

Figure 3-2. Job flow in the System V spooler

Requests are spooled in the */var/spool/lp/requests* directory. The *requests* directory is further subdivided into directories for each print server; on a machine called *printhost*, requests are stored in */var/spool/lp/requests/printhost*:

```
[gast@systemv ~]$ lp words.txt
request id is laser-6 (1 file(s))
[gast@systemv ~]$ su -
# lp -d laser words.txt
request id is laser-7 (1 file(s))
```

```
# ls /var/spool/lp/requests/printhost
1-0   2-0   3-0   4-0   5-0   6-0   7-0
```

Each file contains information about a request:

```
# cd /var/spool/lp/requests/printhost/
# cat 7-0
laser-7
0
root
1
2620
955570050
printhost
# cat 6-0
laser-6
1001
gast
1
1037
955561390
printhost
```

Here's the general format of the print request description in */var/spool/lp/requests*:

```
request ID of job
User ID
User name
group ID
size
Unix time (seconds past the epoch at January 1, 1970)
The host from which the job was sent.
```

Requests are held in */var/spool/lp/tmp/systemname* until printed. For the request *laser-5* on *printhost*, an entry will be made in */var/spool/lp/tmp/printhost/5-0*:

```
# cd /var/spool/lp/tmp/printhost
# cat 5-0
C 1
D laser
F /root/words.txt
P 20
T words.txt
t simple
U root
s    0000
v 2
```

As in the BSD spooler, each line begins with a letter. The format of the request spool file is similar to the request log. A complete listing of the letters in the request log file is shown in Table 3-5.

Table 3-5. Common Letters in System V Request Spool File

Letter	Meaning
C	Number of copies requested.
D	Destination of the job; either a printer or a class, or the word any.
F	Name of the file printed. If a print request contains multiple files, it will have multiple F lines.
P	Priority of request.
T	Banner page title.
t	Content type in files.
U	Username of request submitter.
s	Flag used for print status; see Figure 3-3.

Requests submitted with lp -c

As discussed previously, System V by default does not copy the file to the spool directory, so changes are printed out. If *lp −c* is used, then the print file is copied to */var/spool/lp/tmp*. The files stored in */var/spool/lp/tmp* have the form:

```
request number-file number
```

When *lp* is used in its default mode, only one file is used in a request, and it is given file number 0. If *lp −c* is used, each print file is also copied into */var/spool/lp/tmp*.

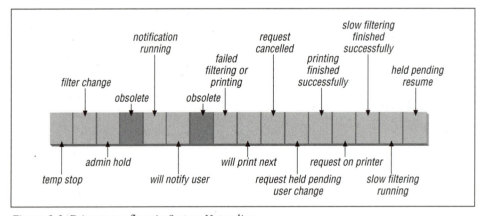

Figure 3-3. Print status flags in System V spooling

In this example, *lp* is used with the *−c* option. As a result, the file *words.txt* will be copied to */var/spool/lp/tmp/printhost/8-1*, and the copied file is used by the spooler.

```
[gast@systemv ~]$ lp -c words.txt
request id is laser-8 (1 file(s))
[gast@systemv ~]$ su -
# cd /var/spool/lp/tmp/printhost
```

```
# ls 8*
8-0 8-1
# cat 8-0
C 1
D laser
F /var/spool/lp/tmp/printhost/8-1
P 20
T 8-1
t simple
U gast
s   0000
v 2
```

Request logging

Requests are logged by *lpsched* in */var/spool/lp/logs/requests*. A typical request log entry is shown in the next example. Like the request spool file, each line begins with a character from Table 3-5:

```
= laser-12, uid 1001, gid 1, size 1037, Wed Apr 12 13:07:30 PDT 2000
z laser
C 1
D laser
F /export/home/gast/words.txt
P 20
T words.txt
t simple
U gast
s 0x0010
v 2
```

The Printer Scheduling Daemon (lpsched)

In the System V world, *lpsched* sends print job data to printers. *lpsched* is analogous to *lpd* in the Berkeley world. *lpsched* monitors spool directories and pick up new requests. *lpsched* must be started at boot time to offer System V print services. On Solaris 7, *lpsched* is started by */etc/rc.d/rc2.d/S80lp*. On Solaris 7, all requests are logged in */var/spool/lp/logs*.

Stopping Print Service (lpshut)

Usage: `lpshut`

lpshut stops print services by killing *lpsched*, like killing all running copies of *lpd* on a BSD system. When *lpshut* is run, jobs are maintained on disk so that when *lpsched* is restarted, queued jobs will be printed. Any requests that were in progress when *lpshut* was run are reprinted from the beginning:

```
printhost:/# lpshut
Line printer scheduler stopped
```

LP Configuration Utility (lpadmin)

lpadmin is the general purpose System V printer-administration tool. Like *lpc* in the BSD spooler, it can take several forms depending on the task being performed.

Adding a new printer

Usage: `lpadmin -p` *printer* `[`*options*`]`

To add a local printer, you must first configure the device that the printer will use. The printer device should be owned by the *lp* user, with permissions of 600. When adding a new printer, you will need an interface script, which is supplied by the printer vendor and placed in */var/spool/lp/model*. When specifying the printer, you can also specify a model name with the *−m* flag to *lpadmin*. The standard model is shipped by Sun with Solaris 7 and provides a vanilla interface. The next example shows how to add a local printer with *lpadmin*; */dev/printer* is a symbolic link to the actual printer device, for the purpose of clarity:

```
printhost:/# chmod 600 /dev/printer
printhost:/# lpadmin -p test2 -v/dev/printer -mstandard
```

Adding a network printer with System V is simple: use the *−s* option to *lpadmin* to specify the server, as shown in this example. Although it is a bit ahead of schedule to mention, the *lpstat* command will tell you if the remote server is responding or not (*deadserver* is a fictitious server that does not exist, which guarantees that it will not respond):

```
printhost:/# lpadmin -p hp1 -s printserver
printhost:/# lpstat -p hp1
printer hp1 is idle. enabled since Apr 12 16:45 2000. available.
printhost:/# lpadmin -p hp2 -s deadserver
printhost:/# lpstat -p hp2
printer hp2 faulted printing hp2-0. enabled since Apr 12 16:47 2000. available.
        server deadserver not responding
```

After adding a printer, you must allow it to accept and print jobs by using the *accept* and *enable* commands.

Setting the default printer with lpadmin -d

Usage: `lpadmin -d` *printer*

To set a printer as the default system printer, run *lpadmin −d* and specify the new default printer as an argument. The effect of this command is that */etc/printers.conf* will have a *_default* line specifying the system default printer:

```
laser:\
        :bsdaddr=printhost,laser,Solaris:
_default:\
        :use=laser:
```

Removing a printer with lpadmin -x

Usage: `lpadmin -x printer`

A printer cannot be removed if it has pending requests. Requests must either be deleted with the *cancel* command or moved to a different queue with *lpmove*.

Getting Status Information (lpstat)

lpstat blends the functionality from both *lpc* and *lpq* in the BSD world. *lpstat* does not perform administrative tasks, but you will run it frequently to determine what administrative action to take with other commands.

Finding the default print job destination: lpstat -d

Usage: `lpstat -d`

lpstat –d prints out the default destination for print jobs:

```
[gast@printhost ~]$ lpstat -d
system default destination: laser
```

Is lpsched running? lpstat -r lets you know

Usage: `lpstat -r`

lpstat –r tells you whether or not the scheduling daemon is running:

```
[gast@printhost ~]$ lpstat -r
scheduler is running
```

Getting printer status information: lpstat -ta

Usage: `lpstat -ta`

lpstat –ta prints out status for each printer on the system. You will see what the device for each printer is, whether the printer is accepting jobs, and whether the printer is busy printing output:

```
printhost:/# lpstat -ta
scheduler is running
system default destination: LaserWriter630
device for HP650C: /dev/null
device for LaserWriter630: /dev/null
device for Phaser: /dev/null
HP650C accepting requests since Oct  4 12:35
LaserWriter630 accepting requests since Oct  4 12:35
Phaser accepting requests since Oct  4 12:34
printer HP650C is idle.  enabled since Aug 18 19:20
printer LaserWriter630 is idle.  enabled since Oct  5 13:04
printer Phaser is idle.  enabled since Mar  5 14:56
```

Print queue contents with lpstat -o and lpstat -R

Usage: `lpstat -o [-R] [printer]`

With no options, *lpstat* displays only the print jobs submitted by a user. This is only moderately useful because most users want to know what jobs are in the queue around them. *lpstat –o* shows all output jobs on the system:

```
[gast@printhost ~]$ lpstat -o
laser-16                gast             2821    Apr 12 16:11
laser-17                gast            13312    Apr 12 17:57
squiggle-18             root            92352    Apr 12 17:55
```

What is more important to a user, though, is the position of print jobs in the queue, which can be displayed by adding the *–R* option:

```
[gast@printhost ~]$ lpstat -o -R
laser-16                gast             2821    Apr 12 16:11
laser-17                gast            13312    Apr 12 17:57
squiggle-18             root            92352    Apr 12 17:55
1 laser-16              gast             2821    Apr 12 16:11
2 laser-17              gast            13312    Apr 12 17:57
```

lp Revisited: Reordering Jobs with –H

Usage: `lp -i request-ID -H [hold | resume | immediate]`

Preferential job treatment is requested in System V with the *lp* command. By using the *–H* option to *lp*, special handling is requested for a job. A job can be *held*, in which case it will not be printed until it is released for output with *resume*, or it can be moved to the top of a queue with the *immediate* option.

Only *lp* and *root* can use the immediate form of *lp –H*, which moves the specified job to the head of the queue:

```
printhost:/# lp -i laser-17 -H immediate
printhost:/# lpstat -o
laser-17                gast            13312    Apr 12 17:57
laser-16                gast             2821    Apr 12 18:14
```

If a second job is moved to the head of the queue with *–H immediate*, then it will take precedence over the first job moved. If you want to reorder several jobs, move the lowest priority job first and work up to the highest priority.

Deleting Print Requests: cancel

Usage: `cancel request-ID` or `cancel destination`

The *cancel* utility deletes print requests from a queue. *cancel* may be used in two different forms. The first form cancels one specific request ID:

```
printhost:/# lpstat laser
laser-60 root      118   Oct  5 14:30
```

```
laser-61 root       118   Oct  5 14:32
laser-62 root      3643   Oct  5 14:33
laser-63 root       843   Oct  5 14:33
printhost:/# cancel laser-60
laser-60 cancelled
```

The second form of *cancel* deletes all of a user's jobs on the specified destination.

To cancel a print request, *cancel* will talk to the printer daemon. Because Solaris launches the printer daemon with *inetd*, there must be an entry in */etc/inetd.conf* to start *in.lpd* when incoming connections arrive. As a practical matter, *inetd.conf* must contain an entry that looks something like this:

```
printer stream tcp nowait root \
    /usr/lib/print/in.lpd in.lpd
```

Allowing cancel requests from a network

By default, users can only cancel print requests that they made and only from the host on which a request was submitted. (Of course, this limitation does not apply to *root*.) If this is inconvenient, system administrators can set *user-equivalence=true* in */etc/printers.conf* on the print server. When *user-equivalence* is true, users can cancel any job associated with their name from any print client.

On Solaris, */etc/printers.conf* should not be edited directly; instead, *lpset* should be used:

```
printhost:/# lpset -a user-equivalence=true printhost
printhost:/# cat /etc/printers.conf
#
#        If you hand edit this file, comments and structure may change.
#        The preferred method of modifying this file is through the use of
#        lpset(1M) or fncreate_printer(1M)
#
laser:\
        :bsdaddr=printhost,laser,Solaris:
_default:\
        :use=laser:
printhost:\
        :user-equivalence=true:
```

Using enable and disable to Control Printing

Usage: `enable printer`

`disable [-r reason] printer`

enable and *disable* control the submission of jobs from the queue to printers; they are equivalent to *lpc stop* and *lpc start* on the Berkeley spooler. Because they control the flow of jobs from a print server to the print device, both *enable* and *disable* must be run on print servers. Running them on a print client will have no effect. Jobs in progress when *disable* is run will be reprinted from the beginning. When using *disable*, the system administrator may also specify a reason for disabling the printer with the *−r* option. This provides information to print users, so they may choose to *cancel* their requests and resubmit them to a different printer if necessary:

```
printhost:/# disable -r "Out of toner" LaserWriter630
printer 'LaserWriter' now disabled
printhost:/# lpstat -p LaserWriter630
printer LaserWriter disabled since Wed Apr 12 15:16:19 PDT 2000. available.
        Out of toner
printhost:/# enable LaserWriter
printer 'LaserWriter' now enabled
printhost:/# lpstat -p LaserWriter
printer LaserWriter is idle. enabled since Wed Apr 12 15:19:07 PDT 2000.
available.
```

Using accept and reject to Control Queuing

Usage: accept *printer*

reject [−r *reason*] *printer*

accept and *reject* are the System V equivalent of *lpc enable* and *lpc disable*. They control whether new jobs may be submitted to a queue. Like *enable* and *disable*, they must be run on print servers. Here is an example of the usage of *accept* and *reject*:

```
printhost:/# reject -r"Installing new ink cartridges" HP650C
destination 'HP650C' will no longer accept requests
printhost:/# lpstat -a
HP650C not accepting requests since Wed Apr 12 15:31:18 PDT 2000
        Installing new ink cartridges
printhost:/# exit
[gast@printhost ~]$ lp -d HP650C words.txt
HP650C: queue is disabled
[gast@printhost ~]$ lpstat -a
HP650C not accepting requests since Wed Apr 12 15:31:18 PDT 2000
        Installing new ink cartridges
[gast@printhost ~]$ su -
printhost:/# accept HP650C
destination "HP650C" now accepting requests
printhost:/# lpstat -a
HP650C accepting requests since Wed Apr 12 15:35:29 PDT 2000
```

Moving Print Requests with lpmove

Usage: lpmove *request-ID destination*

lpmove *old-destination new-destination*

lpmove has no analog in the BSD spooler; it moves requests between queues; it can only move jobs on the local system, so it must be run on print servers. Some *lpmove* implementations require the administrator to shut down printing before using them. The first form of *lpmove* moves a single print request to a new queue:

```
[gast@printhost ~]$ lp words.txt
request id is laser-63 (1 file(s))
[gast@printhost ~]$ su -
printhost:/# lpmove laser-63 Phaser
total of 1 requests moved to Phaser
```

The second form of *lpmove* takes all the requests for one destination and moves them to another, which makes it convenient for moving requests from a queue you plan to shut down and delete from the print spooler:

```
[gast@printhost ~]$ lp words.txt
request id is laser-63 (1 file(s))
[gast@printhost ~]$ lp more-words.txt
request id is laser-64 (1 file(s))
[gast@printhost ~]$ lp does-he-ever-shut-up.txt
request id is laser-65 (1 file(s))
[gast@printhost ~]$ su -
printhost:/# lpmove laser deskjet
move in progress ...
total of 3 requests moved from laser to deskjet
```

lpmove does not check that the new queue is accepting jobs, but it will not move requests with options the new destination cannot handle.

BSD to System V Translator for System Administrators

Table 3-6 translates printer usage and administration commands between the BSD and System V idioms.

Table 3-6. BSD to System V Print Administration Translations

Task	BSD	System V
Print a file.	lpr *filename*	lp *filename*
Print a file to a specific printer.	lpr -P *printer filename*	lp -d *printer filename*
Changing the default printer for a user.	Set the PRINTER environment variable.	Set the LPDEST[a] environment variable
Change the system default print destination.	Edit */etc/printcap* and add the *lp* alias to the new default printer. Remember to remove it from the old one!	lpadmin -d *printer*
See what is in a print queue.	lpq -P *printer*	lpstat -o *printer*

Table 3-6. BSD to System V Print Administration Translations (continued)

Task	BSD	System V
Delete a pending job.	`lprm` *job-number* (May also use `-P` to specify queue.)	`cancel` *request-ID*
Add a new printer to the system.	Create the */etc/printcap* entry.	`lpadmin -p`
Remove a printer.	Comment out or delete */etc/printcap* entry.	`lpadmin -x`
Stop spooling on a queue.	`lpc disable`	`reject`
Begin spooling.	`lpc enable`	`accept`
Start a printer.	`lpc start`	`enable`
Stop printer.	`lpc stop`	`disable`
Configure remote printing.	Add `rm` and `rp` tags in */etc/printcap*.	`lpadmin -p -S`
Get status information.	`lpc status`	`lpstat`
Main spool location.	*/var/spool/lpd*	*/var/spool/lp*
Location of printer definitions.	*/etc/printcap*	*/etc/lp/printers* & *terminfo* database

a Some System V implementations, such as Solaris, consult both the `LPDEST` environment variable and the `PRINTER` environment variable, with `LPDEST` taking priority.

Microsoft TCP/IP Printing

With Windows NT 4.0, Microsoft has included the TCP/IP Printing Service, which allows Windows NT machines to print to Unix servers running *lpd*, or Unix workstations to print to NT.*

Installing the Microsoft TCP/IP Printing Service

Microsoft TCP/IP Printing is not installed by default, so the first step in using it is to install it. Log on as *Administrator*, go to the *Network* control panel (Start → Settings → Control Panel, then double-click the *Network* icon), click on the *Services* tab, and click Add. The dialog box you will see is shown in Figure 3-4. Select the *Microsoft TCP/IP Printing* item.

When you click OK, Windows copies files from the NT CD-ROM and return you to the *Network* dialog. Under services, there should now be a listing for *Microsoft TCP/IP Printing*. Click Close and restart your system.

---

* As we use it in this section, an NT *workstation* is a machine running Windows NT. It may be running either NT Workstation or NT Server.

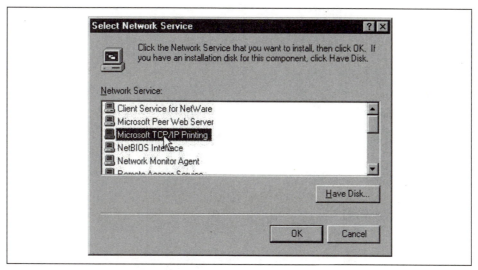

Figure 3-4. Network Service dialog

Printing to Unix from Windows NT

For this example, a Windows NT machine will be configured to print to the *laserwriter* queue on a host named *voyager*. Add a new printer to your Windows system by double-clicking on the *Add Printer* icon in the *Printers* folder. Add a local printer,* and click next. You should now be looking at the port selection dialog of Figure 3-5.

Click on the Add Port button, which will bring up the *Printer Ports* dialog box of Figure 3-6. Select *LPR Port* and click on the *New Port* box.

You will now see the *Add LPR Compatible Printer* dialog box of Figure 3-7. Enter the hostname or IP address in the top text box, and the queue name of the print queue on *voyager* (laserwriter) in the lower box. These two entries correspond to **rm** and **rp** variables in the *printcap* file on a Unix host with a BSD spooler.

After clicking OK, you will return to the Port dialog, but with the newly defined port checked off, as in Figure 3-8. When you click Next, it will be time to choose the driver for the remote printer.

Selecting a driver is similar to selecting a driver for any other printer on Windows. Find the correct driver in the familiar selection box of Figure 3-9 and click Next.

Now you will be asked to enter a name for this printer. It is a good idea to give some sort of descriptive name. You can also choose to have this printer be the default for the system. Once you have entered a name and selected the appropriate

---

* This is exactly the opposite of what you would expect since we are going to print to a remote printer!

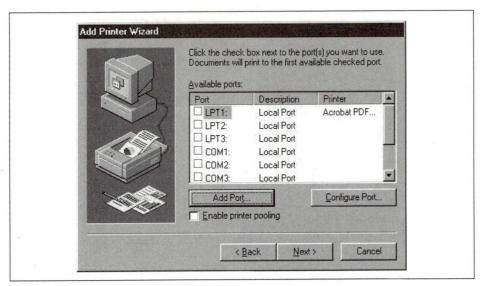

Figure 3-5. Port selection dialog

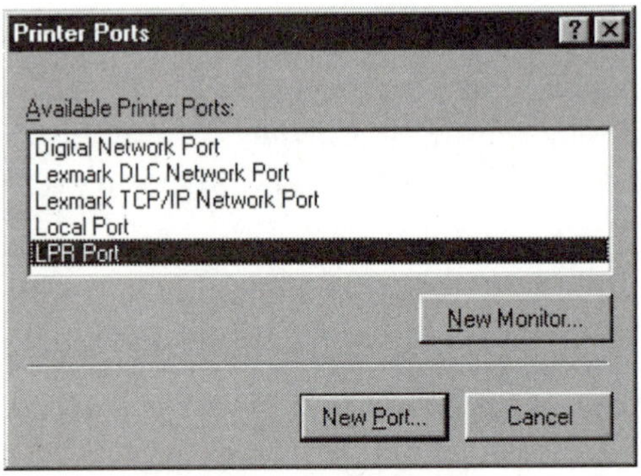

Figure 3-6. Printer Ports dialog

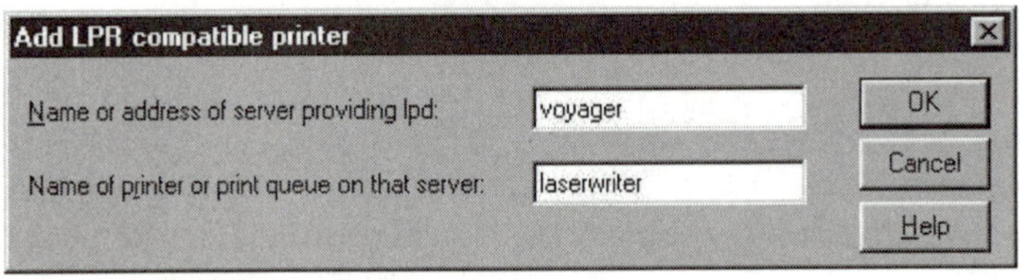

Figure 3-7. Add LPR Compatible Printer dialog

radio button for default printer, click Next. You will be asked if you would like to
share this printer with other Windows systems and, if so, the name by which this
printer should be known. Make your choice and click Next.

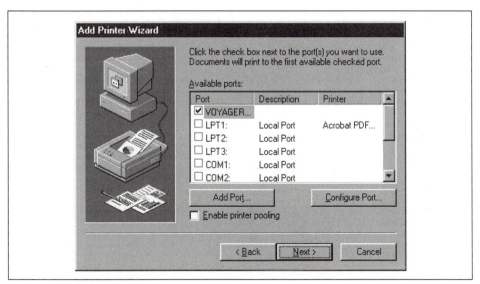

Figure 3-8. New lpd server defined in Port dialog

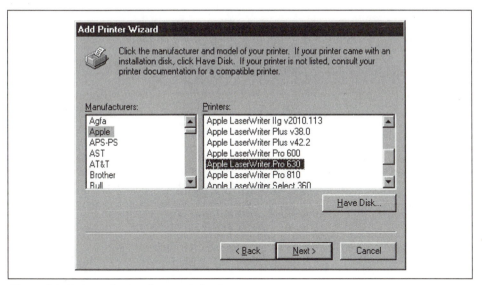

Figure 3-9. Driver selection for new lpd printer

Finally, you will be asked if you would like to send a test page to the new printer. Select Yes, and then click Finish. If all goes well, a test page will appear out of your printer with all sorts of useful information about the device and the drivers. You should have a new icon in your *Printers* folder. You may use this printer to submit jobs to a remote *lpd* server.

Printing to Windows NT from Unix

In order for Unix clients to print to a Windows NT server, the server side of *Microsoft TCP/IP Printing* needs to be installed and running on your NT machine.

Like other NT services, you may start or stop this service either using the command prompt or using the Windows NT GUI. To use the GUI, double-click on *Services* in the Control Panel. You should see a dialog box similar to Figure 3-10; select the *TCP/IP Print Server* service from the list and click Start. The service is configured to be started manually by default. If you want the service to start automatically at boot time, click the *Startup* button and select the *Automatic* setting.

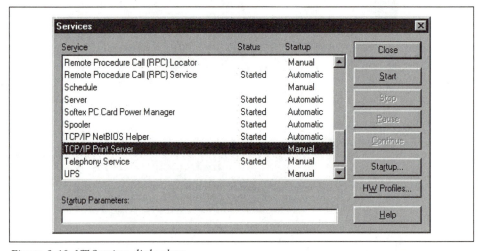

Figure 3-10. NT Services dialog box

Alternatively, you can use the command line to start and stop the service. TCP/IP print service can be started and stopped with *net start lpdsvc* and *net stop lpdsvc*, respectively.

To a Unix client, the Windows NT print server looks like a standard remote printer, so there has to be an entry in the client's */etc/printcap* file.

Extending the Berkeley Spooler with Print Filters

If the previous chapter laid the foundation of our architecture, this chapter supplies the scaffolding. Moving beyond plain text requires, as with so much else in the Unix world, a touch of scripting. The Berkeley spooler can be configured to call *filter scripts* for each print job to customize the behavior of each printer queue based on local needs. With filter scripts, print queues can process jobs in different ways depending on the content of those jobs.

Remote Printers

Local area networks were built to share expensive peripherals among a group of users. One result is that the *lpr* software supports printing to remote printers just as easily as to a local printer. Users invoke the same print commands they would for locally attached printers, but due to system administrator magic in the *printcap* file, the job is printed remotely.

Of course, it is not really magic at all—just specify the name of the remote machine and the name of the queue in the remote */etc/printcap* with the rm and rp attributes, respectively. lp should be set to */dev/null*. Here's how to set up a local queue to forward print jobs to the *laser* queue on *printers.fofz.com*:

```
lp|remote-printer:\
    :sd=/var/spool/lpd/remote-printer:\
    :rm=printers.fofz.com:\
    :rp=laser:\
    :lp=/dev/null:\
    :sh:
```

To allow printing to a server, list clients that are allowed to submit jobs in the server's */etc/hosts.lpd* or */etc/hosts.equiv*. We suggest using *hosts.lpd* because *hosts.equiv* also controls remote login privileges.

Ethernet Printers

The increasing complexity of print jobs has increased the size of the data for the average job. Modern page-description languages, combined with desktop publishing, have rendered serial and parallel communications inadequate. Transporting jobs from the print server to the printer requires higher speed communication. As a result, large, expensive, and fast printers offer the option of an Ethernet interface.

Printers that support LPD

Many Ethernet-equipped printers support the LPD protocol. You can easily use the `rm` and `rp` options to submit jobs directly to those printers over Ethernet. Typically, printers that support LPD supply several queues. For example, most HP printers have a queue named *raw* to accept raw page-description language input, such as HP PCL or PostScript. A basic configuration for such a printer is shown here:

```
lp|remote-hplj:\
      :sh:\
      :lp=/dev/null:\
      :sd=/var/spool/lpd/remote-lj:\
      :rm=lj.fofz.com:\
      :rp=raw:
```

Older HP printers and JetDirect cards do not support LPD. Instead, clients connect directly to the print engine on port 9100. The client opens a TCP stream and sends the print job through the socket to the print engine. On the stock Berkeley spooler, there is no way to support such a protocol without print filters because LPD does not support connecting to an arbitrary TCP port. When using print filters, though, a script can supply the interface to printer hardware, making the use of odd protocols possible.*

Print Filters

The Berkeley spooler allows system administrators to specify arbitrary programs to act on print jobs. The only restriction is that filter programs use standard input and standard output for their input and output, respectively. By allowing arbitrary, user-defined programs to interact with print jobs, there is no restriction on what can be done. Individual files in a job can be processed by an input filter, as shown in Figure 4-1.

Early versions of *lpr* supported application filters. By specifying the appropriate flag on the command line, *lpr* would run the appropriate application to translate

---

* System V separates processing the job data from the printer interface by calling two separate scripts. An *interface script* defines how the spooling daemon should interact with the printer hardware, while filter scripts manipulate only job data.

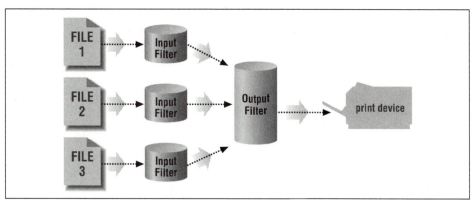

Figure 4-1. Print filters in the Berkeley spooler

the job file to a format understood by the printer. Magic filters* have supplanted application specific filters because there is no need for command line flags, and there are far fewer user education requirements. With magic filters, *lpd* determines what application to run from the file type. No user intervention (or knowledge) is needed.

The Mystery of Strange Output

A standard Unix text file ends each line with the newline character. Unfortunately, many printers will interpret newline characters as directives to "advance the paper one line" and nothing more. The printer advances the paper, but the print head is not returned to the beginning of the line, resulting in a piece of paper with lines of text that resemble a staircase:

```
Line 1.
        Line 2.
                Line 3.
```

Sending PostScript files to a non-PostScript printer results in even stranger output. Rather than what you expect from the application, pages and pages of PostScript code spew forth from the printer. Raw PostScript is printed when clients send jobs to non-PostScript printers. Avoiding this problem is simple, though, as we will see in the next section.

---

* Filters that can automatically determine the action to take based on the type of file they are acting on are generally known as magic filters. The "magic" referred to is the ability to determine a file's type using its "magic" number.

Solution: Print Filters

Strange output is often the result of improper processing. For text files, the instructions sent to the printer should end each line with both a carriage return to return the print head to the left margin and a line feed to advance the paper one line. For PostScript, jobs should be passed to PostScript printers unchanged, but translated to the printer's native language if PostScript is unsupported by the destination.

The designers of the Berkeley spooler anticipated changing technology by allowing system administrators to specify helper programs, called print filters, to process the input and output. Print filters are programs that take the print job on standard input, do some processing, and send out a modified print job on standard output.

A simple script for destaircasing

To eliminate the staircase effect, a filter script needs to replace the newline character at the end of each line with a carriage return plus a newline. This can be accomplished with this short Perl script:

```
#!/usr/local/bin/perl
#
# destaircaser perl script
#
while(<STDIN>) {
    chop $_; # remove last character (the newline)
    print "$_\r\n";# insert carriage return and replace the newline
};
# Some text printers may not end the job automatically, so you may need
# to add a form feed at the end of the job.
print "\f";
```

After saving the above Perl script in */var/spool/lpd* as *destaircaser.pl* and making it executable (*chmod 755 destaircaser.pl*), add an `if` line to */etc/printcap* telling *lpd* to run *destaircaser.pl* on each print job, as in Example 4-1.

Example 4-1. Using destaircaser.pl

```
lp|sc|staircaser|:\
    :sd=/var/spool/lpd/sc:\
    :mx#0:\
    :lp=/dev/lp0:\
    :if=/var/spool/lpd/destaircaser:\
    :sh:
```

A more complicated example: virtual PostScript printers

When dealing with PostScript files and non-PostScript printers, Ghostscript is your salvation. Ghostscript is a full PostScript interpreter that takes a set of PostScript commands and creates bitmapped output that can be sent to a printer in its native language. The Ghostscript home page is *http://www.cs.wisc.edu/~ghost/*.

Ghostscript supports many, but not all, common printer languages. Check the supported hardware list on the Ghostscript home page. Even if support for a printer is not explicit, the printer may emulate a printer that is fully supported. For example, one of the authors owns an HP LaserJet 6P. This printer does not appear on the supported list, but the *ljet4* driver produces HP PCL output that can be understood and printed by the 6P.* If you need help selecting a Ghostscript driver, see Greg Taylor's Printing HOWTO Support Database at *http://www.picante.com/~gtaylor/pht/printer_list.cgi*.

 HP's PCL is supported on all HP printers and is a de facto standard for non-PostScript laser printers. Many non-HP printers support PCL through emulation. Older dot-matrix printers are often compatible with the Epson control language.

Interpreting PostScript is inherently dangerous because you are essentially running a program of potentially unknown or hostile origin. To eliminate many of the headaches, the authors of Ghostscript include a flag, *–dSAFER*, to prevent most of the bad stuff.

Print filters cannot accept command line arguments. Passing command line arguments requires the use of a wrapper script. The next example shows a simple wrapper script to run the main Ghostscript executable *gs* with an argument to specify the driver used:

```
#!/bin/sh
gs -dSAFER -sDEVICE=ljet4 -sOutputFile=- -
```

The trailing dash is the input file for the *gs* executable; it specifies that input should be taken from standard input.

 PostScript interpretation can be CPU-intensive, so you may wish to establish a dedicated Ghostscript server.

---

* Both the LaserJet 4 series and the LaserJet 6 series use PCL level 5e.

Running a filter for remote printers

lpd does not run the input filter for jobs sent to remote printers. Unfortunately, printers with built-in *lpd* support do not apply any filters. To send a PostScript file to a PCL printer, Ghostscript must first process the job. Running a local filter before forwarding the job to a remote printer requires the use of two queues. One queue is exposed locally to applications. Jobs submitted to the first queue are processed by the input filter and forwarded to the second queue by the filter script. The second queue forwards the job on to the remote printer. Here is an example of how to run an input filter for a remote printer:

```
lp|lj6:\
    :sh:\
    :lp=/dev/null:\
    :sd=/var/spool/lpd/lj6:\
    :if=/var/spool/lpd/send-to-remote-lj6:
lj6-remote:\
    :sh:\
    :lp=/dev/null:\
    :sd=/var/spool/lpd/lj6-remote:\
    :rm=printers:\
    :rp=raw:
```

send-to-remote-lj6 translates PostScript to PCL and then submits the PCL data to the *lj6-remote* queue on the machine *printers*. One possible implementation is shown in this example:

```
#!/bin/sh
gs -q -dSAFER -sDEVICE=ljet4 -sOutputFile=- - | lpr -Plj6-remote
```

Older Ethernet printers with no lpd support

For printers that accept raw print jobs on a TCP port, use the *netcat* utility to send the contents of the job to remote socket. Instead of using *lpr* to forward the job to the remote printer, use *netcat* as shown here:

```
#!/bin/sh
gs -q -dSAFER -sDEVICE=ljet4 -sOutputFile=- - | nc printer.fofz.com 9100
```

A footnote: HylaFAX

The *sendfax* program distributed with *HylaFAX* can take a PostScript file and transmit it via faxmodem. By specifying a print device of */dev/null* and using a filter that runs *sendfax*, print servers become fax servers. *HylaFAX* is available from *http://www.hylafax.org*.

Print Filters for Organizations on a Budget

In some cases, even the flexibility of custom scripts and programs will not save the day. Fitting printers with host-based rendering into the Unix spooling regime forces the use of dirty hacks.

Printers that cannot be attached to Unix servers

Some printers on the market require the use of Microsoft Windows. Vendors of these printers take intelligence out of the printer and write a software driver to replace that functionality. The advantage is cost, but the disadvantage is that some vendors only write software drivers for Windows. If somebody "saved" money by purchasing a printer that can only be used with drivers for Microsoft Windows, filters and job redirection can still allow the use of a central Unix print server.

Unix servers can accept PostScript jobs from the network and submit them to a Windows queue by using Samba.* Secondary Windows rendering servers then submit the PostScript data to the Windows version of Ghostscript, and the vendor's GDI driver then renders the job for the print engine. Compared to purchasing a printer with an on-board rendering engine, this strategy is lacking. Jobs must hop through two print servers, which means two points of failure. (One of those points even runs Windows!) Inexpensive parallel-port printers that can be used by Unix are easy to find, and do not cost substantially more than a Windows-only printer, especially after adding up the value of time spent on the care and feeding of the Windows-only printer and the Windows server host.

HP's Printing Performance Architecture

HP's Printing Performance Architecture (PPA) is a special case of a printer that can't be attached to a Unix print server. Like other Windows-specific printers, PPA moves the rendering step from the printer itself to a host computer, cutting the cost of hardware. PPA drivers exist only for Windows operating systems, so Unix hosts cannot talk directly to PPA printers.

Although not aesthetically (or technologically) pleasing, print filters allow enough translation to send PostScript jobs to PPA printers. First, Ghostscript renders the jobs into Portable Bit Map (PBM) graphics files. Next, use Tim Norman's PBM-to-PPA package, which translates PBM data into PPA printer-specific bitmaps. The package is freely available under the GPL from *http://www.httptech.com/ppa*. (In the end, you could also decide your time is valuable enough to buy a PCL or PostScript printer, too.)

---

* Nothing prevents submitting jobs to a Macintosh queue using *netatalk*, except that it is silly to send a job to a Macintosh server when the Unix server could send a job directly to a network printer using the AppleTalk protocols.

Magic Filters

Building a universal print server requires universal print filters. A print queue should be generic and respond to the data submitted, rather than requiring users to know the details of filter configuration. To return to the ideal print server, jobs should just print.

Baby Steps: Application Specific Filters

Some versions of *lpr* have application specific filters, which allow users to choose specific handling of job files. After informing *lpr* that the job is of a particular type, *lpr* will run helper programs to translate the job to a format understood by the printer. When users have the ability to select the appropriate command line options, application specific filters are adequate. Even for experienced users, however, application specific filters are cumbersome. For flexibility and ease of use, magic filters were developed.

Magic Filters: Application Specific Filters on Steroids

Magic filters use the magic number* of the input file to determine the input file type and run the appropriate programs to ensure that the output from the queue is intelligible to your printer hardware. Magic filter scripts fork sub-programs, which may be either scripts or binary programs, to process the output. Magic filters are not complicated—they are only a way to associate a set of file types with the methods for processing them.

Magic filters have several advantages over application-specific filters. Scripts and applications just run *lpr* without concerning themselves with setting the appropriate command line flags. Only one magic queue is needed. In addition to saving time setting up the Unix queues in the first place, it also means that additional software packages are easier to configure because they only need to print to one queue. Last but definitely not least, magic filters make the administration task easier by centralizing job processing logic on the print server.

Installing APS Filter

One widely used magic filter package is Andreas Klemm's APS Filter. It has an easy menu-driven installation that automatically checks for prerequisites and sets up */etc/printcap* and the spool directories.

---

* See the man page for *file(1)*.

Before attempting to install APS Filter, Berkeley-style printing must be installed and configured. For use with non-PostScript printers, Ghostscript is a necessity. There are two versions of Ghostscript on the market. Aladdin Ghostscript contains the most current drivers and is free for non-commercial use, which prevents its inclusion in many OS distributions. Aladdin Software gives older versions to the Free Software Foundation to distribute as GNU Ghostscript. To use a new printer with a new printer language version, an upgrade to the commercial version of Ghostscript is necessary:

1. Get the source. APS Filter is available from *ftp://metalab.unc.edu/pub/Linux/ system/printing*. Get the tar file and move it to */usr/local/lib* and uncompress it.

2. Choose a Ghostscript driver. Simply run the *SETUP* shell script in */usr/local/lib/ apsfilter* and follow the menu prompts. For help, consult your printer's documentation for language support info, the Ghostscript web site, or Greg Picante's PHT Support Database.

3. Configure the parallel-port interface. Setting up the printer interface is exactly the same as it is for an unfiltered queue. To find out which parallel-port to use, you can look at the kernel's boot messages to find the parallel-port at I/O port 0x378, which is *LPT1:* under MS-DOS. To check what parallel-port devices may be installed, look in the kernel boot messages and search for the string *lp*:

   ```
   FreeBSD:~$ dmesg | grep lp
   lpt0 at 0x378-0x37f irq 7 on isa
   lpt0: Interrupt-driven port
   lp0: TCP/IP capable interface

   [root@linux ~]# dmesg | grep lp
   lp1 at 0x0378, (polling)
   ```

4. Choose paper and color. In the U.S., choose *letter*. The rest of the world should choose *A4* or *A3* as appropriate. Whether or not your printer supports color should be obvious.

5. APS Filter finishes the rest. APS Filter will build *a2ps* and *rewindstdin*, two support utilities, if they do not exist on the system. Finally, the setup routine will set up queues and */etc/printcap* for you.

How APS Filter Works

Like many other text processing tools, APS Filter is just a Perl script. In this case, the key to the Perl script is the queue name. APS Filter names queues in a particular way to aid in determining how to invoke helper programs such as Ghostscript.

A queue name looks like this: *aps-ljet4-letter-auto-mono*. The first part, *ljet4*, is the name of the Ghostscript printer driver. The second part, *letter*, is the paper size.

The third part is *auto*, *raw*, or *ascii*, depending on whether the queue will print the text as ASCII, dump it raw into the print engine, or attempt to process it according to the type of file it is. Finally, the last part tells whether the queue is color or black and white. APS Filter will assign the *lp* name to the auto queue so print jobs are automatically directed there.

The queue name

The first part of the queue name is always the letters *aps* and has no further effect on processing. The second part tells APS Filter which Ghostscript driver to use so that Ghostscript speaks the appropriate (non-PostScript) printer language. The third part tells APS Filter what size the paper is, which is used for passing options to Ghostscript. Examples would be *letter* for U.S. letter size paper and *A4* for A4 size paper. The *auto |raw |ascii* setting determines how APS Filter will process the job. *raw* jobs are sent directly to the printer engine without any processing. *ascii* jobs are destaircased, and *auto* jobs are processed according to magic number. You can send text jobs to an *auto* queue, which is why the queue names in the APS Filter-generated *printcap* file will assign the *lp* name to the automatic queue. The *color |gray |mono* setting tells APS Filter whether or not the printer supports color.

The queue name *aps-ljet4-letter-auto-mono* would use the LaserJet4 (PCL 5) driver to print a black and white image on US letter size paper, and would be able to interpret a wide variety of file formats.

Troubleshooting APS Filter

When troubleshooting filtering scripts, you should use the same techniques as for any other script or program. Validate the input at intermediate steps and check the error log files. On the BSDs and some Linux distributions, logs are stored in */var/log/ messages* and */var/log/lpd-errs* in addition to the log file kept at the location specified in */etc/printcap*. Some Linux distributions may keep system messages in */usr/ adm* or */var/adm*.

It may help to set the *PRINT_TO_FILE* variable in */usr/local/lib/apsfilter/bin/ apsfilter* to "True" to save paper during testing and troubleshooting.

If you attempt to use a Ghostscript driver that is not compiled into your Ghostscript executable, an error message similar to this will be generated:

```
Unknown Device: lj5gray
```

5

The Next Generation Berkeley Spooler: LPRng

In spite of our great fondness for the Berkeley spooler, we must admit that its age clearly shows—the stock Berkeley spooler has been in use longer than many of its users have been working with computers. Recent developments have led to one potential successor: LPRng. LPRng began life as a PLP, a reimplementation of the Berkeley spooler free of the AT&T Unix license. In the early 1990s at San Diego State University in California, Patrick Powell redesigned and rewrote the PLP code base to build a print server package that could stand up to the rigors of an academic environment.* Due to the number of changes that were made, the package was renamed LPRng in honor of its venerable ancestor.

LPRng supports the LPD protocol as described in RFC 1179, but adds several nifty features. System V command emulation enables system administrators to replace System V spoolers with Berkeley spoolers while retaining compatibility with System V print commands. Several configuration file options make it easier to manage large sites or improve scalability.

Perhaps the main strength of LPRng, though, is that it can be used to provide a unified interface to the print spooler on several different operating systems. For administrators who are more familiar with the Berkeley spooler, it offers the opportunity to replace System V spoolers with Berkeley spoolers, but such an ambitious project should not be taken lightly.

---

* That was not a joke. No better test of accounting exists than to use it in an attempt to collect money from students who don't have any.

Compiling and Installing LPRng

The first step in using any software package distributed in source form is compilation and installation. Several modern Linux distributions have, however, adopted LPRng as the standard print spooler.

Compiling Your Own Binaries

On other operating systems, especially those descended from System V, building from source is required. LPRng is freely available in source form under the GNU General Public License from *ftp://ftp.astart.com/pub/LPRng*. The latest stable distribution will be stored as *LPRng-stable.tgz*. Documentation is distributed from the same site in the file *LPRng_DOC-latest.tgz*. As this chapter was written, the latest version of LPRng was 3.6.12.*

Unpacking the source

The source is distributed as a compressed tar file. Uncompress and unpack it with *tar* and *gzip*, as shown here:

```
bastet:~/lprng$ gunzip LPRng-stable.tgz
bastet:~/lprng$ tar -xf LPRng-stable.tar
LPRng-3.6.12/
LPRng-3.6.12/src/
. . .etc. . .
```

Configuring for your system

One of our favorite trends in free software for Unix systems is the use of the GNU autoconfiguration package. Software developers include a script that runs many small test programs to determine what library calls are available and where other software is installed. GNU *autoconf* reduces configuration to running the *./configure* script in the top-level source directory. You will see a large number of tests. Here is the start of the procedure on a Sun running Solaris 7:

```
bastet:~/lprng$ cd LPRng-3.6.12
bastet:~/lprng/LPRng-3.6.12$ ./configure
creating cache ./config.cache
checking host system type... sparc-sun-solaris2.7
checking target system type... sparc-sun-solaris2.7
checking build system type... sparc-sun-solaris2.7
checking for mawk... no
checking for gawk... no
checking for nawk... nawk
checking for perl... /usr/bin/perl
. . . other tests skipped . . .
```

---

* This is a clear illustration of the rapid evolution of open source software. It is no longer sufficient to speak of current versions as books are written because several revisions may appear during the course of composing a book.

By default, LPRng will be installed in */usr/local*, but the target can be set by supplying the *–bindir* option to the *configure* script, or by editing the *Makefile* after running the *configure* script.

Compiling the code

The next step is to run *make* to build the software. Minor confusion exists because GNU *make* and Berkeley *make* are slightly different.

With GNU *make*, run *make clean all*. For BSD *make*, specify the BSD *Makefile* instead by using the *–f* option on the command line: *make -f Makefile.bsd clean all*. Here is the beginning of the procedure for Solaris 7:[*]

```
bastet:~/lprng/LPRng-3.6.12$ gmake clean all
gmake MAKETARGET=clean src man po
gmake[1]: Entering directory `/export/home/gast/LPRng-3.6.12'
gmake -C src clean
gmake[2]: Entering directory `/export/home/gast/LPRng-3.6.12/src'
rm -f *.o *.core *.a ? core lpc lpd lpq lpr lprm lpf lpraccnt pclbanner psbanner
checkpc lp lpstat lpbanner monitor ../lpd.conf sserver sclient
gmake[2]: Leaving directory `/export/home/gast/LPRng-3.6.12/src'
gmake -C man clean
gmake[2]: Entering directory `/export/home/gast/LPRng-3.6.12/man'
gmake[2]: Nothing to be done for `clean'.
gmake[2]: Leaving directory `/export/home/gast/LPRng-3.6.12/man'
gmake -C po clean
gmake[2]: Entering directory `/export/home/gast/LPRng-3.6.12/po'
gmake[2]: Nothing to be done for `clean'.
gmake[2]: Leaving directory `/export/home/gast/LPRng-3.6.12/po'
gmake[1]: Leaving directory `/export/home/gast/LPRng-3.6.12'
gmake -C src all
gmake[1]: Entering directory `/export/home/gast/LPRng-3.6.12/src'
gcc -g -O2 -g -Wall -DHAVE_CONFIG_H -DLOCALEDIR=\"/usr/local/share/locale\" -DLPD_
CONF_PATH=\"/usr/local/etc/lpd.conf\" -DLPD_PERMS_PATH=\"/usr/local/etc/lpd.perms\
" -DPRINTCAP_PATH=\"/usr/local/etc/printcap\" -DLPD_PRINTCAP_PATH=\"/usr/local/
etc/lpd_printcap\" -DFORCE_LOCALHOST=\"1\" -DREQUIRE_CONFIGFILES=\"1\" -I.. -I./
include   -c -o lpc.o ./common/lpc.c
. . . lots of other stuff skipped. . .
```

Installation

As *root*, run *make* again to install the binaries to the location specified in the *Makefile*. If your system uses a BSD derived version of *make*, use *Makefile.bsd*:

```
bastet:~/lprng/LPRng-3.6.12$ su -
Password:
Sun Microsystems Inc.   SunOS 5.7       Generic October 1998
# gmake install
gmake MAKETARGET=install src man po
```

---

[*] When GNU *make* is installed on Solaris systems, it is often named *gmake* to distinguish it from the version of *make* shipped with the operating system.

```
gmake[1]: Entering directory `/export/home/gast/LPRng-3.6.12'
gmake -C src install
gmake[2]: Entering directory `/export/home/gast/LPRng-3.6.12/src'
echo "SETUID_ROOT IS SUID_ROOT_PERMS, PERMS 04755 -o root";
SETUID_ROOT IS SUID_ROOT_PERMS, PERMS 04755 -o root
for i in /usr/local/bin /usr/local/sbin /usr/local/sbin /usr/local/libexec/
filters; do \
  if [ ! -d $i ] ; then ./mkinstalldirs $i ; fi; \
done;
mkdir /usr/local/sbin
mkdir /usr/local/libexec/filters
../././install-sh -c -s -m 04755 -o root lpq /usr/local/bin
../././install-sh -c -s -m 04755 -o root lprm /usr/local/bin
../././install-sh -c -s -m 04755 -o root lpr /usr/local/bin
../././install-sh -c -s -m 04755 -o root lpstat /usr/local/bin
../././install-sh -c -s -m 04755 -o root lpc /usr/local/sbin
 . . . more skipped  . . .
```

Installation ends with the installation of skeleton *lpd.perms* and *lpd.conf* files in
/usr/local/etc.

Replacing the Existing Spooler

When replacing an existing spooler, begin by removing your old spooler software.

Kill the old daemon

The spooler daemon on BSD systems is *lpd*:

```
# kill `ps -aux | grep lpd | grep -v grep | awk '{print $2}'`
```

System V uses the *lpsched* daemon, and requires slightly different flags to *ps*:

```
# kill `ps -ef | grep lpsched | grep -v grep | awk '{print $2}'`
```

Replace the vendor-provided printing programs with the LPRng programs

First, check your system's man pages to find the name of the programs that make up
your print system. To search the disk for the *lpr* program, use the find command:

```
# find / -type file -name lpr -print
```

After running the find command, rename the existing program *lpr*, and then link
lpr to the LPRng *lpr*:

```
# mv /usr/bin/lpr /usr/bin/lpr.orig
# ln -s /usr/local/bin/lpr /usr/bin/lpr
```

Modify system startup scripts

System startup scripts launch the print spooler daemon on boot. On BSD systems,
look for the command that starts *lpd* in */etc/rc* and replace it with a line that runs

the LPRng *lpd* instead. Alternatively, remove that line entirely and run the LPRng *lpd* in */etc/rc.local*.

On System V, print services are frequently started at run level 3. Look for the script that starts *lpsched* and delete it (or at least rename it). You also need to track down and delete the S and K links to this script, which are probably in */etc/init.d/ rc3.d*. We'll replace this with a script that starts the LPRng *lpd*. The very basic script in Example 5-1 provides a jumping off point for further customization. For example, some administrators first check that the System V daemons are stopped before starting LPRng daemons.

Example 5-1. LPRng Startup Script for System V init

```
#!/bin/sh
    case "$1" in
        start)    echo "Starting lpd";
                  /usr/local/sbin/lpd;
                  ;;
        stop)     echo "Shutting down lpd";
                  kill `ps -ef | grep lpd | grep -v grep | awk '{print $2}'`
                  ;;
        *)        echo "Usage: lpd {start|stop}"
                  exit 1
                  ;;
    esac
```

After customizing the script, put it in */etc/init.d/lprng* and create a link to the new LPRng startup script in */etc/init.d/rc3.d*, such as */etc/init.d/rc3.d/S77lprng.*

Some System V based Unix flavors may also fire up a print daemon in */etc/inetd. conf*. If a line such as the following exists in */etc/inetd.conf*, remove it:†

```
    printer stream tcp nowait root /usr/lib/print/in.lpd in.lpd
```

Replace System V print services

If the LPRng programs are invoked with the System V name, they will act like the System V programs. Installing System V emulation allows system administrators to provide both BSD and System V interfaces to the printing system while only maintaining one software package.

If *lpr* is run as *lp*, it will use *lp* syntax. The same goes for *lpq* when run as *lpstat*, and for *lprm* when run as *cancel*. To enable System V emulation, make a set of

---

* The System V boot process is too complex to be explained here; for a detailed discussion, see *Essential System Administration*, by Æleen Frisch (O'Reilly).

† The line is in fact an excerpt from *inetd.conf* on Solaris 7. In Chapter 4, *Extending the Berkeley Spooler with Print Filters*, we noted that Solaris has started using Berkeley-style spooling. What better demonstration than a spooling daemon with *lpd* in the name?

symbolic links for the System V names, as shown in Example 5-2. (The LPRng installation will perform that step for you.) For completeness, create the System V names in the standard place, */usr/bin*, as well as */usr/local/bin*.

Example 5-2. Replacing System V Binary Names with LPRng Binaries

```
# cd /usr/local/bin
# ln -s lpr lp
# ln -s lpq lpstat
# ln -s lprm cancel

# cd /usr/bin
# mv lp lp.dist
# ln -s /usr/local/bin/lp lp
# mv lpstat lpstat.dist
# ln -s /usr/local/bin/lpstat lpstat
# mv cancel cancel.dist
# ln -s /usr/local/bin/cancel cancel
```

When replacing the System V binaries, update the documentation as well. Replace the vendor's *lp*, *lpstat*, and *cancel* man pages with the respective man pages from the LPRng distribution, as in Example 5-3.

Example 5-3. Replacing System V man Pages on Solaris 7

```
# cd /usr/share/man
# cd man1
# cp /usr/local/man/man1/lp.1 .
# cp /usr/local/man/man1/lpstat.1 .
# cp /usr/local/man/man1/cancel.1 .

# cd ../cat1
# mv lp.1 sysv-lp.1
# mv lpstat.1 sysv-lpstat.1
# mv cancel.1 sysv-cancel.1

# cd ../sman1
# mv lp.1 sysv-lp.1
# mv lpstat.1 sysv-lpstat.1
# mv cancel.1 sysv-cancel.1
```

Solaris notes

On Solaris, remove */var/spool/cron/crontabs/lp* to prevent it from running. To uninstall System V printing, run the commands in Example 5-4.

Example 5-4. Removing System V Spooling from Solaris 7

```
# /etc/init.d/lp stop
Print services stopped.
# /usr/sbin/pkgrm -n SUNWpsu
Removal of <SUNWpsu> was successful.
# /usr/sbin/pkgrm -n SUNWscplp
```

Example 5-4. Removing System V Spooling from Solaris 7 (continued)

```
Removal of <SUNWscplp> was successful.
# /usr/sbin/pkgrm -n SUNWpcu
Removal of <SUNWpcu> was successful.
# /usr/sbin/pkgrm -n SUNWpsr
Removal of <SUNWpsr> was successful.
# /usr/sbin/pkgrm -n SUNWpcr
Removal of <SUNWpcr> was successful.
# /bin/rm -f /var/spool/cron/crontabs/lp
```

On Solaris, you must also create the */var/run* directory for the LPRng *lpd* to store lock information.

Configuring LPRng

LPRng configuration is, for the most part, a superset of classic *lpr* configuration. LPRng uses standard *printcap* syntax extensively, but some of the additional options may be confusing at first.

Compatibility with the Berkeley Spooler

Configuration files used with the plain vanilla Berkeley spooler are almost completely compatible with LPRng. The only options from the stock Berkeley spooler software that cannot be used with LPRng are used for configuring serial ports for use with serial printers. Classic Berkeley printcap syntax uses the *fc, fx, xc,* and *xs* parameters to configure serial ports. These parameters describe a series of binary flags used to configure the serial-port. LPRng configures serial ports by using *stty*. In addition to being more friendly, *stty* is available on both System V and BSD, which allows the same *printcap* to be used with both System V and BSD. Conversion of BSD serial-port configurations to LPRng serial-port configurations is detailed in the LPRng documentation.

Much of the LPRng *printcap* syntax makes it incompatible with standard *lpr* syntax, though. LPRng does not require backslashes at the end of each *printcap* line to continue it onto the next line; it uses keywords that are sometimes more than two characters long; and it supports a variety of extended options that are not present on stock *lpr*. In our experience, there is no reason to go back to *lpr* after making use of some of the advanced options covered in the next few pages.

Printing Directly to Remote Printers

A major hassle with stock Berkeley LPR is that the *lpr* client program is dumb. It dimly follows orders, depositing jobs in spool directories and pestering *lpd* to do the hard part. Job routing is done by *lpd*, so any host providing or using print service must run *lpd*. Each host running *lpd* must be configured by providing an appropriate *printcap*.

LPRng's *lpr* is quite a bit smarter. It can send a job directly over a TCP connection to a remote *lpd* process, so there is no need to run *lpd* on every host, and no need to configure *printcap* files for every host. Eliminating *printcap* configuration for the print clients makes distributing *printcap* files much simpler because only servers need *printcap* files. LPRng *lpr* allows the user to specify the hostname and printer on the command line, as in the following examples:

```
$ lpr -Pprinter@server file
$ lpr -Plaser@printhost words.txt
```

System administrators can use the *PRINTER* environment variable to set defaults. For the simplest setup, assign a default value to the variable. More complex scripts could test the hostname and assign a default printer based on the hostname, IP address, or any other piece of system information.

LPRng allows a *printcap* file to use the *printer@server* extension as the `lp` capability, eliminating the need for the stock Berkeley LPR `rp` and `rm` capabilities. Printing to a specified remote port is supported by using a `%` in the `lp` capability. Because LPRng can print directly to a remote port, there is no need to fork a copy of *netcat* for the sole purpose of opening a TCP socket. Busy servers that handle lots of jobs may see substantial resource savings by using this option instead of forking *netcat* processes to achieve the same result. These extensions are illustrated here:

```
# Classic Berkeley-style
remote-classic:\
     :rp=raw:rm=server:

# LPRng extension identical to the above
remote-lprng:
     :lp=raw@server

# Use % to go to a non-standard port
remote-9100:
     :lp=raw@server%9100
```

In the previous examples, the LPRng *lpr* program will not need any help from *lpd*, so there is no need to run *lpd* on the client host.

Enhanced Banner Pages

In addition to the standard *lpr* attributes, LPRng adds some extended options for improved banner printing. As with *lpr*, the *bl* line describes the short banner line used for banner page generation. The default *bl* value is:

```
$-'C:$-'n Job: $-'J Date: $-'t
```

When expanded by LPRng, a file named *book.ps* will be given the banner line:

```
gast:A Job: book.ps Date: Mon Sep 06 12:27:03 PST 1999
```

To print a much more interesting banner, you can specify an external banner generation program in the LPRng *printcap*, which works like a filter. As input, the banner program takes the short banner line, as customized by *bl*,* and it will write its output to standard output, which goes directly to the printer, bypassing any filters. Because the output of the banner program is not filtered, it must generate output appropriate for the printer. Of course, if you prefer, you can specify the *sb* flag in *printcap* to only print the short banner.

External banner programs are specified with *bp*, *bs*, and *be*. *bp* specifies a specific banner program, while *bs* is used exclusively for start banners and *be* is used for ending banners. To print the banner at the end of a job, use the *bl* option as you would with *lpr*.

Filtering for Remote Queues: Bouncing a Job

One problem discussed in Chapter 4 is the difficulty of filtering a job before it is passed to a remote queue. Rather than use a double queuing strategy, LPRng allows the system administrator to run filters for remote printers without extra hassle.

Good: bounce queues

As explained previously, processing a job before forwarding it to a remote server requires two queues with the classic Berkeley software. Setting up two queues just to run a filter is something which would be good to eliminate. If you have a large number of queues, a typo in a *printcap* file or script may cause a large number of users to lose the ability to print.

LPRng introduced the bounce queue, which runs filters on the input and then sends the processed job to the bounce queue. To specify a bounce queue, use the `bq` capability. Jobs will first be processed by the queue in the `lp` capability and filtered by the specified print filter. After filtering, the job will be sent to the queue specified by `bq`. In Example 5-5, the *lj6* queue filters jobs locally and sends the results to the *lp* queue on the server named *spooler*. When using bounce queues, the host doing the processing must have a queue directory to hold temporary files, so the `sd` capability must be set.

---

* The LPRng version of *printcap* has several more variables than the generic BSD *printcap*. Check the man page for the LPRng *printcap* for a full description.

Example 5-5. Bounce Queue Configuration

```
lj6:
    :lp=lj6@localhost
    :bq=lp@spooler
    :sd=/var/spool/lpd/lj6
    :if=/usr/local/lib/filters/apsfilter
```

Better: bouncing with lpr

Configuring a queue in the style of Example 5-5 requires that *lpd* be run on the client host. Running *lpd* processes on every host that prints imposes administrative overhead that is not necessary with LPRng. The LPRng *lpr* program can apply the input filter before passing the job to a server if the *lpr_bounce* capability is specified in the *printcap* file, as in Example 5-6. If *lpr_bounce* is specified, no local spool directory or local *lpd* process is required.

Example 5-6. Bouncing with lpr

```
lj6:
    :lpr_bounce
    :lp=lp@spooler
    :if=/usr/local/lib/filters/apsfilter
```

Omnibus printcap Files

Real administrative scalability comes from distributing one configuration widely. LPRng includes tools to allow a single *printcap* file to be distributed to many end hosts and parsed differently.

Separating client and server information

LPRng allows the *printcap* file to divide information into two classes: information for use by the *lpd* daemon, and information that is used by the LPRng clients, such as *lpr*. In the LPRng *printcap* file, the tag *server* indicates that the *printcap* entry is for use only by *lpd* and not by any of the clients. For example, the *printcap* file in Example 5-7 will result in the *lpd* server printing locally to */dev/lp0*, while *lpr* will attempt to print to *printer1* on *printhost*.

Example 5-7. Division of Client and Server Configuration with the server Tag

```
printer1:
        :lp=printer1@printhost

printer1:
    :server
    :lp=/dev/lp0
```

Sharing common attributes

If you have several printers with shared attributes, you can avoid extra typing by taking advantage of the *tc* tag, which allows you to define a common base configuration that can be further customized. Options specified in the *tc* sections will be overridden by any options in the *printcap* configuration. *printcap* entries starting with the period, underscore, or @ will be ignored by LPRng except for use by the *tc* tag. For example, if you would like to suppress the header page and remove the maximum job size limit for all printers, you can set up a common section with those commands and include them in other *printcap* definitions. Furthermore, you can specify multiple add-in sections with a single *tc* attribute. Example 5-8 also makes use of the LPRng extension *%P*, which is replaced by the name of the printer when the file is parsed.

Example 5-8. Sharing Common Attributes in the LPRng printcap

```
.common:
    :sh
    :mx=0
    :sd=/var/spool/lpd/%P

.notsocommon
    :if=/usr/local/lib/filters/apsfilter

printer1:
    :tc=.common
    :lp=/dev/lp0

printer2:
    :tc=.common,.notsocommon
    :lp=/dev/lp1
```

When expanded by LPRng, the configuration file of Example 5-8 will be processed as if it were the configuration file shown in Example 5-9.

Example 5-9. After Processing

```
printer1:
    :sh
    :mx=0
    :sd=/var/spool/lpd/printer1
    :lp=/dev/lp0

printer2:
    :sh
    :mx=0
    :sd=/var/spool/lpd/printer2
    :if=/usr/local/lib/filters/apsfilter
    :lp=/dev/lp1
```

Using entries on some hosts only

By using the *oh* option in the LPRng *printcap*, you can specify that a *printcap* entry is valid only on the hosts specified in the *oh* tag. If the host does not match the *oh* pattern, the entry will be ignored. The *oh* attribute can be set to an IP network, specified either by IP address and mask length (*192.168.1.0/24*) or by IP address and subnet mask (*192.168.1.0/255.255.255.0*). You may also use a wildcard pattern on the domain name (**.eng.fofz.com*). Multiple specifications can be separated with commas.

One potential use of the *oh* option is to set the default printer based on the IP address or domain name of the client. In Example 5-10, the default printer for hardware engineering is *plotter*, while the default printer for the marketing department is *psychedelic*.

Example 5-10. Using the oh Tag to Set the Default Printer

```
lp:
    :oh=*.eng.fofz.com
    :lp=plotter@printers.fofz.com
lp:
    :oh=*.mkt.fofz.com
    :lp=psychedelic@printers.fofz.com

plotter:
    :server
    :lp=raw@plotter.fofz.com%9100

psychedelic|This one does colors, man!:
    :server
    :lp=raw@psychedelic.fofz.com%9100
```

A Logical Queue with Multiple Physical Devices

LPRng allows you to set up a logical main print-queue with several possible destinations, much as System V allows a class to have several component destinations. The *printcap* options used for this are *ss* and *sv*. The main queue is set up with the *sv* option, which lists the queues connected to actual physical printers. *Service queues*, which drain jobs from the main queue, use the *ss* option to indicate the main queue from which it takes jobs. Example 5-11 shows a *printcap* that exposes a queue named *lasers* to its clients, but the *lasers* queue distributes jobs to the printers *lj-1* and *lj-2*.

Example 5-11. Logical Queue with Multiple Devices

```
.common-base
    :sd=/usr/spool/%P
    :rw
    :mx=0
```

Example 5-11. Logical Queue with Multiple Devices (continued)

```
    :lf=/var/log/%P-log
    :if=/usr/local/lib/filters/apsfilter
    :ss=laser

lasers
    :lp=lasers@printers
lasers|lj
    :server
    :sv=lj-1,lj-2

lj-1|LaserJet #1
    :server
    :tc=.common-base
    :lp=raw@lj-1%9100

lj-2|LaserJet #2 .
    :server
    :tc=.common-base
    :lp=raw@lj-2%9100
```

Distributing printcap Files

LPRng makes it significantly easier to distribute printer information to a network, especially because *lpd* must only be run on those hosts that communicate with printers. Print clients can just be pointed at the print servers with *lp* entries in the LPRng *printcap*. Clients will then spool jobs over TCP sockets to the servers. If necessary, you can configure clients to bounce filtered jobs to servers in the *printcap* file. One potential strategy for distributing *printcap* information is to write a single large *printcap* file (using the *tc* and *ob* options) and distribute it to all print clients on your network periodically using *rdist* or *sdist*.

If you have a network, though, why not use it? Rather than pushing out information to clients, let them fetch it from a central database.

NIS

First, set up NIS with the *printcap* information distributed as a map.* The first step in setting up NIS is to remove any *printcap* entries that use the *lpr* syntax of *option#value* because the databases used to store NIS maps will interpret # as the start of a comment and will truncate the rest of the line. If the line is truncated, no values will be stored in the NIS map. LPRng supports the use of *option=value*, which is far more readable.

Next, in *lpd.conf,* you need to specify the program to get *printcap* information from. LPRng defines a simple interface to the external program: on standard input,

---

* For help with NIS, we recommend Hal Stern's *Managing NFS and NIS* (O'Reilly, 1991).

specify the name of the printer you would like *printcap* information for. The program must supply the *printcap* information for that print name on its standard output. NIS commands require several arguments, so a script is necessary to assemble the arguments into a complete command. Example 5-12 shows an NIS argument marshalling script.

Example 5-12. Getting printcap Entries from NIS

```
#!/bin/sh
# filename: /usr/local/lib/printcap-by-name
# Get printcap info from NIS for first argument
read printer
ypmatch "$printer"printcap.byname
```

Then, in */etc/lpd.conf*, configure LPRng to call this script to get a *printcap* entry:

```
printcap path |/usr/local/lib/printcap-by-name
```

LDAP

To distribute the *printcap* file via LDAP, take the same approach. After putting printcap information into a directory, revise *printcap-by-name* to assemble the *printcap* entry from data stored in the directory. We will return to this problem in more detail later.

More Fun with Filters

Included in the LPRng distribution is *lpf*, a simple filter which translates linefeeds to carriage return plus linefeed, exactly like the *destaircaser* Perl script in the filter chapter. A collection of LPRng compatible filters is maintained at *ftp://ftp.astart.com/pub/LPRng/FILTERS*.

Hewlett Packard Printers

The *CTI-ifhp* filter was originally developed at the Computer Technology Institute of Patras, Greece to support ASCII, PostScript, and PJL print jobs from their heterogeneous network. An additional challenge faced by the authors was the need to support the downloading of a variety of Greek fonts to printers. *CTI-ifhp* also has hooks into accounting packages.

PostScript Printers

The *psfilter* package is much like *CTI-ifhp*, but for PostScript printers. It supports the same accounting methods, so administrators need to learn only one package and develop one set of scripts.

APS Filter, Revisited

apsfilter_LPRng is a modified version of the APS Filter package described in the last chapter. To install it, though, you will need to get your own copies of *a2ps*, Ghost-script, and *pnm*. Setup is, for obvious reasons, similar to setting up APS Filter in Chapter 4.

When installed, *apsfilter_LPRng* takes advantage of some LPRng extensions to sim-plify the *printcap* file. APS Filter depends on the name of the print queue to deter-mine what options to pass to subprograms and what subprograms to run. The *force_queuename* option and the *qq* option work in tandem to create front-end queues for APS Filter that tie into a single back-end queue. When used together, the name of the queue in *force_queuename* is recorded in the control file by the LPRng software. When APS Filter processes the job, the job appears to have come from the queue named by the *force_queuename* parameter even though all jobs are processed by one back-end queue.

By setting the queue name on a submitted job, you can supply APS Filter with the queue name it is expecting so it can do its magic, even though all jobs are actu-ally submitted to the back-end queue, which leaves a natural place to do account-ing. In Example 5-13, also note that the *server* option hides the *back end* queue from print clients.

Example 5-13. apsfilter_LPRng Configuration

```
ascii|LJ6-ascii-mono
 :qq
 :lp=backend@printserv
 :force_queuename=aps-LJ6-letter-ascii-mono

raw|LJ6-raw
 :qq
 :lp=backend@printserv
 :force_queuename=aps-LJ6-letter-raw

auto|lp|LJ6-auto-mono
 :qq
 :lp=backend@printserv
 :force_queuename=aps-LJ6-letter-auto-mono

backend:
 :qq
 :lp=/dev/lp0
 :server
 :sd=/var/spool/backend
 :lf=log
 :af=acct
 :if=/usr/local/lib/filters/apsfilter
```

Accounting

Printer accounting is a difficult task because the imposition of accounting serves as a motivation to subvert the accounting procedures. The accounting routines in LPRng were developed for an academic environment, which is the most demanding proving ground for code that collects small amounts of money. Accounting is frequently subject to diverse local requirements, so this section sketches out a basic outline of the accounting mechanisms built into LPRng.

How a Job Is Processed

LPRng accounting facilities are hooked into the processing of print jobs in several places. Understanding the accounting facilities requires a knowledge of the job processing procedure. Here's how LPRng processes jobs:

1. Open the accounting file specified with the *af* option in *printcap*.

2. Open the printer device. If the printer is specified as a remote printer, open a socket to the remote *lpd*. If it is a hardware device, lock the device and open it for writing.

3. If an output filter is specified, run the filter. Send standard output of the output filter to the printer device. Save the file descriptor for the standard input of the output filter. For clarity, we refer to this as the *output file descriptor* because output from other filters is written to that descriptor.

4. Print a banner page if one is set up in *printcap*. (Refer to "Enhanced Banner Pages" earlier in this chapter for details.) The banner page is written directly to the output file descriptor. It is *not* processed by the input filter, but is processed by the output filter.

5. To process a data file, write a magic character sequence to the output filter to suspend it.* While the output filter is suspended, launch a copy of the input filter and feed the data for the print job to it. The input filter will process the data and write its output to the output file descriptor. *lpd* waits for the input filter to exit. If the input filter exits successfully, reactivate the output filter.

6. Repeat the previous step for each additional data file.

7. Print a trailing banner if specified.

8. Close the output filter, mark the job as completed, and erase any temporary files from the spool directory.

---

* Technically, output filters can only be suspended if the job is of type *f* (formatted text), *l* (leave control characters in the job), or *p* (print text like *pr*). However, most jobs are one of these types.

Using Accounting Scripts

Accounting with *CTI-ifhp* or *psfilter* is straightforward. When the input and output filters start and end, information is written to a log file. LPRng includes a Perl script that can be called with the *as* and *ae* options in the *printcap* file to produce an accounting log. Each filter records its beginning and end in a file, along with the printer's page count. Each pair of lines looks like Example 5-14, which can easily be parsed by Perl, or *sed* and *awk*, or yet another text processing tool.

Example 5-14. Format of Log Lines in Accounting File

```
start -ppagecount -Ff -kjob -uuser -hhost -R...
end  -ppages -qpagecount -Ff -kjob -uuser -hhost -R...
```

At the beginning, the output filter will stamp the start of a job with *–Fo* and the input filter will record a pair for each file in the job with *–Ff.* At the very end of the job, the output filter will generate a final line for the log. A typical job might look something like Example 5-15.

Example 5-15. Typical Accounting File Entry

```
1 start -p120 -Fo -kcfA017pauli -ugast -hpauli -R...
2 start -p121 -Ff -kcfA017pauli -ugast -hpauli -R...
3 end  -p1 -q122 -Ff -kcfA017pauli -ugast -hpauli -R...
4 start -p122 -Ff -kcfA017pauli -ugast -hpauli -R...
5 end  -p3 -q125 -Ff -kcfA017pauli -ugast -hpauli -R...
6 end  -p5 -q125 -Fo -kcfA017pauli -ugast -hpauli -R...
```

The log snippet of Example 5-15 describes a single job with two data files in it, most likely as the result of *lpr file1 file2*. To make sense of the output, you need to break it down line by line:

1. The output filter is started for job 17 submitted to the server from user *gast* on host *pauli.* The initial printer page count is 120.

2. An input filter is started for the first data file in the job. The printer page count is 121 because the banner page has been printed on page 121. Because the banner page does not get processed by the input filter, there is no *–Ff* pair for the banner page.

3. The input filter for the first data file in job 17 ended normally after printing one page, leaving the printer page count at 122.

4. A second input filter started for the second data file in the job. The printer page count is still 122 because nothing is printed in between files in a job.

5. The second input filter terminated after printing three pages (123, 124, and 125).

6. The output filter terminated after printing five pages.

If the output filter terminated unexpectedly, then we would have seen the next job start without ever seeing the end of job 17, as in Example 5-16.

Example 5-16. What Happens When Output Filters Die

```
start -p120 -Fo -kcfA017pauli -ugast -hpauli -R...
start -p121 -Ff -kcfA017pauli -ugast -hpauli -R...
end  -p1 -q122 -Ff -kcfA017pauli -ugast -hpauli -R...
start -p122 -Ff -kcfA017pauli -ugast -hpauli -R...
start -p125 -Fo -kcfA039laplace -utodd -hlaplace -R...
start -p126 -Ff -kcfA039laplace -utodd -hlaplace -R...
```

In the previous example, we can still assume that user *gast* printed five pages, but that he attempted to hang the printer to avoid paying for the last three. A program parsing the accounting log needs to handle all the cases of missing entries that may happen at your institution.

II

Front-End Interfaces to Unix Queues

6

Connecting Windows to Unix Servers: Let's Samba

Completing the first section of this book has laid the foundation and built the structural frame for our architecture. Although the Unix print system is the technological core of our architecture and serves as the hub for all print jobs, it is probably not useful to your Windows network clients.

Most desktops run a flavor of Microsoft Windows, making print service for Windows a high priority. To provide services to Windows clients from the Unix server platform, we use the Samba open source software package,* initially developed by Andrew Tridgell, who was later joined by many volunteers.

Introduction to the Server Message Block Protocol (SMB)

Microsoft Windows networking is based on the *Server Message Block* (SMB) protocol.† SMB networking has two types of entities: *servers* and *clients*. Clients request the use of *resources*, such as files and printers, from SMB servers.

SMB and its transport protocol, NetBIOS, were designed to function in small, chaotic network environments without full-time administrators. SMB networking copes with servers randomly powering up and joining the network and leaving the network as

---

* You can configure an NT server to print to Unix queues using the Microsoft TCP/IP Printing Service (see Chapter 3, *Exploring the Spooler*) and then share those printers with your Windows clients.

† Current versions of Microsoft's SMB implementation may refer to SMB as the Common Internet File System (CIFS). Microsoft has extended SMB to make it an Internet-capable file sharing platform. A CIFS specification has been submitted as an Internet Draft to the IETF.

they are powered down or crash. At the time the IETF standardized NetBIOS over TCP/IP, PCs were commonly powered down (or crashed) abruptly and would not gracefully release the NetBIOS names they had claimed.

NetBIOS, TCP/IP, and the SMB Protocol Stack

SMB uses NetBIOS as its transport protocol. NetBIOS can be run directly over a link layer, or over network layer protocols such as IPX/SPX or TCP/IP. Most organizations have now adopted TCP/IP as the preferred protocol suite, so this book focuses on NetBIOS over TCP/IP. The SMB protocol stack is shown in Figure 6-1.

Although originally developed as a means of connecting a small workgroup on a LAN before TCP/IP was widely deployed, NetBIOS has successfully adapted to changing network environments since its inception. NetBIOS over TCP/IP, which is occasionally called *NBT*, consists of three services, which are documented in RFC 1001 (Concepts and Methods) and RFC 1002 (Detailed Specifications):

NetBIOS Name Service
> Analogous to DNS, the NetBIOS Name Service maps NetBIOS names to IP address and allows applications to communicate using NetBIOS computer names. NetBIOS name services are run over UDP on port 137.

NetBIOS Datagram Service
> Unreliable best-effort delivery is handled by the NetBIOS Datagram Service. Because datagram service is not intended to be reliable, it is implemented over UDP on port 138.

NetBIOS Session Service
> When reliable streams are required, NetBIOS sessions are established over TCP on port 139.

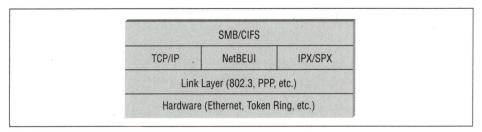

Figure 6-1. The SMB protocol stack

Faking SMB with Samba

At the time this book was being written, Samba was available for all of the commonly used Unix flavors, and efforts were underway to port to several other operating systems, including VMS, Novell NetWare, and MVS.

Samba is a full-featured implementation of SMB services that supports sharing of files and printers to any SMB client. Samba is extremely flexible. If the Unix philosophy is small, configurable Lego-like* pieces with no hard-coded defaults that place limitations on your imagination, then Samba is SMB networking done by disciples of Unix philosophers. Instead of obfuscated hard-coded behavior, nearly every feature in Samba can be adjusted at runtime by appropriate changes to its configuration file.

Although Samba is a very capable file server, those capabilities are beyond the scope of this book. This chapter only describes using Samba as a print server. At various points, we may describe interesting things that you can do with Samba's file-serving capabilities, but we will not provide detailed instructions. For more information on Samba, see *Using Samba*, by Robert Eckstein, David Collier-Brown, and Peter Kelly (O'Reilly and Associates, 1999).

Compiling and Installing Samba

Samba source code is freely available on the Internet. The master site, *http://www.samba.org*, will lead you to a mirror site. Binary distributions are readily available from many sites, but programs that require heavily privileged operation are better built from source. As this book was written, Samba 2.0.6 was the current shipping version.

The source package comes as a compressed archive. When uncompressed, there will be directories with documentation, example configurations, and the source code itself. Like most modern open source packages, Samba supports the GNU autoconfiguration system. Autoconfiguration scripts allow software maintainers to build scripts to detect various configuration and operating system settings so that system administrators building software do not have to know the intimate details of every system call of every OS they run.

Start off by uncompressing the archive file:

```
[root@krypton src]$ ls
RPM/    linux-2.2.13/ samba-2.0.6.tar.gz
linux@
[root@krypton src]$ tar -xzf samba-2.0.6.tar.gz
RPM/    linux-2.2.13/ samba-2.0.6.tar.gz
linux@ samba-2.0.6/
[root@krypton src]$ cd samba-2.0.6
[root@krypton samba-2.0.6]$ ls
```

---

* Have you ever noticed how many network engineers and Unix system administrators loved Legos as children? We wonder if there is grant money to study this question....

```
COPYING    README              Read-Manifest-Now  WHATSNEW.txt  examples/  source/
Manifest   README-smbmount  Roadmap              docs/          packaging/  swat/
[root@krypton samba-2.0.6]$ cd source
[root@krypton source]# ls
Makefile.in       config.guess*       include/       nmbd/        rpc_server/
ubiqx/
acconfig.h        config.sub*         install-sh     param/       rpcclient/
utils/
aclocal.m4        configure*          internals.doc  parsing.doc  script/
web/
architecture.doc  configure.developer*  lib/         passdb/      smbadduser*
change-log        configure.in        libsmb/        printing/    smbd/
client/           cvs.log             locking/       rpc_client/  smbwrapper/
codepages/        groupdb/            mem_man/       rpc_parse/   tests/
```

Autoconfiguration scripts are usually called *configure*. Reasonable security practices keep the current working directory out of the command execution path, so preface *configure* with *./*. When run, *configure* prints out the results of many tests:

```
[root@krypton source]$ ./configure
creating cache ./config.cache
checking for gcc... gcc
checking whether the C compiler (gcc -O ) works... yes
checking whether the C compiler (gcc -O ) is a cross-compiler... no
checking whether we are using GNU C... yes

[lots of output omitted]

checking configure summary
configure OK
updating cache ./config.cache
creating ./config.status
creating include/stamp-h
creating Makefile
creating include/config.h
```

Running the *configure* script builds all the *Makefile*s needed to compile the software, then you can just run *make*:

```
[root@krypton source]$ make
Using FLAGS =  -O -Iinclude -I./include -I./ubiqx -I./smbwrapper  -DSMBLOGFILE="/
usr/local/samba/var/log.smb" -DNMBLOGFILE="/usr/local/samba/var/log.nmb" -
DCONFIGFILE="/usr/local/samba/lib/smb.conf" -DLMHOSTSFILE="/usr/local/samba/lib/
lmhosts"   -DSWATDIR="/usr/local/samba/swat" -DSBINDIR="/usr/local/samba/bin" -
DLOCKDIR="/usr/local/samba/var/locks" -DSMBRUN="/usr/local/samba/bin/smbrun" -
DCODEPAGEDIR="/usr/local/samba/lib/codepages" -DDRIVERFILE="/usr/local/samba/lib/
printers.def" -DBINDIR="/usr/local/samba/bin" -DHAVE_INCLUDES_H -DPASSWD_
PROGRAM="/bin/passwd" -DSMB_PASSWD_FILE="/usr/local/samba/private/smbpasswd"
Using FLAGS32 =  -O -Iinclude -I./include -I./ubiqx -I./smbwrapper  -
DSMBLOGFILE="/usr/local/samba/var/log.smb" -DNMBLOGFILE="/usr/local/samba/var/log.
nmb" -DCONFIGFILE="/usr/local/samba/lib/smb.conf" -DLMHOSTSFILE="/usr/local/samba/
lib/lmhosts"   -DSWATDIR="/usr/local/samba/swat" -DSBINDIR="/usr/local/samba/bin"
-DLOCKDIR="/usr/local/samba/var/locks" -DSMBRUN="/usr/local/samba/bin/smbrun" -
DCODEPAGEDIR="/usr/local/samba/lib/codepages" -DDRIVERFILE="/usr/local/samba/lib/
printers.def" -DBINDIR="/usr/local/samba/bin" -DHAVE_INCLUDES_H -DPASSWD_
PROGRAM="/bin/passwd" -DSMB_PASSWD_FILE="/usr/local/samba/private/smbpasswd"
```

```
Using LIBS = -ldl  -lcrypt
Compiling smbd/server.c

[lots of compiling and linking messages omitted]

Compiling utils/nmblookup.c
Linking bin/nmblookup
Compiling utils/make_printerdef.c
Linking bin/make_printerdef
```

The Resulting Pieces

After the build finishes, there will be several executables:

smbd

> The SMB server daemon. Although some things are configured at compile time, most compile-time defaults can be overridden in the main configuration file, *smb.conf.*

smbstatus

> Shows current connections to the SMB server.

nmbd

> Provides NetBIOS name services. It listens for name queries and responds to them. It also contains experimental code to operate as a WINS* server.

nmblookup

> A command line program used to query the NetBIOS name service. It is useful as a general troubleshooting tool for SMB networking.

smbclient

> A command line interface to SMB servers. It presents an FTP-like interface to SMB servers. Because it accepts a wide variety of command line arguments, it is useful for troubleshooting.

testparm

> Checks a configuration file for syntactic errors so that the file can be tested before it is used. Acquire the habit of running *testparm* before using a configuration file live.

make_printerdef

> Used in the process of setting up automatic driver installations for Windows clients.

make_smbcodepage

> Creates code pages so you can use international character sets with Samba.

smbrun

> A glue program that runs shell commands for *smbd.*

---

* WINS is the Microsoft Windows Internet Naming Service. It is similar to DNS in that WINS maps NetBIOS names to IP addresses.

Installation and Basic Configuration

Run *make install* to create the Samba directory structure under */usr/local/samba*.
Use an account with appropriate permissions to write to the installation directories:

```
[root@krypton source]$ su -
Password:
[root@krypton source]# make install
Installing bin/smbd as /usr/local/samba/bin/smbd
Installing bin/nmbd as /usr/local/samba/bin/nmbd
Installing bin/swat as /usr/local/samba/bin/swat
[lots of other installation messages omitted]
```

Choosing a start-up method

Samba can either be started in response to incoming connections by the *inetd*
super-server, or the *smbd* and *nmbd* daemons can be run as daemons. Running
from *inetd* saves memory when neither *smbd* or *nmbd* are being used, but the
trade off is a slower initial response time as *inetd* launches the appropriate daemon to service the connection. Memory and disk space are cheap and getting
cheaper, so run Samba in daemon mode.

To start Samba on a system with System V-style *init*, use a script like Example 6-1
in your */etc/init.d* tree. Once you've installed this script in *init.d*, you should make
S and K links to it from the appropriate directory—the name is up to you, but it
should be something like */etc/init.d/rc3.d/S97Samba.**

Example 6-1. System V init Script to Start and Stop Samba

```
# Script to start and stop Samba on SVR4

case $1 in

'start')
# you may need to change these pathnames to match your
# own installation!
   /usr/local/samba/bin/smbd -D
   /usr/local/samba/bin/nmbd -D
   ;;
'stop')
   kill `ps -ef | grep smbd | grep -v grep | awk '{ print $1 }'`
   kill `ps -ef | grep nmbd | grep -v grep | awk '{ print $1 }'`
   ;;
*)
   echo "Usage: /etc/init.d/samba {start | stop}"
```

A Berkeley-style script like Example 6-2 would be placed in */etc/rc.d/rc.samba.*

---

* See *Essential System Administration,* by Æleen Frisch (O'Reilly), for a detailed discussion of System V
booting.

Example 6-2. Berkeley-Style Samba Startup Script

```
# Start Samba
/usr/local/samba/bin/smbd -D
/usr/local/samba/bin/nmbd -D
echo "starting samba..."
```

To start Samba from *inetd*, */etc/services* must have entries for NetBIOS services and */etc/inetd.conf* must have commands for those services. Add the NetBIOS ports to */etc/services* with lines like the following:

```
netbios-ns      137/udp
netbios-ns      137/tcp
netbios-dg      138/udp
netbios-ssn     139/tcp
```

After defining port numbers in */etc/services*, add the associated daemons to */etc/ inetd.conf.* The format of *inetd.conf* may differ slightly from operating system to operating system, so check system documentation. Some implementations of *inetd* limit the length of the command line, which may require the use of a wrapper script:

```
netbios-ns      dgram   udp  wait    root  /usr/local/samba/bin/nmbd
netbios-ssn     stream  tcp  nowait  root  /usr/local/samba/bin/smbd
```

Permissions on /dev/null

When *smbd* runs external commands, it uses */dev/null* as standard output. If */dev/ null* is not world writeable, the output from helper programs may cause *smbd* to die unexpectedly.

Configuring Samba for Print Service

Print service is a pretty simple task—the client opens up a pipe to the server and stuffs the file into it. The server prints the file and deletes the job file.

Configuration File Variables

Samba's flexibility is due in large part to configuration file variables. By using variables, Samba can be adapted to a wide variety of host systems. Samba's behavior can also be customized based on the value of these variables by including them in parameter values. The common configuration file variables for print service are shown in Table 6-1.

Table 6-1. Samba Configuration Variables Useful for Print Service

Variable	Meaning

%m	Expands to the NetBIOS client name. One debugging trick using %m is to log each client in its own file, using something like the following configuration snippet:
	`; log each client separately`
	`    log file = /usr/local/samba/var/log.%m`

Table 6-1. Samba Configuration Variables Useful for Print Service (continued)

Variable	Meaning
%p	The Unix printer queue.
%s	The full pathname of the print file.
%j	The job identifier on the Unix server.
%U	The *session username*, which is the username requested by the client in the SMB connection setup dialog. It may be overridden by the server. When a client connects to a guest service on a Samba server, the *session username* is the requested username, but the *service username* is the name of the guest account used to provide access to the service. (Samba provides the lowercase %u option to refer to the service username.) %U is often used when many users need to access a shared resource and the server assigns the same user ID to all of them.[a]
%L	Expands to the NetBIOS name of the server. Most SMB implementations only allow servers to have one NetBIOS name, but Samba allows each physical server to have several NetBIOS names. Use this option to create several logical SMB servers, each with a different configuration and each tied to a different NetBIOS name. See the section on *Virtual NetBIOS Servers* for more details.

[a] This is often the case for print servers. For the daring, you can set up a Samba server to interact with the NFS automater and store user profiles in home directories on Unix servers. See *smb.conf* man page for the %N variable.

I Command You: Out, Out, Print Job!

After *smbd* accepts a job and stores it in a temporary file, it needs to know how to get the bits on the disk to the printer. Half of this task is defining your Unix print-queue correctly, and the other half is informing *smbd* about those queues.

At the most basic level, printing with Samba is a simple matter of using the correct print command for your spooler. Performing the basic task of printing a temporary file and deleting it calls for commands like the following. Explicitly deleting the temporary file on System V is required because *lp* lacks the equivalent of the *–r* option to *lpr*:

```
BSD$ lpr -r -Plogjam info.txt
SYSV$ lp -dlogjam info.txt; rm info.txt
```

If Samba were to offer up the *unix-logjam* queue to a Windows network, the configuration entry might look something like Example 6-3.

Example 6-3. Basic Configuration to Serve a Queue to Windows

```
[logjam]
   printer = unix-logjam
   comment = a laser printer somewhere
   printing = LPRNG
   print command = /usr/bin/lpr -r %s
   printable = yes
   path = /var/spool/printing
```

To share a printer, you need to tell Samba what its name is and how to use it. The *printer* option is used to tell Samba to share the Unix printer *unix-logjam* as *SAMBA**logjam* to Windows clients. The comment field associates a free-form text line with the printer, which is displayed as detailed information in the Windows Network Neighborhood.

To configure Samba to operate a queue, set the `printing` variable, which gives Samba a reasonable set of defaults for your printing subsystem. Typically, `printing` is set to BSD or SYSV, though in the previous example we set it to LPRng; its effects are discussed in detail in a later section. Defaults set by `printing` can be overridden.

The option `printable = yes` serves the obvious purpose of informing Samba that the share is a printer. If no path is specified, then Samba will use a default of */tmp*, which may not be adequate for a busy server if */tmp* is allocated a small disk slice. The path for a print share is where *smbd* puts the print job file before running the `print command`. Like */tmp*, the spool directory should be world writeable with the sticky bit set. With that set of permissions, any user can write to the directory, but only owners can delete files. To create a suitable spool directory, use commands such as:

```
[root@krypton]# mkdir -p /usr/spool/samba
[root@krypton]# chmod a+rwxt /usr/spool/samba
[root@krypton]# ls -l /usr/spool | grep samba
drwxrwxrwt   2 root     root          1024 Mar 30 18:00 samba/
```

Configuring the print interface the easy way: choosing a spooler

As you might have gathered from the first part of the book, there are different ways to print on different kinds of Unix systems by using the `printing` configuration option. You can select BSD, System V, or LPRng. Other options exist for more exotic print servers, like AIX and HP-UX.

Default values for printing options are set by the `printing` value. Table 6-2 shows the default values for each possible setting of `printing`; default variables make heavy use of the variables in Table 6-1. Setting the printing type also helps Samba to interpret error codes and status information from your print system.

Table 6-2. Defaults Defined by the printing Variable in smb.conf

smb.conf Option	BSD, LPRNG/PLP, AIX	SYSV, HP-UX
`print command`	*lpr −r −P%p %s*	*lp −c −d%p %s; rm %s*
`lprm command`	*lprm −P%p %j*	*cancel %p−%j*
`lpq command`	*lpq −P%p*	*lpstat −o%p*
`lppause command`	Not defined	*lp −i %p−%j −H hold*
`lpresume command`	Not defined	*lp −i %p−%j −H resume*

Table 6-2. Defaults Defined by the printing Variable in smb.conf (continued)

smb.conf Option	BSD, LPRNG/PLP, AIX	SYSV, HP-UX
queue pause	Not defined	HP-UX: *disable %p* SysV: *lpc stop %p*
queue resume	Not defined	HP-UX: *enable %p* SysV: *lpc start %p*

Manual configuration of the print interface

Printing options may be set individually. Printing operations are carried out with the credentials of the Unix user specified by the administrator, or by the guest user if no specific user is specified. That user account must have the print command in its execution path. For this reason, many Samba administrators override the default settings with fully qualified pathnames (*/usr/bin/lpq* rather than simply *lpq*).

Guest account

Printing services may be offered without user authentication. When services are not authenticated, *smbd* operates with the user identity of the guest account. Windows network operations are also performed with guest account privileges. The default is *nobody*. However, on some Unix systems, user *nobody* does not have permission to print or make network connections. If *nobody* lacks sufficient privileges, create an account and give it the required permission.

On many systems, *nobody* is often assigned the user ID 65,535. This UID is extremely dangerous when used with Samba! When represented as a binary number, 65,535 is a sequence of sixteen 1's. However, a sequence of sixteen 1's in two's complement arithmetic is –1.

Because SMB networking services are offered over privileged ports, Samba needs to start up as *root* to bind to those ports. After binding to the low-numbered ports, Samba uses the setreuid() system call to change UID to give up *root* privileges in favor of the UID of the user making the connection.

Calls to setreuid() will not change the UID if the new UID is –1, which is exactly what happens with a UID of 65,535. Thus, if you use a guest account (or have any other account) with a UID of 65,535, connections made to that account via Samba will run with *root* privileges. This is very, very bad. Don't let this happen to you!

A Simple Configuration for a Print Server

smb.conf is the master configuration file for Samba. By default, it is stored in */usr/local/samba/lib*. Both *smbd* and *nmbd* will use the information in the file. The file

is broken into *sections*. One section holds global parameters, and other sections are
for network shares. Sections have parameters to set options; a global parameter
would be the NetBIOS name of the computer, while a network share parameter
might be the Unix directory to share. Samba comes with several thoroughly documented example configurations. Here are some final printer configuration options:

`printcap file = ` *`filename`*

> The *printcap* file is where Samba learns the names of printers this server runs
> queues for. On Berkeley-derived systems that use a *printcap* file, setting this
> parameter is straightforward. It is usually */etc/printcap*, although some LPRng
> systems may use */usr/local/etc/printcap*. On System V-based platforms, use
> `printcap file = lpstat`, which will make Samba run *lpstat* to determine
> the names of all attached printers.

`lpq cache time = ` *`n`*

> To avoid overloading the Samba machine with requests for a list of pending
> print jobs, Samba caches the output of the *lpq* command for *n* seconds. The
> default is 10, which should be sufficient for most sites. For large sites, how-
> ever, a higher setting is useful to limit the amount of CPU time *lpq* consumes.

The `[printers]` *section*

> Samba can automagically determine all the printers on a system if a global
> `[printers]` section is included in the configuration file. In essence, the
> `[printers]` section supplies defaults for each network printer you may
> choose to share. One important point to bring up is that if a printer in *printcap*
> has the same name as a Unix user, the user home directory will be processed
> first and the printer will be that user's home directory, not a printer share.

Example 6-4 shows a simple configuration file that is enough to bring up a Samba
server and share all the printers defined in the *printcap* file. It is not complex—its
only purpose is to illustrate a basic *smb.conf* before moving on to more intricate
configurations.

Example 6-4. Sample Configuration File

```
[global]
    netbios name = ATHENA
    workgroup = BOOKNET
    server string = This is a Samba server

; Automatically load all printers in printcap and share to network
    printcap name = /etc/printcap
    load printers = yes
    printing = lprng

; Samba allows you to fine tune the options on any network sockets allocated
; by the operating system. In particular, disabling the Nagle algorithm
; (RFC 896) seems to offer a large performance gain, in part because
```

Example 6-4. Sample Configuration File (continued)

```
; Microsoft TCP/IP stacks are sometimes slow in acknowledging transmitted
; data. (Think carefully before disabling the Nagle algorithm on a WAN.
; It was developed to prevent congestion collapse across a WAN.) You
; can set any socket  option defined by your OS; see the man page for
; setsockopt() on your system for details.
    socket options = TCP_NODELAY

; Share all printers with guest account "samba," which has permission to
; write to /usr/spool/samba
[printers]
    comment = All Printers
    path = /usr/spool/samba
    public = yes
    printable = yes
    guest ok = yes
    guest account = samba
```

User Authentication

Depending on your security policy, user authentication may be an important part
of offering print services. For a print server, there are two good options: forget the
issue entirely, or work with an existing user database. With Samba, the best way to
accomplish the latter is to plug into a Windows NT domain.

Is authentication really necessary?

Authentication may be disabled by using `public = yes` on selected shares. If policy does not mandate authentication of print jobs, this may be a viable option.

Password Caching on Windows Clients

Do not cache passwords. Older passwords are stored in a weak form in
username.pwl files on the disk. Even if passwords are changed, Windows for
Workgroups may remember the older password. After deleting the *.pwl* file,
the user is allowed to enter the new password. Disabling password caching has
a security benefit as well because the encryption algorithm used to protect the
passwords was flawed, and several freely available utilities were written to
quickly extract passwords from *.pwl* files.

NT domain integration

If user authentication is required, the best way is to add new Samba servers into
Windows NT domains. Add a machine entry on the NT primary domain controller
(PDC) in the Windows NT Server Manager for Domains. Be sure to use the Samba
server's primary NetBIOS name rather than a NetBIOS alias.

Next, tell Samba about the PDC by running *smbpasswd* as *root*, supplying the domain name with the *–j* option and the PDC with the *–r* option. For example, to add a Samba server to the NT domain *BOOKDOM* with a PDC named *bookpdc*, run this command:

```
[root@krypton]# smbpasswd -j BOOKDOM -r bookpdc
```

To take advantage of the NT domain controller, add the `security = domain` parameter to the `[global]` section of *smb.conf.* Working in the NT security model requires knowledge of the domain controller to pass authentication requests to. Domain controllers must be specified with the `password server` parameter. Either specify domain controllers by NetBIOS name or use `password server = *` to find domain controllers through WINS:

```
[global]
   security = domain
   workgroup = BOOKDOM
; List PDCs and BDCs, or you can resolve them via WINS by using "*"
   password server = *
```

Even if an NT domain is used for authentication information, users must have valid Unix accounts to use services.

Intriguing Future Possibilities

The Samba team is currently in the process of implementing several features that can allow Samba to replace a Windows NT domain controller. This new code offers a potentially interesting opportunity. For example, Samba can use the information in NIS and NFS to store Windows profiles and logon scripts on NFS exported home directories.

Eventually, it may be possible to make a Samba server the authentication server for an entire institution or workgroup using this feature. Samba's password synchronization features can keep SMB network passwords the same as Unix passwords. Other Unix functionalities, such as NIS or Kerberos, combined with Pluggable Authentication technology, can be used to set up flexible authentication mechanisms for the entire company.

Virtual SMB Servers with Samba

Many Internet service providers will host web sites on *virtual servers*. Virtual servers appear as distinct servers, but may co-exist on a single physical machine. Virtual HTTP servers are quite common; virtual SMB servers were rare until Samba offered the opportunity to create them. Figure 6-2 illustrates how Samba might be used to offer virtual SMB service.

One potential use of virtual SMB servers is to build print servers that have names corresponding to geographic locations. A small company with offices in San Francisco and San Jose could have print services run on one machine in the server room at the main location. For simplicity, this example will have only two printers: *SF**SF-COLOR*, and *SJ**SJ-LASER.**

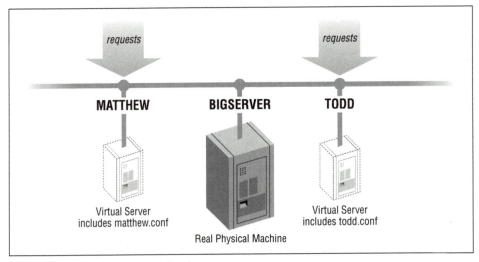

Figure 6-2. Virtual servers with Samba

Adding *SF* and *SJ* to the `netbios` aliases in *smb.conf* creates the *SF* and *SJ* virtual servers. To configure shares on a per virtual server basis, use the `include file` parameter with `%L` (see Example 6-5). Each server's shares are then configured in a separate file. When clients connect to the *SF* server, the `include file` parameter will include *sf.conf.* Shares specific to the San Francisco location and the *SF* server are then stored only in *sf.conf* and not in the main *smb.conf.*

Example 6-5. Using %L for Virtual NetBIOS Service

```
[global]
    netbios name = BIGSERVER
    netbios aliases = SF SJ
    include file = /usr/local/samba/lib/%L.conf
```

On startup, Samba would read */usr/local/samba/lib/sf.conf* (Example 6-6) and */usr/local/samba/lib/sj.conf* (Example 6-7). Samba uses the configuration in *sf.conf* and lists only the *SF**SF-COLOR* printer share. *sf-color* must be defined in the *printcap* file (Example 6-8), of course. When a user submits a job to *SF**SF-COLOR*, the

---

* An SMB share is often written using the Universal Naming Convention (UNC): *SERVER**SHARENAME.*

temporary file is stored in */var/spool/public*. *lpd* will then send the job to the *raw* queue on *sf-color.printers.corp.com*.

Example 6-6. sf.conf

```
[sf-color]
    printable = yes
    comment = San Francisco color printer
    path = /var/spool/public
```

Example 6-7. sj.conf

```
[sj-laser]
    printable = yes
    comment = San Jose laser printer
    path = /var/spool/public
```

Example 6-8. printcap

```
sf-color:
    :sh:\
    :mx#0:\
    :rm=sf-color.printers.corp.com:\
    :rp=raw:
sj-laser:
    :sh:\
    :mx#0:\
    :lp=/dev/lpt0:\
    :if=/usr/local/print/magicfilter:\
    :sd=/var/spool/lpd/sj-laser:
```

Automatic Driver Installation for Windows

Windows machines need to install print drivers to produce output. Windows printer drivers translate the GDI screen output into printer language. Distributing drivers can be a major annoyance on a network of any size. When Windows connects to a remote printer, it can download and install appropriate drivers from the remote machine. Samba implements the automatic driver installation feature. This example illustrates setting up an HP LaserJet 6P, but there is nothing exotic about this choice.

Step 1: The printer driver share

Create a public *PRINTER$* share that is world readable.* It is a simple process, requiring only a few lines in *smb.conf*:

```
[printer$]
    path=/usr/local/samba/print-drivers
```

---

* SMB shares with names ending in *$* do not show up on browse lists.

```
public=yes
writeable=no
```

Step 2: Windows driver installation

Install the Windows driver on a Windows machine. Many print drivers must now be installed to easily obtain the individual component files.

Step 3: Create the Samba printer definition

To determine what files are used by your print driver, consult Windows system information files. Get these four files (older Windows 95 clients only had the first two) and transfer them to your Samba server:

```
C:\WINDOWS\INF\MSPRINT.INF
C:\WINDOWS\INF\MSPRINT2.INF
C:\WINDOWS\INF\MSPRINT3.INF
C:\WINDOWS\INF\MSPRINT4.INF
```

For printers released into the marketplace after a Windows release, look for the *OEM*.INF* file on the installation disk.

On the Samba server, put all the *MSPRINT.INF* files together so that you have one big file filled with printer information. Samba uses this information to create its *printer definition*. The printer definition is a structured way of informing the client which files it must copy to install the driver. Samba's printer definition is created with *make_printerdef*, a program that takes two arguments: the repository of printer information and the name of the printer. Example 6-9 illustrates using *make_printerdef*.

Example 6-9. Using make_printerdef to Determine the Files in the Windows Driver

```
[root@krypton]# ls
MSPRINT.INF  MSPRINT2.INF  MSPRINT3.INF  MSPRINT4.INF
[root@krypton]# cat *INF > msprint.inf
[root@krypton]# /usr/local/samba/bin/make_printerdef msprint.inf "HP LaserJet 6P"
Found:PCL5EMS2.DRV.BIDI
End of section found
CopyFiles: @PCL5EMS2.DRV,@PJLMON.DLL,UNI,FINSTALL
Datasection: UNI_DATA
Datafile: PCL5EMS2.DRV
Driverfile: PCL5EMS2.DRV
Helpfile: UNIDRV.HLP
LanguageMonitor: PJL Language Monitor

Copy the following files to your printer$ share location:
PCL5EMS2.DRV
PJLMON.DLL
UNIDRV.DLL
UNIDRV.HLP
ICONLIB.DLL
```

Example 6-9. Using make_printerdef to Determine the Files in the Windows Driver (continued)

```
FINSTALL.DLL
FINSTALL.HLP


HP LaserJet 6P:PCL5EMS2.DRV:PCL5EMS2.DRV:UNIDRV.HLP:PJL Language Monitor:EMF:PCL5EMS2.
DRV,PJLMON.DLL,UNIDRV.DLL,UNIDRV.HLP,ICONLIB.DLL,FINSTALL.DLL,FINSTALL.HLP
```

The last two lines printed out are the Samba printer definition. You can peel off the last two lines by using shell I/O redirection:

```
[root@krypton]# /usr/local/samba/bin/make_printerdef msprint.inf "HP LaserJet 6P" \
>> printers.def
Found:PCL5EMS2.DRV.BIDI
End of section found
CopyFiles: @PCL5EMS2.DRV,@PJLMON.DLL,UNI,FINSTALL
Datasection: UNI_DATA
Datafile: PCL5EMS2.DRV
Driverfile: PCL5EMS2.DRV
Helpfile: UNIDRV.HLP
LanguageMonitor: PJL Language Monitor

Copy the following files to your printer$ share location:
PCL5EMS2.DRV
PJLMON.DLL
UNIDRV.DLL
UNIDRV.HLP
ICONLIB.DLL
FINSTALL.DLL
FINSTALL.HLP

[root@krypton drvinst]# cat printers.def
HP LaserJet 6P:PCL5EMS2.DRV:PCL5EMS2.DRV:UNIDRV.HLP:PJL Language Monitor:EMF:
PCL5EMS2.DRV,PJLMON.DLL,UNIDRV.DLL,UNIDRV.HLP,ICONLIB.DLL,FINSTALL.DLL,FINSTALL.
HLP
```

Step 4: Populate the PRINTER$ share

make_printerdef prints instructions to copy over files to the *PRINTER$* share. Those files will most likely be found in *C:\WINDOWS\SYSTEM*. Put the printer definition file in the *PRINTER$* share directory. If there is already a *printers.def* file, append the new printer definition to the existing file.

Step 5: Modify the Samba configuration

Finally, you need to add three options to *smb.conf*:

`printer driver`

> The printer driver tells clients what type of printer is attached and what driver they should be using.

`printer driver file`

> The printer driver file tells clients which files must be installed to support the driver named by the previous parameter.

```
printer driver location
```
To find the files specified by the previous parameter, the client will look in the location specified by this parameter.

Putting it all together, you'll get an *smb.conf* file that looks something like this:

```
[global]
    . . .
    printer driver file = /usr/local/samba/print-drivers/printers.def
    . . .

[Lazer]
    path = /tmp
    comment = Matthew's printer
    browseable = yes
    printer = yes
    public = yes
    writable = no
    create mode = 0700
    printer driver = HP LaserJet 6P
    printer driver location = \\%L\PRINTER$

[printer$]
    path=/usr/local/samba/print-drivers
    public=yes
    writeable=no
```

Troubleshooting

If everything in life went smoothly, there would be no need for help desks, customer support engineers, and maybe not even computer books. As with any other computer software, though, problems do occur.

Network Problems

Before doing complicated troubleshooting and attempting to track down esoteric problems, start simple. Make sure that network interfaces are attached to the network and configured properly. Check IP addresses, subnet masks, and DNS server information. If Samba is run in daemon mode, check that the daemons are running and are bound to the appropriate ports with *netstat*. If Samba is run from *inetd*, make sure that Samba starts when requests are received. Run the *testparm* utility to check the configuration, and check that any log and lock directories specified exist. To be sure network connectivity is established, ping between the hosts that are not communicating correctly.

Proper interface detection

Because SMB networking depends heavily on broadcasts, it is essential that Samba know the IP broadcast addresses of any network interfaces in your server. Although it makes a good effort at detecting them, interface autodetection may fail and you will need to manually tell Samba about your network interfaces. Check the *nmb.log* file to see the interfaces that *nmbd* detected automatically. The interfaces parameter in *smb.conf* tells Samba about network interfaces and subnet masks. For example:

```
interfaces = 10.1.0.0/255.255.0.0 192.168.1.0/255.255.255.0
```

Do not bind the hostname to 127.0.0.1 in /etc/hosts

If it is possible to ping other computers, but not possible to establish SMB sessions, the problem may be that your hostname is bound to 127.0.0.1 in */etc/hosts*. If the hostname resolves to 127.0.0.1, SMB traffic is sent over the loopback interface, not to the network. To fix this, move the hostname to a non-loopback address.

Name resolution problems

The *nmblookup* tool supplied with Samba is useful for testing the NetBIOS name resolution process. Make sure that you can look up the Samba server by searching for the NetBIOS name __SAMBA__, as well as the name of the other client, as in the following example:

```
[gast@gell-mann]$ nmblookup __SAMBA__
Added interface ip=10.2.0.94 bcast=10.2.0.255 nmask=255.255.255.0
Sending queries to 10.2.0.255
10.0.2.94 __SAMBA__<00>
[gast@gell-mann]$ nmblookup feynman
Added interface ip=10.2.0.94 bcast=10.2.0.255 nmask=255.255.255.0
Sending queries to 10.2.0.255
10.0.2.91 feynman<00>
```

To check that the interfaces are configured correctly, use *nmblookup* to determine what hosts on the local subnet are running SMB servers:

```
[gast@gell-mann]$ nmblookup -d 2 '*'
Got a positive name query response from 10.2.0.94 ( 10.2.0.94 )
Got a positive name query response from 10.2.0.91 ( 10.2.0.91 )
Got a positive name query response from 10.2.0.92 ( 10.2.0.92 )
10.2.0.94 *<00>
10.2.0.91 *<00>
10.2.0.92 *<00>
```

User Account Problems

"This server is not configured to list shared resources" message

If you receive the error message "this server is not configured to list shared resources" from a Windows client, run *smbclient –L SERVER* from a Unix machine. If this does not return a list of shares, you should check that the guest account exists in */etc/passwd* and does not have a UID of 65,535.

Trapdoor UID systems

Samba depends on switching user IDs as it runs to implement its security policy. Some operating systems, most notably SCO Unix, have a *trapdoor UID system* in which a process is allowed to change its user ID only once. This would be used to start a process as *root* to bind to a low numbered privileged port, and then change to an unprivileged user. With a trapdoor UID system, the OS enforces security by preventing processes from reassuming *root* privileges.

Samba daemons enforce access control by running as the user on whose behalf the request was made, so the Samba daemon has the privileges that a logged-on user would have. Unfortunately, the daemon depends on being able to switch UIDs from *root* to any authorized user and back. (After staring at the changing output of *top* long enough, it is possible to see the Samba daemons change UIDs.) Trapdoor UID systems will prevent Samba from switching UIDs. As frustrating as a trapdoor UID system may be, it only limits functionality. It does *not* introduce any security problems.

Printing Problems

Many printing problems are caused by misconfigured permissions on spool directories. See Chapter 3 to fix this. Make sure that the guest account has permission to print. To test this, assign the guest account a password, log in, and attempt to print something from the command line. If printing from the command line succeeds, look somewhere else. One common problem is that *smbd* is unable to locate the print commands when they are not specified with a fully qualified path.

Raw PostScript

Raw PostScript is printed when the print subsystem does not read the file type. Check *printcap* and the filter programs to make sure they are correctly identifying the file as PostScript. Run *file* on the print file to verify that the operating system is correctly identifying the file type.

Some PC drivers insist on sending *Ctrl-D*, the end of file character, as the first output character. Write a Perl filter script to strip off this character and replace it with the PostScript magic sequence (%!) or use the `postscript = true` option in *smb.conf.*

Testing Samba

Isolating Samba's queuing features from the Unix spooler is often a productive line of inquiry. Samba's responsibility is to accept the data to be printed and submit that data to the Unix spooler. To verify Samba's operation, use *cp* as the print command to copy the print data to a known location. One simple debugging setting is `print command = cp %s /tmp/tmp.print`. After submitting a print job from a Windows client, make sure that */tmp/tmp.print* exists, and then attempt to print *tmp.print* with *lp* or *lpr*.

Other Help and Filing Useful Bug Reports

If the steps in the previous section fail, follow the procedure in *Diagnosis.txt* in the *docs* directory of the Samba distribution. If that does not solve the problem, get help from the *comp.protocols.smb* newsgroup, but only after doing the appropriate legwork. Complex problems may benefit from the use of *tcpdump-smb*, an enhanced version of *tcpdump* with additional SMB decode support. Subtle bugs may require system call traces for resolution; see *Tracing.txt* for details.

Configuration File Templates

CEPS is a management layer that was originally developed by Cisco, but is now open source. CEPS was designed to manage large numbers of distributed configuration files. Part of the management scalability of CEPS stems from the use of a template *smb.conf* used on all Samba servers. In the template, CEPS variables are indicated by double percent signs (`%%CEPS_VARIABLE%%`). This section will look at each part of the Cisco *smb.conf.template*. You may not want to use CEPS yourself, but the template idea is interesting and worth exploring as you develop your own printing solutions.

As previously discussed, the *nobody* account often makes a poor guest account because it lacks appropriate privileges to spool files and write to the printer devices. The default permissions on RedHat's *lp* devices is to be writeable only by the *daemon* group, which includes users *root*, *bin*, and *daemon*. Of these, the *daemon* user was the least privileged user available set up out of the box, and since these machines are only print servers, compromising a specially set up printer account can lead to the same denials of service that compromising the *daemon* account can lead to.

The Cisco *smbprint* script is not the Samba *smbprint* script. Cisco's *smbprint* is distributed as part of CEPS:

```
[global]
;  Information about our print spooling software
   printing = bsd
```

```
printcap name = /etc/printcap
load printers = yes
guest account = daemon
log file = /var/log/samba
lock directory = /var/lock/samba
share modes = yes
dead time = 3
lpq cache time = 30
lpq command = /usr/bin/lpq -P'%p'
print command = /usr/local/ciscolp/bin/smbprint '%p' '%m' '%U' '%s' '%L'
lprm command = /usr/bin/lprm -P'%p' -U'%U' '%j'
```

Windows networking depends on maintaining accurate browse lists of network resources. Building and distributing browse lists can consume a fair amount of memory and CPU time. Given the comparatively slim resources available to Cisco's print servers, browsing is turned off:

```
;  Don't become a master browser anywhere to save resources
   os level = 0
   domain master = False
   preferred master = False
   local master = False
```

To aid WINS servers in building browse lists, Cisco's Samba servers are configured to send unsolicited announcements to the WINS servers with the **remote announce** parameter:

```
;  Force remote browsing to work
   remote announce = %%SMB_ANNOUNCE%%

   server string = Cisco print server (Linux & Samba)
   wins proxy = False
   wins support = False
   wins server = 171.68.235.228
   workgroup = %%SMB_DOMAIN%%

;  Parameters to automatically install print drivers on Win95
   printer driver file=/usr/local/ciscolp/etc/printers.def
   printer driver location=\\%L\!DRIVERS\INSTALLS
```

The next lines are the heart of Cisco's Samba scalability. Based on the NetBIOS name and aliases that are used, different printers will be included in the server list. Each NetBIOS server name has associated configurations stored in */var/spool/ ciscolp/conf/smbconf.d*. After dissecting *smb.conf.template*, we will explore this scalability mechanism:

```
netbios name = %%SMB_NBNAME%%
   netbios aliases = %%SMB_NBALIAS%%

include = /var/spool/ciscolp/conf/smbconf.d/%L.conf
```

Finally, two disk shares hand out printer drivers and up-to-date information for Windows print users:

```
[!drivers]
    comment = PostScript printer drivers
    browseable = yes
    public = yes
    writeable = no
    printable = no
    path = /usr/local/ciscolp/pcfiles

[!readme]
    comment = Up to date information on printers
    browseable = yes
    public = yes
    writeable = no
    printable = no
    path = /usr/local/ciscolp/pcfiles/readme
```

Using the server name to scale administration

If a printer is named *PRINT-FOO,* and also is known by the NetBIOS aliases of *PRINT-BAR* and *PRINT-BAZ,* then the NetBIOS name and the aliases in the *smb.conf template* will cause Samba to read in *print-foo.conf, print-bar.conf,* and *print-baz.conf.** CEPS generates *print-*.conf,* which is where the actual printer share configuration is stored. Example 6-10 shows a typical *.conf* file.

Example 6-10. print-.conf*

```
[printer1]
    comment = Loc: Cube 73, Contact: John Doe, 555-1212
    path = /tmp
    browseable = yes
    printable = yes
    public = yes
    writeable = no
    create mode = 0700
    printer driver = Adobe HP LaserJet 5Si/5SiMX
```

Detailed Information on Parts of smb.conf.template

Three aspects of *smb.conf.template* are worthy of further comment.

Print commands

The print command is a script named *smbprint.* It is a custom-written script that calls *lpr,* but with several enhancements. If a printer is unknown, the script will send email to users requesting contact information. If the print request came from

---

* Technically, these names play a bit fast and loose with the rules. The important conclusion that you should take away from reading this is that including files with *%L.conf* in *smb.conf* makes your job as an administrator much easier.

an NT Server, the script sends instructions to the user to change their print-queue from the NT Server to the Samba server. It filters output from known bad drivers, or print-queues that do not exist any more.

Because of the large number of users demanding print services (especially in printer-happy departments), the `lpq cache time` was made much larger than the default time of ten seconds to avoid overloading the server with *lpq* requests. The **dead time** parameter can help reduce the server load by disconnecting inactive clients. By default, disconnection is disabled. Cisco enabled this option and set it to three minutes.

Windows networking interaction

Disabling browsing saves processing power on the print servers. Servers use WINS to resolve names, but do not serve information via WINS. All print servers are configured to give Windows clients the appropriate print driver.

When WINS servers crash, they lose the name/address mappings they have accumulated. Acquiring name mappings places an additional load on the network as names are re-resolved and stored. The **remote announce** parameter is used to overcome this barrier. **remote announce** causes Samba to send service advertisements directly to the IP addresses and workgroups specified. On large networks, it can be directed at WINS servers so that the Samba server's NetBIOS name, aliases, and IP address are continuously registered with Windows name services.

User authentication

To allow new printers to be added quickly and streamline the process of adding users to the network, Cisco's team decided not to force user authentication because there was no reason to deny printing to users already on the network. Not maintaining a user database helps administrators spend more time improving the system. Table 6-3 reviews common options on print servers.

Table 6-3. Commonly Used smb.conf Options on Print Servers

Option	Scope	Value	Default Value	Description
[printers]	Global		N/A	A special share that automatically creates print-queue entries. If a [printers] share exists, Samba creates a share for each printer in the *printcap* file. Note: When a share wasn't explicitly created in *smb.conf*, Samba processes [homes] and then [printers]. If a printer has the same name as a user, processing terminates with [homes]. Users expecting to connect to a print service will connect to a disk service instead.

Table 6-3. Commonly Used smb.conf Options on Print Servers (continued)

Option	Scope	Value	Default Value	Description
printing	Global	BSD, LPRNG, SYSV, or HPUX	Based on server OS	Tells Samba the "personality" of the underlying Unix spooler. This variable controls defaults for queue and job manipulation programs and helps Samba to interpret status and error codes. Other values of printing are possible, but for print servers, one of the listed values is likely to be used.
print command	Share	Fully qualified path (string)	See Table 6-2	After the print file is received and stored on the local disk, the print command is run to enter the print file into the spooler.
lprm command	Share	Fully qualified path (string)	See Table 6-2	Command to delete a single job from a print-queue.
lpq command	Share	Fully qualified path (string)	See Table 6-2	Command to list contents of a queue.
lppause command	Share	Fully qualified path (string)	See Table 6-2	Command to pause printing for a specific job. It is only set if printing is set to SYSV.
lpresume command	Share	Fully qualified path (string)	See Table 6-2	Command to resume printing for a specific job. It is only set if printing is set to SYSV.
queuepause command	Share	Fully qualified path (string)	See Table 6-2	Pauses the print-queue, not just a single job. Default setting is generally correct.
queueresume command	Share	Fully qualified path (string)	See Table 6-2	Resumes a print-queue, not just a single job. Default setting is generally correct.
netbios name	Global	String	Server hostname	Sets the primary NetBIOS name of the server. Changing the value of this option is generally not a good idea.
netbios aliases	Global	String	Not set	Used to create virtual servers. Multiple virtual servers may be created by separating names by spaces.
workgroup	Global	String	Set to compiled-in default	Defines the workgroup or domain the server belongs to.
security	Global	Domain, server, user, or share	Samba 2.0: user Samba 1.9: share	Sets security model to be used. Most likely, this will be set to user or domain.

Table 6-3. Commonly Used smb.conf Options on Print Servers (continued)

Option	Scope	Value	Default Value	Description
`password server`	Global	NetBIOS server name (string)	Not set	Sets authentication server to be used. May be set to * to resolve password servers via NetBIOS name services.
`server string`	Global	String	Samba plus the version number	Comment string for the server in the Windows Network Neighborhood.
`path`	Share	Fully qualified directory (string)	Not set	Print shares must store temporary files. Any directory should be world writeable and use the "sticky bit" to control access to file owners.
`public` or `guest ok`	Share	Boolean	No	No authentication is required when set to **yes**. Anonymous connections are made using the `guest account`.
`printable` or `print ok`	Share	Boolean	No	`printable=yes` must be set, or Samba will treat the share as a disk share.
`guest account`	Share	Unix account name (string)	`nobody`	Unix account used for guest access to share. `nobody` frequently lacks permission for many operations and is often replaced by `ftp` because the `ftp` user is set up for secure anonymous access.
`printer driver`	Share	String	Not set	String sent to clients to tell them what driver to load.
`printer driver file`	Share	Fully qualified pathname (string)	Not set	Location of driver definition file used in automatic driver installation on Windows clients.
`printer driver location`	Share	Network pathname (string)	Not set	Network pathname that holds printer driver and definition files; frequently set to \\%L\PRINTER$ or similar.
`lpq cache time`	Global	Number of seconds to cache status information from the *lpq* command	10	Queue information is saved for the number of seconds specified by `lpq cache time`. If queue listings take large amounts of time to maintain, increase this parameter.
`postscript`	Share	Boolean	No	Prepends %! to the print file, which forces print system to see job as a PostScript file.
`load printers`	Global	Boolean	No	If set to yes, each printer in *printcap* is shared.

Table 6-3. Commonly Used smb.conf Options on Print Servers (continued)

Option	Scope	Value	Default Value	Description
`printcap name` or `printcap`	Global	Fully qualified pathname (string)	System dependent: */etc/qconfig* (AIX) */etc/printcap* (BSD/LPRng) *lpstat* (SYSV)	Location of printer configuration file.
`min print space`	Share	Integer	0	Amount, in kilobytes, of free space required before printing.

7

Connecting Macintosh Networks to Unix Servers

The Unix programming environment allows the development of specialized servers for nearly any network protocol suite. To prevent Windows users from having all the fun, the Research Systems Unix Group at the University of Michigan developed *netatalk*, an implementation of the AppleTalk protocol suite for Unix systems. *netatalk* was later refined and extended by Adrian Sun to include many other goodies. Like Samba, *netatalk* also makes an excellent file server for its clients, although we will not devote much time to these capabilities. This chapter is for Macintosh network administrators what the previous chapter was for Windows network administrators.

The AppleTalk Protocol Suite

Sometimes, all that keeps network administrators sane is that all protocol suites have the same structure, so that once you know one networking protocol, you know them all, to a certain degree. This section is a brief overview of the protocol. In many respects, AppleTalk networking is easy on a network administrator because of the automatic configuration routines built into AppleTalk. If you need more detail on any part of the AppleTalk suite, the comprehensive overview is *Inside AppleTalk*, by Gursharan Sidhu, Richard Andrews, and Alan Oppenheimer (Addison Wesley, 1990).

Alphabet Soup

The AppleTalk protocol stack, as it relates to printing, is shown in Figure 7-1.

At the link layer, AppleTalk runs over *LocalTalk* and Ethernet-like media. (For simplicity, and because of the dwindling Token Ring installed base, we will just call it

Ethernet here.) Over Ethernet, AppleTalk frames are transmitted using 802.3 SNAP encapsulation, which is different from the standard IP encapsulation.* Like IP, AppleTalk includes a method for dynamically translating network layer addresses to link layer addresses called AARP, the AppleTalk Address Resolution Protocol.

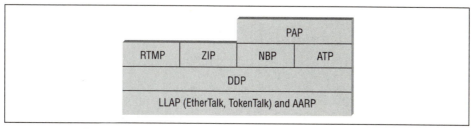

Figure 7-1. AppleTalk protocol stack

The core of AppleTalk networking is the Datagram Delivery Protocol (DDP). Like IP, DDP provides connectionless best-effort delivery of packets on an AppleTalk internetwork. DDP addresses have a 16-bit network number and an 8-bit host identifier. Network numbers zero and 65535 are reserved (65535 is used for zone broadcasts), and networks 65280 through 65534 are used for startup purposes. For normal operation, network numbers 1 through 65279 are used. DDP is relatively simple, and leaves reliability and sequencing to higher level protocols, such as the AppleTalk Transaction Protocol (ATP). ATP also provides transaction identifiers for client/server communications.

DDP is a routable protocol. Routing tables are built by a distance vector protocol called RTMP, the Routing Table Maintenance Protocol. Like most distance vector routing protocols, RTMP's structure will be familiar to network administrators who have used IP's Routing Information Protocol (RIP). For user convenience, Apple-Talk networks can be divided into zones, which allow users to associate zone names with resources. Dynamic resource name binding and registration are handled by the Name Binding Protocol (NBP), and inter-zone name coordination is handled by the Zone Information Protocol (ZIP).

Compiling and Installing netatalk

netatalk is a Unix implementation of the AppleTalk protocol suite. It was originally developed by the University of Michigan Research Systems Unix Group to support the University of Michigan campus network. Later modifications by Adrian Sun improved portability and added AppleShareIP support. Modern versions of *netatalk* run on BSD-derived systems, Linux, Solaris, and SunOS.

---

* For Ethernet encapsulation details, see *Ethernet: The Definitive Guide*, by Charles Spurgeon (O'Reilly, 2000).

netatalk servers must have network interface cards that support hardware level multicasting because many of the AppleTalk support protocols transmit data-link layer multicast frames. In practice, this is a trivial requirement. All modern Ethernet boards support Ethernet multicasting. Operating system support for multicasting is also required.

Preparing to Build netatalk

Building *netatalk* from source is not a complex operation, but a few conditions must be met before you begin. AppleTalk is a separate protocol suite with its own OSI layer 3 (network) protocol, so you must compile support for that protocol stack into the kernel. Additionally, *netatalk* requires a separate cryptographic library and TCP connection control sofware.

AppleTalk kernel modifications

DDP is the core of native AppleTalk networking. Building a Macintosh network without DDP is like building a Unix network without IP. *netatalk* depends on the OS kernel to provide DDP protocol support.

BSD. Add the line *options NETATALK* to the kernel configuration file and rebuild the kernel. Nothing is displayed after rebooting to indicate that AppleTalk support has been added.

Linux. Run *make config* in the kernel source tree and say yes at the *AppleTalk DDP?* prompt. After installing the new kernel, check to see if the kernel supports AppleTalk by searching for it in the kernel messages after boot:

```
# dmesg | grep Apple
AppleTalk 0.17 for Linux NET3.035
```

If nothing appears, the kernel does not support AppleTalk. AppleTalk support may have been built as a module. Find *appletalk.o* and use *insmod* to insert it into the running kernel.

Solaris. *netatalk* includes a kernel module to use with Solaris. To make the kernel aware of the module, edit */etc/netconfig*. Add the following line to */etc/netconfig* to support DDP:

```
ddp tpi_clts - appletalk ddp /dev/ddp -
```

After modifying *netconfig*, build the AppleTalk kernel module. Compile and install the Solaris kernel module by running *make kinstall*. *make* will put the driver into */usr/kernel/drv* and */usr/kernel/strmod* and then run *add_drv ddp* to start using the AppleTalk kernel module. Although not strictly required, some versions of Solaris may require more file descriptors to run a busy *netatalk* server.

Install a DES library

Using scrambled passwords between the Macintosh and the *netatalk* server requires a DES library. An excellent choice is Eric Young's *libdes*, available at *ftp://ftp.psy.uq.oz.au/pub/Crypto/DES/libdes.tar.gz*. (Eric Young also wrote *SSLeay*, the precursor to *OpenSSL*.)

After retrieving the source, untar it and run *make gcc* (other options are available, depending on the operating system, but we suspect most readers use *gcc*):

```
[root@krypton]# tar -xzf libdes.tar.gz
[root@krypton]# cd des
[root@krypton]# make gcc
make -f Makefile CC=gcc CFLAGS="-O3 -fomit-frame-pointer -DRAND -DTERMIO     -O3
-fomit-frame-pointer" all
make[1]: Entering directory `/root/atalk/des'

[lots of build messages skipped]

gcc -O3 -fomit-frame-pointer -DRAND -DTERMIO        -O3 -fomit-frame-pointer -o des_
opts des_opts.o libdes.a
make[1]: Leaving directory `/root/atalk/des'
```

The build process creates the *destest* program, which will test the compiled code:

```
[root@krypton des]# ./destest
Doing ecb
Doing ede ecb
Doing cbc
Doing desx cbc
Doing ede cbc
Doing pcbc
Doing cfb8 cfb16 cfb32 cfb48 cfb64 cfb64() ede_cfb64() done
Doing ofb
Doing ofb64
Doing ede_ofb64
Doing cbc_cksum
Doing quad_cksum
input word alignment test 0 1 2 3
output word alignment test 0 1 2 3
fast crypt test
```

If the binaries pass *destest*, either install the package or optimize before installation. As part of building *deslib*, the *des_opts* program is compiled. Running it prints out recommendations for compile time flags:

```
[root@krypton des]# ./des_opts
Doing des_encrypt_u4_cisc_idx  's for 10 seconds
7160323 des_encrypt_u4_cisc_idx  's in 10.00 second

[ other run results omitted ]

des_encrypt_u4_cisc_idx   bytes per sec =   5728258.40 (  1.4uS)
des_encrypt_u16_cisc_idx  bytes per sec =   5949475.20 (  1.3uS)
```

```
des_encrypt_u4_risc1_idx  bytes per sec =  5137001.60 (  1.6uS)
des_encrypt_u16_risc1_idx bytes per sec =  3359066.40 (  2.4uS)
des_encrypt_u4_risc2_idx  bytes per sec =  5189824.45 (  1.5uS)
des_encrypt_u16_risc2_idx bytes per sec =  3092923.20 (  2.6uS)
des_encrypt_u4_cisc_ptr   bytes per sec =  5412998.40 (  1.5uS)
des_encrypt_u16_cisc_ptr  bytes per sec =  5499091.20 (  1.5uS)
des_encrypt_u4_risc1_ptr  bytes per sec =  4880884.00 (  1.6uS)
des_encrypt_u16_risc1_ptr bytes per sec =  5767096.80 (  1.4uS)
des_encrypt_u4_risc2_ptr  bytes per sec =  4652663.20 (  1.7uS)
des_encrypt_u16_risc2_ptr bytes per sec =  4984191.20 (  1.6uS)
options     des ecb/s
16  c i    743684.40 100.0%
16  r1 p   720887.10  96.9%
 4  c i    716032.30  96.3%
16  c p    687386.40  92.4%
 4  c p    676624.80  91.0%
 4  r2 i   648728.06  87.2%
 4  r1 i   642125.20  86.3%
16  r2 p   623023.90  83.8%
 4  r1 p   610110.50  82.0%
 4  r2 p   581582.90  78.2%
16  r1 i   419883.30  56.5%
16  r2 i   386615.40  52.0%
-DDES_UNROLL
```

In this case, *des_opts* recommends recompiling on this machine with the option
–DDES_UNROLL. After recompiling with the recommended options set, install the
software with *make install*.

TCP Wrappers

netatalk will not compile unless TCP Wrappers* is installed. TCP Wrappers also
has some security benefits.

Building netatalk

The source for *netatalk* is freely available and is currently distributed by Cobalt
Networks. The University of Michigan RSUG distributed all the versions prior to 1.4
beta 2. Adrian Sun's enhancements are distributed as the *netatalk+asun* version; as
of the writing of this book, the current version was *netatalk-1.4b2+asun2.1.3*,
available from *ftp://ftp.cobalt.com:/pub/users/asun/release*. Uncompressing the tar
file is simple:

```
[root@krypton]# tar -xzf netatalk-1.4b2+asun2.1.3.tar.gz
[root@krypton]# cd netatalk-1.4b2+asun2.1.3
```

---

* TCP Wrappers is a security program that "wraps" other programs such as *telnetd* or *ftpd*, and controls
access to them. The access control is based on the client's source IP address or domain name.

Edit DESTDIR in the root-level *Makefile*. The *netatalk* directory hierarchy will be installed at that point. Unless you have strong reasons for doing so, the default of */usr/local/atalk* is fine. If you chose to install *deslib*, you need to set the DESTDIR variable to its location.

Linux-specific notes

The build process is simplified if you use Linux 2.0 or later. Earlier versions of Linux require you to check the location of some system header files and install them if needed. Because you should be using Linux 2.0 for reasons too numerous to list here, readers wishing to use old and decrepit versions of Linux are referred to the *netatalk* documentation.

For Linux customizations, edit *sys/linux/Makefile* in the source directory. If you use RedHat or another Linux distribution that uses Pluggable Authentication Modules (PAM), you need to add *–DUSE_PAM* to the DEFS variable and *–lpam –ldl* to the AFPLIBS variable. Modern distributions based on the GNU C Library, Version 2 should not use the *–DNEED_QUOTACTL_WRAPPER*. For Linux 2.2, you can use the *–DSENDFILE_FLAVOR_LINUX* to reduce the overhead when sending or copying files.

Finding a home for deserving binaries

Building the executables is a simple matter of running a *make* in the top level source directory. Provided that you have defined everything correctly, the process should be relatively fast and bug free. Installation of the binaries is accomplished with *make install*. The build process creates the following pieces:

atalkd

> The daemon that implements RTMP, NBP, ZIP, and AEP. As you might guess, it is necessary for AppleTalk networking.

aecho

> Sends AppleTalk echo packets to the target. It is like the familiar ping command, but for AppleTalk networks.

afpd

> Implements the AppleTalk Filing Protocol (AFP), over both DDP and TCP/IP. If you are running an AppleShareIP server, you do not need to run *atalkd*. AFP over AppleTalk requires some services provided by *atalkd*.

papd

> A Printer Access Protocol (PAP) server. It accepts print jobs from AppleTalk clients and feeds them to the underlying Unix spooler.

nbplkup

Provides AppleTalk Name Binding Protocol services and functions much like *nslookup* for AppleTalk networks.

Edit /etc/services

netatalk currently implements AppleTalk's RTMP, NBP, AEP, and ZIP. Adrian Sun added support for AppleShare IP, which uses TCP as its network layer transport. To define all of these, add the following lines to */etc/services*:

```
rtmp 1/ddp      # AppleTalk Routing Table Maintenance Protocol
nbp  2/ddp      # AppleTalk Name Binding Protocol
echo 4/ddp      # AppleTalk Echo Protocol
zip  6/ddp      # AppleTalk Zone Information Protocol

afp-tcp 548/tcp # AppleTalk Filing Protocol over TCP
afp-tcp 548/udp
```

Configuring automatic startup

Copy *rc.atalk.redhat* to */etc/rc.d/init.d/atalk.init* on RedHat 5.2 and later to automatically start *netatalk* on boot. You may need to edit *atalk.init* to define *SBINDIR* and *BINDIR*.

When a Linux machine boots, a message such as *eth0: Setting Rx mode to 1 addresses* appears as the IP address is assigned to the system's network interface. When running *netatalk*, DDP addresses will cause additional network addresses to be assigned and the Ethernet card may become responsible for two or three network addresses as the *atalkd* daemon starts. DDP addresses are reported by the *ifconfig* command on Linux. The automatic address assignment procedures have assigned the DDP address 280.138 to *eth0*. The first part of the address is the AppleTalk network number; the latter part is the host. The following example shows an Ethernet card running under Linux that has EtherTalk enabled:

```
[gast@asimov]$ /sbin/ifconfig eth0
eth0      Link encap:Ethernet  HWaddr 00:20:AF:35:FB:C0
          inet addr:10.2.0.11  Bcast:10.2.0.255  Mask:255.255.255.0
          EtherTalk Phase 2 addr:280/138
          UP BROADCAST RUNNING MULTICAST  MTU:1500  Metric:1
          RX packets:99 errors:0 dropped:0 overruns:0 frame:0
          TX packets:96 errors:0 dropped:0 overruns:0 carrier:0
          collisions:0
          Interrupt:11 Base address:0x220
```

Configuring netatalk

Compared to configuring Samba, *netatalk* is a breeze. AppleTalk has extensive automatic configuration procedures to automatically number network interfaces by using a *seed router.*[*] Only the seed router needs to be manually configured; other routers learn network numbers from the seed router.

Configuring the daemon: atalkd.conf

atalkd.conf must be set up for systems that cannot reliably get an interface list from the kernel, most notably Solaris. Each line in *atalkd.conf* configures one interface. If there are other AppleTalk seed routers on the network, only the interface name is required. On a Solaris server, *atalkd.conf* is as simple as the network interface to bind *atalkd* to:

```
# atalkd.conf on Solaris when seed routers are present
le0
```

Other configuration options may be specified on each interface. Table 7-1 describes the options that may be used.

Table 7-1. atalkd.conf Configuration Options

Option	Description
–seed	Run *atalkd* as a seed router for the network. If *atalkd* is run as a seed router, it supplies configuration information to any other routers on the network, so all other fields must be fully specified. If *–seed* is not used, all other configuration information may be overridden by the local seed information.
–phase number	number is either 1 or 2, and defaults to 2.
–net range	For single homed servers, range should be set to 1-65279, which corresponds to the range of operational networks. For seed routers, range should be set to the smallest network range possible; network numbers should be supplied by the local AppleTalk network administrator.
–addr net.host	If the address is specified but the network is not, a range of 1 is assumed. *atalkd* caches the last assigned address in *atalkd.conf* with the *addr* parameter. See the subsequent section "Address caching and the dual role of *atalkd.conf*."
–zone name	name specifies the zone name for the interface.

Options are set on a per-interface basis. Add any options to the end of the line. If *atalkd* is not a seed router, though, it is better to leave the configuration to the automatic configuration processes. Some versions of *atalkd* will crash if the configuration disagrees with the seed configuration. Here is a sample configuration:

```
de0 -phase 2 -net 280-281 -addr 280.197
```

---

[*] AppleTalk networks depend on seed routers to provide some initial information to any other routers attached to the same cable. Seed routers are configured with a range of DDP network numbers. Based on the seed information, other routers can automatically configure themselves.

AppleTalk routers and zone names

To have a network with zones, there must be an AppleTalk router somewhere on the AppleTalk network. Unix machines running *atalkd* can be AppleTalk routers if you configure *atalkd* to bind to multiple interfaces. Multiple interface configuration is a logical extension of single interface configuration: use multiple lines, with one line for each interface. A very simple AppleTalk router that relies on other routers for seed information looks like this:

```
# AppleTalk router seeded by other AppleTalk routers
eth0 -phase 2
eth1 -phase 2
```

To assign zone names to physical networks, *atalkd* must be run as a seed router. When using the *-seed* option to run *atalkd* as a seed router, the network range and address must be configured. After all, if you do not seed the seed router, how is it going to seed the rest of the network? Here is a sample multi-zone *atalkd.conf* file:

```
eth0 -seed -phase 2 -net 1-3 -addr 2.4 -zone Brobdingnag
eth1 -seed -phase 2 -net 5-9 -addr 4.4 -zone Lilliput
```

Address caching and the dual role of atalkd.conf

In addition to configuring AppleTalk networking, *atalkd.conf* also serves as the DDP address cache. AppleTalk nodes obtain DDP addresses from AppleTalk routers as part of network initialization. To make restarting more efficient, nodes will save the last AppleTalk address assigned by the router. When reinitialized, nodes attempt to retain the last assigned address. When a single interface *netatalk* server starts, *atalkd* rewrites *atalkd.conf* to accept any address for its next initialization. *atalkd.conf* will save the current DDP address, but the network range that *atalkd* accepts will be extended over the full range of network addresses allowed by AppleTalk. Don't be surprised if the *-net* option is extended to 1–65535 like this:

```
eth0 -phase 2 -net 1-65535 -addr 2.4
```

Password Configuration

Macintosh networks have no centralized administrative facilities, which eliminates most of the password synchronization headaches inherent in SMB networking. AppleTalk networks have no central user database or authentication mechanism; each server requests a username and password and then authenticates users. Flexibility comes with a price, though. AppleTalk networks have no central authentication servers.

netatalk does not add anything to this administrative model except the underlying flexibility of Unix. PAM allows you to centralize user accounts somewhere else, such as a NIS server. Authentication for AppleShare servers can then be based on information stored in a large-scale user database.

Sharing a Printer: papd.conf

/usr/local/atalk/etc/papd.conf configures the PAP software. Sharing a printer already set up as a Unix queue is straightforward. *papd.conf* looks like a *printcap* file. The printer name for the Macintosh network, which must be 32 characters or less, is associated with the Unix spooler by using the options described in Table 7-2.

Table 7-2. papd.conf Options

Option	Description
pr	Names the Unix queue to submit jobs to.
op	All jobs submitted to *papd* are entered into the Unix spooler by the same user, which is specified by *op*.
pd	Macintosh print files are all PostScript files, and *pd* allows the system administrator to select a PPD file for the printer. For more information on PPDs, see the sidebar, "What Exactly Is a PPD File?"

The following *papd.conf* shows how to share the queue named *laser* to an Apple-Talk network as *Lumberjack* and enters all jobs as user *lpadmin*, a generic Unix printer-administration account (the PPD file for the printer is stored at */usr/local/atalk/ppd/laser.ppd*):

```
# papd.conf
#
# This file shares the "laser" printer to the Mac network
Lumberjack:\
        :pr=laser:\
        :op=lpadmin:\
        :pd=/usr/local/atalk/ppd/laser.ppd:
```

pr may also be used to specify a pipe to hand the job to. Printing to a pipe is often necessary when using *netatalk* with LPRng. In the following example, *pr* does not specify a printer name, but opens a pipe to an *lpr* command to submit the job to *laser*:

```
Lumberjack:\
        :pr=|/usr/bin/lpr -Plaser:\
        :op=lpadmin:\
        :pd=/usr/local/atalk/ppd/laser.ppd:
```

Sending Macintosh jobs to network printers

One attractive feature of our architecture is that the Unix spooler hides any printer interface details from higher level applications. If a printer can be given a Unix

---

What Exactly Is a PPD File?

PostScript is a baroque language, to say the least. Different printers and man-ufacturers will produce hardware with different capabilities. PostScript printer description (PPD) files enumerate printer capabilities. *papd* uses the PPD to accurately report printer capabilities to remote Macintosh clients. If the wrong PPD is used, documents may be printed incorrectly, or some printer features may be unavailable. A generic PPD can be used when a printer-specific PPD is not available.

Frequently, PPD files are bundled with printer hardware. If not, PPD files are often available from printer vendor web sites, as well as from the Adobe web site at *http://www.adobe.com/prodindex/printerdrivers/macppd.html* and the Adobe FTP site at *ftp://ftp.adobe.com/pub/adobe/printerdrivers/mac/all/ppdfiles.*

For consistency, it is important to use the same PPD file on the client Macintosh and the print server. You can do this by copying the file over to the server from the client Mac. PPD files for *netatalk* should be stored as plain text files.

---

queue, then *netatalk* can send jobs its way. As an example, take a laser printer that accepts jobs to a queue named *raw* with the LPD protocol. A *printcap* file for that printer would look something like this:

```
scotsman:\
  :lp=/dev/null:\
  :sd=/var/spool/lpd/laser:\
  :mx#0:\
  :rp=raw:\
  :rm=haggis.corp.com:
```

Any jobs submitted to the *scotsman* queue are sent by *lpd* to the *raw* printer on *haggis.corp.com*. Getting the job in the queue is the responsibility of *papd*. An associated *papd.conf* file would look like this:

```
MacLaser:\
  :pr=scotsman:\
  :pd=/usr/local/atalk/ppd/haggis.ppd:
```

Jobs sent by Macintosh clients to the *MacLaser* printer are received by *papd* and placed in the *scotsman* queue. Although not part of the example files presented, the *scotsman* queue may use print filters to process the output. By using GhostScript, for example, a non-PostScript printer may be used by Macintosh clients.

Zone information in papd.conf

To advertise a printer in a zone other than the default zone, the zone must be specified in *papd.conf.* Put *@zone* on the end of the printer name to change the advertisement. Example 7-1 show how to share the *Deforester* printer in the *Brobdingnag* zone and the *MacLaser* printer to the *Lilliput* zone:

Example 7-1. papd.conf in a Multi-Zone Network

```
# papd.conf
#
# This file shares printers in two different zones

Deforester@Brobdingnag:\
        :pr=ljet4-letter-auto-mono:\
        :op=lpadmin:\
        :pd=/usr/local/atalk/ppd/ljet4.ppd:
MacLaser@Lilliput:\
        :pr=scotsman:\
        :op=lpadmin:\
        :pd=/usr/local/atalk/ppd/haggis.ppd:
```

Configuring Macintosh Clients

Macintosh clients obtain AppleTalk network information from the nearest seed router on boot, which makes AppleTalk configuration simple. To see how easy configuration is, call up the AppleTalk control panel. Go to the *Apple* menu in the upper left hand side of the screen, and select the AppleTalk control panel from the *Control Panels* menu, as shown in Figure 7-2.

The AppleTalk control panel in Figure 7-3 is used to select a zone on a multi-zone network. If only one zone is available, then only that zone will be displayed.

Client Driver Configuration from the Chooser

For this example, we will use Apple's LaserWriter 8 driver. LaserWriter 8 is a fairly modern driver that has eliminated many of the headaches previously associated with the LaserWriter 7 driver. One key LaserWriter 8 feature is its ability to use PostScript printer description (PPD) files to adjust driver configuration on the fly. For more on PPDs, see the sidebar in the previous section.

On a multi-zone AppleTalk network, the Chooser is separated in half, with services and zones appearing on the left and services appearing on the right, as in Figure 7-4. To use a printer, select LaserWriter 8 on the left hand side, and select the zone you want to see resources for. Based on responses to name queries sent to the network, the Chooser builds a list of LaserWriter 8 resources in the selected zone. The *papd.conf* in Example 7-1 showed two queues in different zones; this example configures the *Deforester* queue's client driver.

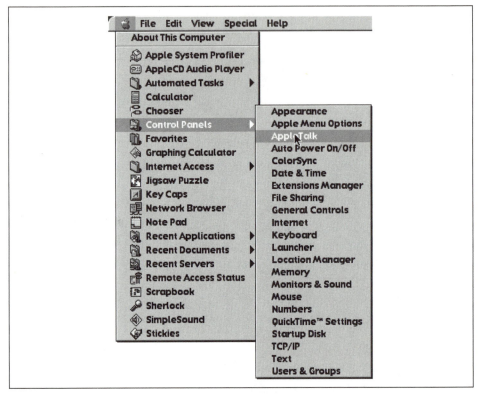

Figure 7-2. Selecting the AppleTalk control panel

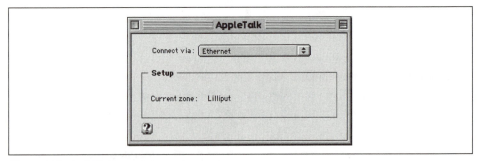

Figure 7-3. AppleTalk control panel

Setting up the client spool

Before the *Deforester* queue has been created, the button below the resource list is a Create button. Click it to bring up the LaserWriter 8 configuration box. The first step is to select a PPD. When entering the PPD selection dialog box, the Finder automatically starts in the Printer Description subfolder of the system folder, as shown in Figure 7-5. There are three choices to determine which PPD to use.

1. Use the generic PPD.

2. Use a PPD already in the Printer Descriptions folder.

3. Select an alternate PPD from the printer vendor by clicking on Select.

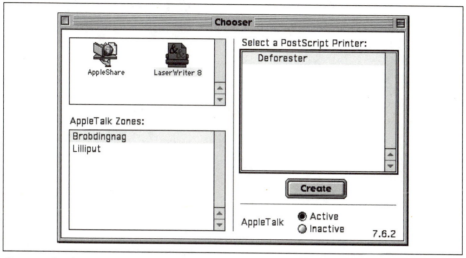

Figure 7-4. Selecting a printer in the chooser

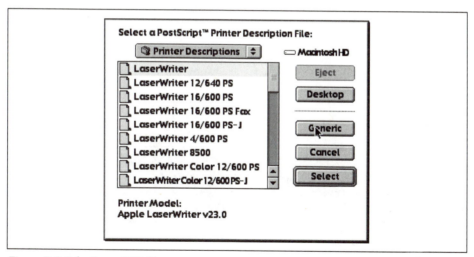

Figure 7-5. Selecting a PPD file

Using the generic PPD works, but it will not take advantage of any special hardware features. As the sidebar noted, PPDs are widely available from printer vendors. Figure 7-6 shows the alternate PPD selection screen operating on a folder of PPDs downloaded from the Hewlett-Packard web site.

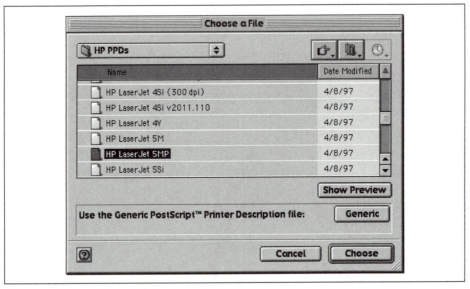

Figure 7-6. Choosing a vendor's PPD

After selecting a PPD, it is possible to view printer information, as shown in
Figure 7-7. The printer information is merely a summary of the information that
comes from the PPD on the *netatalk* server, supplied by *papd*.

It is a good idea to use the same PPD on the *netatalk* server and the
client. You can use *netatalk*'s file sharing capabilities to set up network drives to share PPDs for your printers, and instruct users to use
the relevant PPD, based on the printer's name.

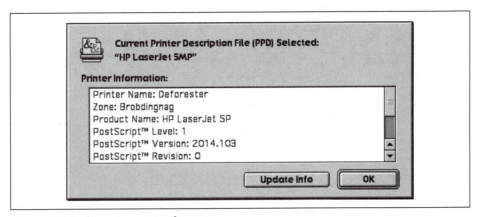

Figure 7-7. Looking at printer information

After the client has selected a PPD, the client side print spool is created, and a small spool icon is placed next to the printer name in the Chooser, as shown in Figure 7-8.

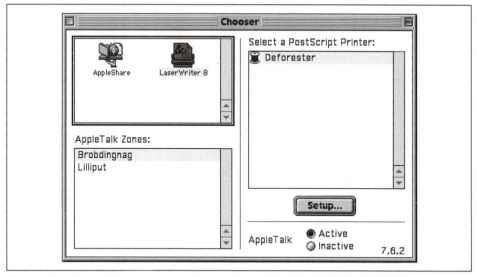

Figure 7-8. The spool icon shows the client side spool has been configured

Client Configuration and Status Reporting

The client is now fully configured to use the *netatalk* queue. The printer will appear on the desktop and is available to have jobs dragged and dropped onto it. If it is the only printer, it will also be surrounded by a bold line to indicate that it's the default system printer.

Many applications have a page setup dialog. Based on the PPD file, different options will appear when the page setup dialog is called up, as shown in Figure 7-9.

Double-clicking on the printer icon on the desktop brings up a printer queue, so the user can see pending jobs. The LaserWriter 8 driver maintains a local spool and assembles PostScript print jobs in the background. When it has finished creating the PostScript job, the LaserWriter 8 driver then sends the job to the *netatalk* server. In Figure 7-10, the LaserWriter driver is still assembling the PostScript job and has not yet sent it to the *netatalk* queue.

When the job is finally sent to the *netatalk* queue, it will be listed in the box at the top of queue display, as shown in Figure 7-11. At this point, some status information will be displayed. For *netatalk* servers, the status information from the print subsystem is displayed.

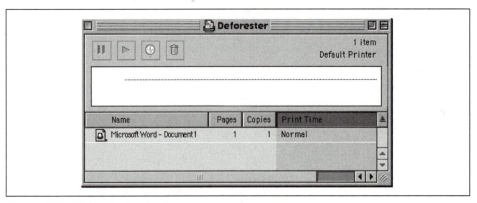

Figure 7-9. Configuring printer settings

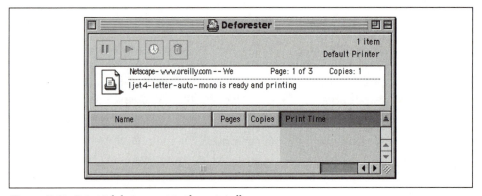

Figure 7-10. Jobs in the local print-queue

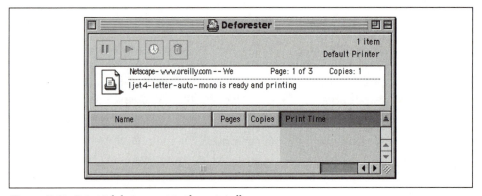

Figure 7-11. Print job being sent to the netatalk server

After the job is sent to the *netatalk* queue, you can use Unix queue monitoring tools to see it:

```
[root@asimov]# lpq
hplj6 is ready and printing
Rank    Owner    Job Files                            Total Size
active lpadmin    5   Microsoft Word - Document1       7756 bytes
1st    lpadmin    6   ...                              415749 bytes
```

Troubleshooting netatalk

As with Samba, try to trace problems through the path the print jobs take. Check the configuration of the client and make sure the client is correctly connected to the server before troubleshooting the application daemons and the *lpd* system.

Problems with atalkd

Generally speaking, most problems that keep the *netatalk* daemons from starting are AppleTalk networking problems, not application layer problems. If *atalkd* starts, the other application daemons, *afpd* and *papd*, will usually also start without difficulty. If AppleTalk networking is unavailable, though, *atalkd* will not start, and the application daemons cannot follow.

atalkd starts slowly

atalkd is a complete AppleTalk router and maintains many complicated internal data structures. It may take several seconds to start, add DDP addresses to all the network interfaces, and set up the AppleTalk routing table.

Too many routes/iface (Linux)

The Linux kernel imposes a limit on the number of AppleTalk routes per interface that can be installed in the AppleTalk routing table. The limit is 4096 networks per interface with kernels before Version 2.2.11. If the network range assigned to an interface is larger than 4096, *atalkd* will not start. To get around this, either decrease the network range or upgrade the kernel.

"AppleTalk not up! Child exited with 1."

This is a generic error message indicating that AppleTalk networking is not available. It may be that kernel support for DDP is not loaded, or that you have already initialized the kernel's DDP data structures and need to reinitialize them. If the *netatalk* server is connected to an Ethernet switch, see the "Vanishing Zones, General Performance Problems, and Intermittent Service" section later in this chapter.

Restarting atalkd is ineffective

On some platforms, the kernel code for DDP does not function correctly after *atalkd* is restarted. The AppleTalk code must be reinitialized. On Linux, remove the AppleTalk module from the kernel, reload it, and then restart *atalkd*:

```
asimov# rmmod appletalk
asimov# insmod appletalk
asimov# atalkd &
```

Other platforms require rebooting because DDP is statically linked into the kernel and cannot be reinitialized from scratch.

Lack of Connectivity

MacPing is a Macintosh program that uses the AppleTalk Echo Protocol (AEP) to send hello packets over the AppleTalk network. Like its IP counterpart, it is a good, quick test of connectivity.

Versions of *tcpdump* supplied with many Unix flavors can capture and decode AppleTalk packets, which can be used to verify that a conversation is taking place over the network.

Only the Guest Can Log In

This situation is typically due to broken authentication. Recompile *netatalk* with the *–DSHADOWPW* added to the compile flags. Problems may also occur if users are using shells that are not in */etc/shells*.

Jobs Spool, but Are Not Printed

When jobs are spooled correctly but do not come out of the printer, there can be a variety of culprits. *papd* submits the job to the Unix spooler. By using a command as the *pr* option in *papd.conf*, you check that the file is received correctly, and then go through the appropriate diagnostics for your print spooler.

Use the LaserWriter 8 driver

The LaserWriter 7 driver for MacOS is trouble-prone for a variety of reasons, some of which have nothing to do with *netatalk*. Apple's LaserWriter 8 driver is much more stable.

lpd job transfers

Stock BSD *lpd* does not transfer files to a remote printer unless the control filename is longer than 13 characters. The broken version of *lpd* is shipped with RedHat 6.0; a patch is incorporated into RedHat 6.1. To apply the patch without a full reinstallation, upgrade to the *lpr-0.39* package on RedHat systems. The problem occurs because *papd* sends a temporary file with a long name to the *lpd* spool area.

Although this problem has long been fixed, it is an excellent example of the power of source code. The reason for the broken *lpd* behavior can be found in *sendjob.c*. The following code fragment shows how a key temporary file is named. In line 2, positions 8 through 13 of the filename are replaced with X. In line 3, *mktemp()* should replace those 6 X's with a unique string, but *mktemp()* will only replace the X's and create the temporary filename if they are at the end of the string. If the original filename is longer than 13 characters, *dup_cfpname* will not end in a string of X's and *mktemp()* will fail:

```
 1 dup_cfpname = strdup(file);
 2 memcpy((dup_cfpname+7), "XXXXXX", 6);
 3 mktemp(dup_cfpname);
 4 tmpmask = umask(007);
 5 dup_cfp=fopen(dup_cfpname, "w");
 6 umask(tmpmask);
 7 if (dup_cfp == NULL)
 8 {
 9   syslog(LOG_ERR, "Can't create temp cfp file %s", dup_cfpname);
10   return(OK);
11 }
```

Line 2 is supposed to replace the last 6 characters in *dup_cfpname* with X, so instead, use the following line:

```
memcpy((dup_cfpname + (strlen(dup_cfpname) - 6)), "XXXXXX", 6);
```

Truncated Jobs

Print jobs may be truncated when printing through a queue served by *netatalk* if they reach the maximum file size. If jobs are truncated, increase the maximum file size or lift the limit altogether. Removing the limit may be the best course of action if your user community regularly generates very large print jobs.

Vanishing Zones, General Performance Problems, and Intermittent Service

If the client Macintosh or *netatalk* server is connected to a switch running the spanning tree protocol (IEEE 802.1d), a wide variety of problems may occur. AppleTalk services may be unavailable, degraded, intermittent, or limited to a subset of the available servers. Ports enabled with the spanning tree protocol may drop packets used to acquire DDP address information and discover network resources, resulting in an invalid or incomplete network setup.

If the server is connected to a dedicated switch port, the spanning tree protocol can safely be disabled on that port. Spanning tree prevents bridging loops, which cannot occur if the switch port is only connected to a single host. Depending on the switch manufacturer, you may also be able to configure a *fast convergence* mode that unblocks ports quickly. Refer to your switch manufacturer's documentation.[*]

---

[*] On Cisco switches, use the *portfast* option.

8

Connecting NetWare Networks to Linux Servers

This chapter describes how to open your Unix spooler to NetWare clients. It's a bit more complicated than Samba or *netatalk*, since you don't get to throw out your NetWare print spooler. What you can do is configure a Linux server to take jobs from a NetWare queue. Instead of allowing users to push jobs into Unix queues from NetWare clients, you are configuring a Unix print server to pull jobs from a NetWare queue into a Unix queue of its own. While it may not eliminate NetWare administrative overhead, it does allow you to maintain a single queue point.

IPX and the NetWare Protocol Suite

The Internet Protocol has long been the protocol of choice for dispersed WANs. Before the recent adoption of IP on LANs, the dominant local area network protocol was Novell's Internetworking Packet Exchange (IPX), a proprietary protocol at the heart of NetWare.

Another Helping of Alphabet Soup

Figure 8-1 shows the NetWare protocol stack.

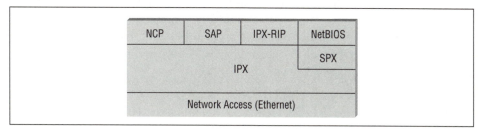

Figure 8-1. NetWare protocol stack

At the link layer, IPX runs over media of several types. Because the focus of this book is building print servers, we need to be concerned only with IPX over Ethernet. Like IP and DDP, IPX provides connectionless best effort delivery services. Reliable streams are provided by the connection-oriented Sequenced Packet Exchange (SPX).

Many NetWare services are built on NCP, the NetWare Core Protocol. Clients use NCP broadcasts to locate servers. NetWare servers announce their services to the network by using the Service Advertisement Protocol (SAP). IPX-RIP builds IPX routing tables for an IPX network.

NDS and Open Source Software

Much of Novell's recent resurgence has been due to its directory services (NDS). Unfortunately, NDS support is lacking in free software. To allow organizations to migrate to NDS-enabled versions of NetWare (4.x and up), Novell developed bindery emulation. In NetWare 3.x, network objects were stored in a registry called the *bindery*. By default, NetWare 4.x and later servers set up an emulation layer to allow *subtrees* of NDS to be accessed by bindery calls. In addition to establishing backward compatibility, bindery emulation allows bindery-aware open source tools to be used on a NetWare network.

In this chapter, we will present examples based on NetWare 4.x for two reasons. First, it is the first version of NetWare to use NDS and run bindery emulation. Second, it was the easiest version of NetWare for us to obtain.

Compiling and Installing ncpfs

ncpfs is a Linux tool primarily used for mounting NetWare shares. However, it includes a program called *pserver* that takes jobs from NetWare queues and prints them to Linux queues on the local host.

Pre-Compilation Tasks

A NetWare server that does not understand IPX won't make much of a NetWare server. Linux has a few key advantages over other Unix variants when it comes to offering NetWare services. Linux, unlike other Unix variants, supports IPX over all of the Ethernet frame types used by NetWare. Furthermore, Linux is the only version of Unix for which all the code to emulate NetWare functions is available.

NetWare emulation programs will depend on the Linux kernel to provide support for IPX. On Linux, run *make config* and say yes to *The IPX Protocol?* prompt. After installing the new kernel, check to see if the kernel supports IPX by searching for it in the kernel messages after boot:

```
# dmesg | grep IPX
Swansea University Computer Society IPX 0.34 for NET3.035
IPX Portions Copyright (c) 1995 Caldera, Inc.
```

Configure IPX networking

The *ipx_interface* command brings up an interface for use with IPX. Before bringing up an interface, find out what Ethernet frame type to use and the IPX network number. The frame type may be *802.3*, *802.2*, *802.2TR*, *SNAP*, or *EtherII*. Be sure to use the same frame type as the NetWare servers on your network to avoid trouble with your NetWare administrator.

In the following example, *eth0* is configured on IPX network 2B, using Ethernet II encapsulation. In this example, *eth0* is also designated as the primary address by the addition of the –*p* option:

```
[root@linux]# ipx_interface add -p eth0 etherii 2b
[root@linux]# ifconfig eth0
eth0      Link encap:Ethernet  HWaddr 00:20:AF:35:FB:C0
          inet addr:10.2.0.11  Bcast:10.2.0.255  Mask:255.255.255.0
          IPX/Ethernet II addr:0000002B:0020AF35FBC0
          UP BROADCAST RUNNING MULTICAST  MTU:1500  Metric:1
          RX packets:3586 errors:0 dropped:0 overruns:0 frame:0
          TX packets:2679 errors:0 dropped:0 overruns:0 carrier:0
          collisions:0
          Interrupt:11 Base address:0x220
```

Assign multi-homed servers an internal network number with the *ipx_internal_net* command.

Compiling ncpfs

The code for *ncpfs* is available from *ftp://ftp.gwdg.de/pub/linux/misc/ncpfs*. The latest version as this book was being written was 2.2.0.

In the root directory of the software distribution, there is a file called *Makeinit* that contains flags for all the compile-time options. *ncpfs* can be built with code for Linux 2.0 or 2.1/2.2, so uncomment the appropriate line. By default, both lines are uncommented, so the binary will work on either version:

```
# Include code for Linux2.0.x
MOUNT2 = 1
# Include code for Linux2.1.x
MOUNT3 = 1
```

The other options in *Makeinit* (NDS support, packet signatures, and so on) are not stable as of this writing, so you probably don't want to enable them unless you can take an active role in debugging.

Finally, simply type *make install* to copy binaries into appropriate system locations.

Configuring Your NetWare Server

pserver doesn't support the latest features of NetWare. You should make your Net-
Ware server as compatible with NetWare 3.x as possible. Packet signatures aren't
supported by *pserver*, and so use bindery emulation until NDS support is stable.

By default, each subtree in NDS gets assigned to a *bindery emulation context*. For
the purposes of illustrating the examples in this chapter, we set up a NetWare
server in the *BOOK* tree and confined our examples to the *fofz* context. A context
is essentially a subtree for which bindery emulation is performed.

To administer a NetWare server, you need to log in to a Windows machine and
run the graphical administration tool from there. Novell makes a network client for
Windows 98 available from their web site, which replaces the default Microsoft
login screen with a Novell login screen. The Novell login screen is shown in
Figure 8-2. In the Novell client login, you get to specify a NetWare server to log in
to and configure. This example will log in to the NetWare server *BOOKSERVER*
and use the NDS subtree *fofz* under the main *BOOK* tree. We'll configure a Linux
machine to take jobs from *BOOKSERVER* and print them using the Linux print system. All these fancy screen shots are the NetWare equivalent of editing *printcap* to
create a queue. They do nothing to the print system on the Windows client itself.

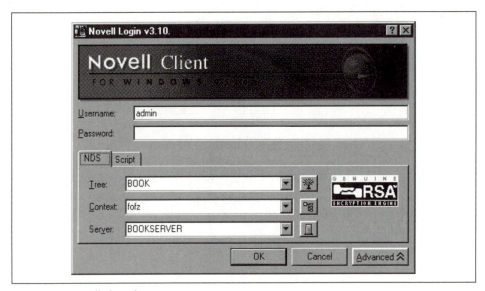

Figure 8-2. Novell client login

After logging in to the server, run the administrative tool *nwadmin. nwadmin* is
stored on the NetWare server, but the NetWare directory is mapped to a local
drive and added to the path when you log in. Running *nwadmin* displays the
objects stored in the part of the directory you logged in to, as shown in Figure 8-3.

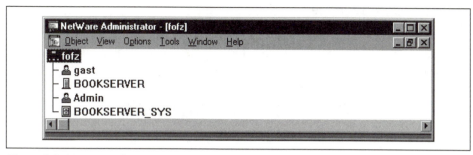

Figure 8-3. Main nwadmin screen

Creating the NetWare Queue

To create a NetWare queue, you must use a NetWare client machine running Windows so that you can use the *nwadmin* administration utility. Although you create this print-queue using a Windows client, it does not configure printing on the Windows client itself. It is only configuring the NetWare server.

Step 1: Creating the NetWare print queue

Print-queues in NetWare have three parts in NDS: a printer object to represent the printer, a queue object to accept jobs, and a print server object linked to both. Create all three, beginning with the print queue. Go to Create, choose Object, and select the *PrintQueue* object type. You will get the screen shown in Figure 8-4.

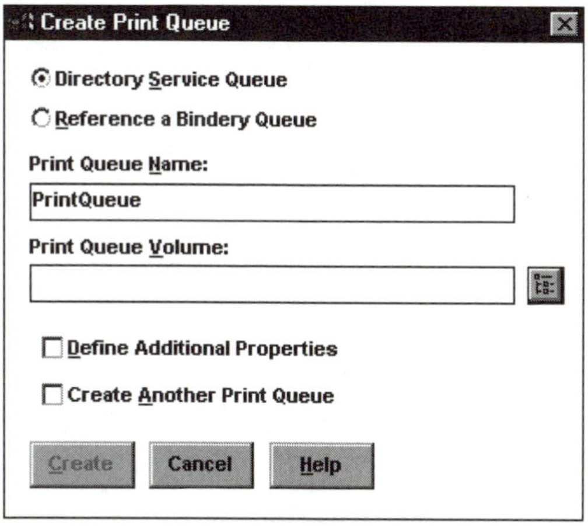

Figure 8-4. Queue creation dialog

Unless you're working with a server that was upgraded from a bindery-based version of NetWare, you have no bindery queues to reference, so you'll want to create an NDS queue. For the volume, select whatever volume has the most disk space.

Step 2: Creating the NetWare printer

Next, create an object for your printer; creating the object brings up the dialog box shown in Figure 8-5. Name the printer, but this time, check the *Define Additional Properties* box to bring up the detailed properties of the new object.

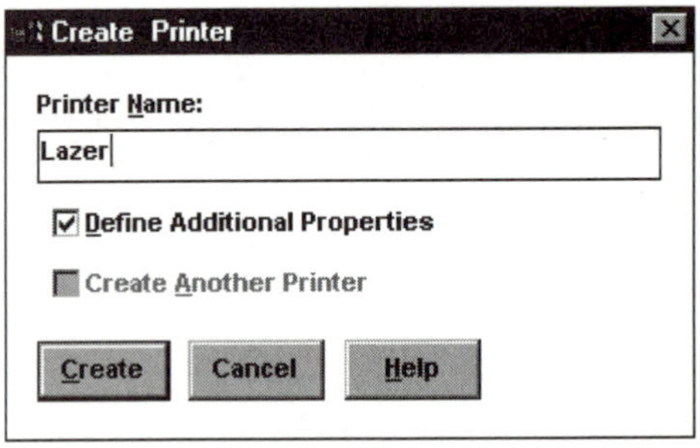

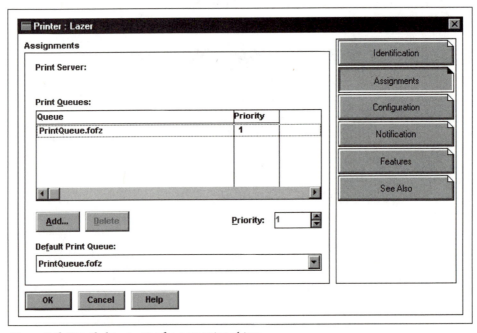

Figure 8-5. Create printer object dialog

After you choose to create the object, you'll want to assign the printer to the print-queue so that jobs printed to the queue will be sent to the new printer. After selecting the *Assignments* tab on the right hand side of the dialog box shown in Figure 8-6, you should add the print-queue you created in step 1.

Figure 8-6. Detailed properties for new print object

Step 3: The NDS print server object

Finally, the printer needs to be assigned to a print server. Create a print server object in NDS, which leads you to a dialog box like Figure 8-7.

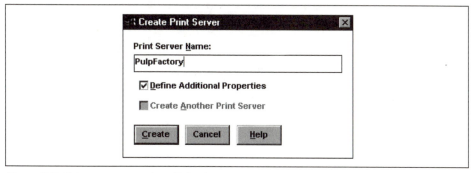

Figure 8-7. Print server creation dialog box

Assign the printer you created in step 2 to it, by using the detailed properties window and the assignments tab, shown in Figure 8-8.

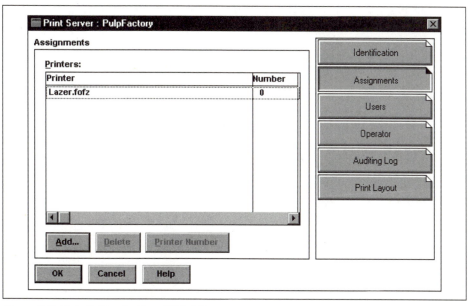

Figure 8-8. Detailed properties of Print Server

Step 4: Load PSERVER.NLM

Once you've configured the NetWare queue, you can run the print server program on NetWare. Go to the NetWare console and type the command LOAD PSERVER in order to load the print server NetWare Loadable Module.

Looking at the NetWare Network from Linux

ncpfs includes a few utilities to poke around the NetWare network. Most commands in the *ncpfs* suite share a common set of command line options, as shown in Table 8-1.

Table 8-1. Common Options for ncpfs Commands

Flag	Description
–S	NetWare server to use
–U	Print server object name, which is presented as a username to the NetWare server
–q	Print-queue name
–P	Password; if no password is required, the *–n* option may be used

slist: Who Are the Servers in Your Neighborhood?

Like Microsoft networking, NetWare includes methods of getting a list of the servers available on the network. The *slist* program prints out the list of NetWare servers, along with their IPX internal network numbers, as shown in the following example:

```
[gast@aluminum ncpfs-2.2.0]$ slist

Known NetWare File Servers                          Network    Node Address
--------------------------------------------------------------------------
BOOKSERVER                                          34AB243C   000000000001
```

pqlist: Excuse Me, Where Can I Get My Print Job Serviced?

Once you've found a server, you can log in as an administrator to see what printer queues are attached to that server, as shown in the following example:

```
[gast@aluminum ncpfs-2.2.0]$ pqlist -S BOOKSERVER -U admin
Logging into BOOKSERVER as ADMIN
Password:

Server: BOOKSERVER
Print-queue name                                    Queue ID
----------------------------------------------------------
Q1                                                  BC000009
```

pqstat: Is My Job There Yet? Is My Job There Yet?

Finally, when a job has been submitted, you can view the contents of a remote NetWare queue with the *pqstat* command, as illustrated by the following example:

```
[gast@aluminum ncpfs-2.2.0]$ pqstat -S BOOKSERVER -U admin Q1
Logging into BOOKSERVER as ADMIN
Password:

Server: BOOKSERVER     Queue: Q1      Queue ID: BC000009
Seq  Name            Description                    Status   Form  Job ID
------------------------------------------------------------------------
  1  ADMIN           No Description                 Active     0   00B2C001
```

Queue Drainage with the pserver Daemon

Now that the queue is set up on NetWare, the Linux server must be configured to pull jobs from the NetWare queue. Create a queue on your Linux server, as described in either Chapter 4, *Extending the Berkeley Spooler with Print Filters*, or Chapter 5, *The Next Generation Berkeley Spooler: LPRng*; an existing queue works fine.

pserver, which takes its name from the NetWare print server program, runs as a daemon and takes jobs from a NetWare queue, which are then put into local queues. Due to some limitations in the NetWare protocol suite, *pserver* must poll the server for new jobs. NetWare does not provide a mechanism for presenting a new print job to another server, or for notifying another server that a job has arrived.

Configuration of *pserver* is straightforward. No files need to be edited because configuration is done entirely through command line arguments. The major command line arguments are familiar at this point from the other *ncpfs* commands, previously described in Table 8-1. For example, to start *pserver* for the print-queue created in the previous section, the command line looks like this:

```
[root@aluminum /root]# pserver -S BOOKSERVER -U PrintServer -q PrintQueue -n
```

Depending on the load on your print server, you may wish to adjust the timeout for *pserver* polls by using the *−t* option.

Interactions with Unix Spooling

Depending on your Unix spooling setup, you may wish to specify the exact command used by *pserver* to submit a job to the Unix queuing system. Each instance of *pserver* is associated with one NetWare queue; multiple NetWare queues require multiple versions of *pserver*. Multiple NetWare queues may be set up for multiple printer devices, though, so you can specify the Linux queue to use with *pserver*'s *−c* option. For example, to send jobs from the *LUMBERJACK* queue on NetWare to the *sawmill* queue on your Linux print server, specify *sawmill* on the *lpr* command line used by *pserver*, as in the following example:

```
root@linux# pserver -S SERVER -U PrintServer -n -q LUMBERJACK -c "lpr -Psawmill"
```

If you wish, you may also use %u in the print command to specify the user. *pserver* must run as root; to have NetWare usernames show up in the Linux queue, simply use the *–u* argument to *lpr*, as in the following:

```
root@linux# pserver -S SERVER -U PrintServer -n -q LUMBERJACK -c \
"lpr -Psawmill -u%u"
```

After getting the options on *pserver* set correctly, you probably want to set it up to start automatically on boot using whatever facilities your system provides.

III

Administration

Using SNMP to Manage
Networked Printers

Things that have "Simple" in their names usually aren't.
—Anonymous System Administrator

Over the past decade, computer software has become increasingly graphically oriented. Sales representatives for any product, even printers, frequently spend large amounts of time talking about whiz-bang GUIs or web-based interfaces to printer managers. Graphical tools are certainly handier than the front-panel tools on most printers, since they tell you more than the front panel ever will and they can be downright useful if you have only a few printers. While the amount of information you can obtain with these tools is impressive, vendor-provided tools are not the only way to obtain this information, as some sales representatives might have you believe. In almost every case, the underlying protocol used to acquire this information is *SNMP*, the Simple Network Management Protocol.

A Simple Introduction to SNMP

SNMP was developed in the late 1980s as a stopgap network management system for the Internet. Although it was intended to be deployed only until a "real" network management protocol could be developed, it has been extended and is now the *de facto* network management protocol on TCP/IP networks. SNMP is a client/server protocol implemented over UDP. SNMP *agents* can run on devices such as routers, computers, and even printers, and report data to a network *management console*. There are only five operations in the protocol. Two get data from an agent, two have an agent set parameters in a device's configuration, and the remaining operation, *trap*, allows an agent to send an immediate notification of a noteworthy event rather than waiting for the next contact from the management console.

Each agent maintains a collection of data about the managed device called the Management Information Base (MIB). The MIB is a hierarchical tree. For example, one part of the MIB will have information about the Internet Protocol software running on a managed device, and another part will have details about the host operating system, and so on. The MIB tree has public branches, which are documented in RFCs and widely supported, and private branches, which are provided by equipment manufacturers and contain a wide variety of information.

Abstract Syntax Notation 1 (ASN.1) Grammar and the MIB Tree

All SNMP data is organized into a tree. Figure 9-1 shows a picture of the MIB tree.

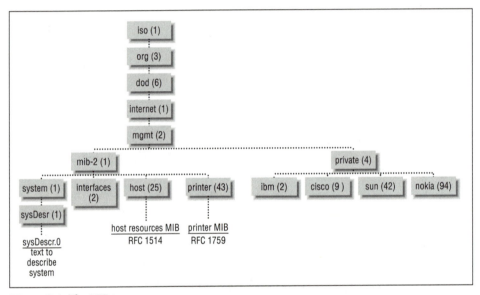

Figure 9-1. The MIB tree

The MIB tree is a set of *objects*, or pieces of data, represented in ASN.1 notation. ASN.1 is used because it allows both easy human interpretation and a compact data representation for sending SNMP over the wire.* The MIB tree used in today's Internet is rooted at *.iso.org.dod.internet*. Because all Internet-related information is stored under this prefix, the prefix is usually omitted in Internet literature.

To provide for compact representation, each branch in the tree is numbered. These numbers are shown on the tree in Figure 9-1. At the first level, *iso* is 1; at

---

* If you looked at the MIB tree and thought it looked like the DNS tree, there is a reason for that. Like DNS, ASN.1 allows different organizations to have control over their subtree.

the second level, *org* is 3. *.iso.org.dod.internet* translates to .1.3.6.1. Like the text prefix *.iso.org.dod.internet*, the numerical prefix .1.3.6.1 is usually omitted when writing object names. Under *.iso.org.dod.internet*, there are two main branches, .1.3.6.1.2 (*iso.org.dod.internet.mgmt*) for the public MIB and .1.3.6.1.4 (*iso.org.dod.internet.private*) for the private MIBs. Each vendor is assigned a unique private MIB number under *.iso.org.dod.internet.private.enterprises*. As shown in Figure 9-1, IBM is assigned enterprise number 2, Cisco is 9, and so on. As this book was written, thousands of enterprise numbers had been assigned.

Strings of dotted numbers are known as *object identifiers* and refer to objects in the MIB. Documenting the mappings of objects such as *.1.3.6.1.2.1.1.1.0* to *.iso. org.dod.internet.mgmt.MIB-2.system.sysDescr.0* is the bulk of the material in MIB RFCs. With slight changes, these RFCs are turned into MIB files and fed into network management systems, like SunNet Manager or HP OpenView.

Data types

RFC 1155 defined the structure of management information (SMI), which evolved into the data types in SNMP. RFC 1155 defined the following types:

INTEGER, OCTET STRING, and NULL
> The ASN.1 primitive types.

Counter
> An unsigned 32 bit integer that can be increased until it reaches its maximum value, at which point it *wraps* around to zero.

DisplayString
> An *OCTET STRING* restricted to the ASCII character set.

IpAddress
> A 4-octet string in network byte order that is used to represent IP addresses and network masks.

TimeTicks
> A non-negative integer that counts time from a noteworthy event, such as the initialization of an SNMP agent. Time is always counted in hundredths of a second.

SNMP MIBs may also define *textual conventions*, which are like user defined data types in other languages. For example, the *PhysAddress* type used to represent Ethernet MAC addresses is an *OCTET STRING*.

MIB Files

MIB files allow SNMP software to construct the MIB tree. In the Unix tradition, MIB files are plain text files that are readable both by the human user and software tools.

Although they have a precise format and may be hard to read at first, it is quite possible to learn some basic syntax and deduce much of the rest from context.

Being able to read MIB files can save lots of busywork when answering pesky questions like "How many of our printers have duplexing units?" One option would be to read the printer manuals and an inventory list, if you have accurate information. A better choice would be to use vendor tools to look at each printer and tally the results. For the best return on work, you could query the MIB of each installed printer and have a script do all the work for you.

Example 9-1 is an excerpt from a MIB file.

Example 9-1. Text File

```
--      mgmt        OBJECT IDENTIFIER ::= { iso org(3) dod(6) internet(1) mgmt(2) }
        org         OBJECT IDENTIFIER ::= { iso 3 }
        dod         OBJECT IDENTIFIER ::= { org 6 }
        internet    OBJECT IDENTIFIER ::= { dod 1 }
        mgmt        OBJECT IDENTIFIER ::= { internet 2 }

        MIB-2       OBJECT IDENTIFIER ::= { mgmt 1 }
        private     OBJECT IDENTIFIER ::= { internet 4 }
        enterprises OBJECT IDENTIFIER ::= { private 1 }

        system      OBJECT IDENTIFIER ::= { MIB-2 1 }
        interfaces OBJECT IDENTIFIER ::= { MIB-2 2 }

sysDescr OBJECT-TYPE
    SYNTAX      DisplayString
    MAX-ACCESS  read-only
    STATUS      current
    DESCRIPTION
            "A textual description of the entity. This value should
            include the full name and version identification of the
            system's hardware type, software operating system, and
            networking software."
    ::= { system 1 }

sysContact OBJECT-TYPE
    SYNTAX      DisplayString
    MAX-ACCESS  read-write
    STATUS      current
    DESCRIPTION
            "The textual identification of the contact person for this
            managed node, together with information on how to contact
            this person. If no contact information is known, the value
            is the zero-length string."
    ::= { system 4 }
```

Like many other types of files, this one begins with a comment. In MIB files, -- at the beginning of a line marks the line as a comment. Also, many MIB files have

comments that resemble the MIB file syntax; MIB compilers for SNMP are programmed to put *iso* (1) at the root of the MIB tree, so that definition is usually left
out. Each line after that defines a branch in the MIB tree.

Because MIB files go down the tree, from least specific to most specific, the easiest way to read a MIB file is from bottom to top. Reading this way helps to avoid
taking the wrong branch in a MIB tree. For example, if you want to know the OID
for *sysDescr*, it is defined as item 1 under *system*. *system* is defined as branch 1
from *MIB-2*, which is item 1 under *mgmt*. Eventually, working backwards to *iso*,
you have *.1.3.6.1.2.1.1.1*.

Step 1: Seeing the branches in the trees

80% of what you need to know about MIB files comes from understanding what
an assignment statement looks like (`::=` is the assignment operator in ASN.1). The
assignment statement assigns an ASN.1 number to an object and identifies its parent branch:

```
object-name some-text ::= { parent-branch-name ASN.1-number-off-parent-branch }
```

For example, *org* is branch 3 under *iso*. In the MIB file shown previously, that is
clearly illustrated by this line:

```
org        OBJECT IDENTIFIER ::= { iso 3 }
```

Some text is either **OBJECT-TYPE** or **OBJECT IDENTIFIER**. **OBJECT IDENTIFIER**s
are branches in the MIB tree, and **OBJECT-TYPE**s are leaves in the MIB tree that
store data.

Step 2: Reading a leaf node's definition

A leaf, indicated by the **OBJECT-TYPE** declaration, has some additional fields associated with it. To define the type of data stored in the object, the **SYNTAX** statement is used. Consider the definition of *system.sysDescr*:

```
sysDescr OBJECT-TYPE
    SYNTAX      DisplayString
    MAX-ACCESS  read-only
    STATUS      current
    DESCRIPTION
            "A textual description of the entity. This value should
            include the full name and version identification of the
            system's hardware type, software operating system, and
            networking software."
    ::= { system 1 }
```

The **SYNTAX** statement tells you that *system.sysDescr* object holds data of type
DisplayString. The **MAX-ACCESS** field does exactly what it sounds like. If the
value of **MAX-ACCESS** is **read-only**, such as with *system.sysDescr*, its value cannot be changed from what the vendor put in the field. Contrast *system.sysDescr*

with *system.sysContact*, which has a MAX-ACCESS of read-write, meaning it can be changed. The DESCRIPTION field is a description of the object, but is not used for any protocol interactions. It is for the RFC author to communicate with the SNMP agent implementor.

There is one slight technical detail about leaf nodes. It would have been slightly more accurate to describe leaf nodes as twigs. The actual data-storing leaf is not *system.sysDescr*, but *system.sysDescr.0*. The reason for the trailing 0 is to accommodate tables easily. In the interfaces table, for example, different interfaces will be given different numbers. The first interface name is stored in *interfaces.ifTable. ifEntry.ifDescr.1*, the second interface name is stored in *interfaces.ifTable.ifEntry. ifDescr.2*, and so on. However, for all practical purposes, you can think of an OBJECT-TYPE as a leaf node.

Step 3: Enumerations

Some objects are by definition constrained to have only one of a handful of values. SNMP allows the definition of enumerated types for these situations. For types that are constantly reused, such as units of measure, enumerations are defined at the beginning of the MIB file. The printer MIB is designed to easily accommodate both metric and English units of measure. The printer MIB authors defined the *MediaUnit* enumeration at the beginning of the MIB to allow other objects to be defined in terms of the *MediaUnit* enumeration:

```
MediaUnit ::= TEXTUAL-CONVENTION
    STATUS current
    DESCRIPTION "Units of measure for media dimensions."
    -- This is a type 1 enumeration.
    SYNTAX INTEGER {
        tenThousandthsOfInches(3),  -- .0001
        micrometers(4)
      }
```

For objects that have a unique set of values, the enumeration is defined with the object. An example is *prtGeneralReset* in the general table of the printer MIB. Status information on whether the printer is resetting is not used in other objects, so the enumeration is defined in the object:[*]

```
prtGeneralReset OBJECT-TYPE
    -- This value is a type 3 enumeration
    SYNTAX    INTEGER {
```

---

[*] Observant readers may have noted that the printer MIB excerpts refer to type 1 and type 3 enumerations. From a technical perspective, the distinction is not important. The Printer Working Group exercises various degrees of control over the different types. Type 1 enumerations are defined as complete within the MIB, so additions require a new RFC. Both type 2 and type 3 enumerations can be added to. The difference is in the degree of oversight by the PWG; additions to type 2 enumerations require approval by the PWG and then the Internet Assigned Numbers Authority (IANA), but additions to type 3 enumerations require only IANA's approval.

```
                    notResetting(3),
                    powerCycleReset(4), -- Cold Start
                    resetToNVRAM(5), -- Warm Start
                    resetToFactoryDefaults(6) -- Reset contents of
                                              -- NVRAM to factory defaults
            }
MAX-ACCESS read-write
STATUS     current
DESCRIPTION
        "Setting this value to 'powerCycleReset', 'resetToNVRAM', or
        'resetToFactoryDefaults' will result in the resetting of the
        printer. When read, this object will always have the value
        'notResetting(3)', and a SET of the value 'notResetting' shall
        have no effect on the printer. Some of the defined values are
        optional. However, every implementation must support at least
        the values 'notResetting' and 'resetToNVRAM'."
    ::= { prtGeneralEntry 3 }
```

The SNMP Protocol

As with any other protocol, understanding how data is transmitted makes your job as a troubleshooter much easier. As the S in SNMP implies, SNMP only has a few operations, and the transmission of SNMP is not complicated. Rather than requiring SNMP software to implement baroque command sets that would be difficult to debug, troubleshoot, test, and extend, the designers of SNMP chose instead to implement a Spartan command set that has only two purposes. The protocol for SNMP makes it possible to retrieve data from the MIB and assign values to objects in the MIB.[*]

A management application sends an SNMP query to a managed device on UDP port 161, usually from an unprivileged port. SNMP messages do not have the same level of structure that many other IP protocols do. The most striking example of this difference is that it is possible to pack several SNMP messages into a single packet on the wire. A query includes the SNMP command and a unique request ID number, as well as a *community name*. For more information on SNMP communities, see the sidebar on SNMP security.

The agent running on the managed device gathers the data from the MIB and respond. If the management application does not receive a response within a set amount of time, it will assume the packet is lost and retry the query. After several queries, the application will time out and report that the device is unreachable.

---

[*] The approach of using a simple protocol with complex endpoint processing was borrowed from the High-Level Entity Management System (HEMS), which is briefly described in RFCs 1021 through 1024.

SNMP Security (Or Lack Thereof...)

In many respects, security is the Achilles' heel of SNMP. Although this is not a book on security, it is important to understand the security implications of what you perpetrate on your network (and co-workers, and support staff, and ...). Enabling SNMP clearly has benefits in terms of efficiency of staff time. Like anything else, this benefit does not come without cost.

You don't want to allow just anybody to set some of the configuration information that we'll describe in this chapter. Unfortunately, SNMP was developed before today's need for strong network security, and does not support one-time passwords, cryptographic authentication, or encryption to prevent snooping and ensure confidentiality.

In SNMPv2, the version currently supported by the bulk of the installed SNMP base, a small measure of security is possible through the use of *communities*. A management application includes a community name in its request. SNMP agents may show different information to different communities and may deny access to any information if the requester is not a member of the appropriate community.

The two major flaws with this are the use of widespread defaults and the lack of protection for community names across the wire. Frequently, the default read-only community name is *public*, and the default read-write community name is *private*. If you do not change these defaults, you may have given anybody with an extremely basic knowledge of SNMP complete access to your SNMP capable devices. Furthermore, there are even some printers that do not allow you to change the SNMP community names.

The lack of protection of community names as they traverse the network is far more serious. SNMP encodes community names before putting them on the wire, but standardized encoding without encryption is equivalent to clear text because network sniffers can easily be programmed to decode community names.

We do not advocate blindly turning off SNMP. Network management software has enabled us to build large networks over the past several years. Many organizations deal with the security problems by enabling SNMP on their private networks and ensuring that it cannot pass across firewalls.

Public MIBs

Public MIBs are standardized in RFCs and implemented (to varying degrees) by vendors. The advantage of public MIBs is that the same piece of information is located in the same place in the MIB tree on each device, no matter which vendor sells the product. If the public MIB is supported by a device, it is possible to read objects and set objects without needing to know any specifics about the brand or model of the device. Therefore, you'll get the best return on your time from using the public MIBs. Presenting the entire set of MIBs used to control printers would be a needless waste of time and paper. Appendix B, *SNMP MIB Objects for Managing Printers*, is a reference of the MIBs most useful for managing printers.

SNMP Tools

Working with SNMP is slightly more complicated than working with some of the more familiar protocols, such as *telnet*, HTTP, and SMTP. SNMP is implemented over UDP, so you cannot telnet to a predefined port and type commands.* Because the data payload of SNMP packets is binary, you must use a more intelligent tool than telnet to decode the response for you. Working with printers frequently does not require the sophistication of the high-end (and high-price) SNMP tools on the market. This section introduces you to some of the common and inexpensive tools that will do much of what you need.

Open Source SNMP Tools

Carnegie Mellon University developed the original set of open source SNMP tools for Unix systems. These tools are now maintained by UC Davis and freely available from *http://www.ece.ucdavis.edu/ucd-snmp*. In addition to an SNMP agent daemon that runs on hosts, the package includes several command line utilities for interacting with SNMP agents on remote devices.

The command *snmpget* does exactly what you would think, given its name: supply an object in the MIB, a community name, and a remote host, and *snmpget* will fetch the value of that object:

```
snmp-nms$ snmpget k2-opsteam public system.sysDescr.0
system.sysDescr.0 = "HP ETHERNET MULTI-ENVIRONMENT,ROM A.03.
15,JETDIRECT,JD24,EEPROM A.05.05"
```

If no leading dot is specified, the UCD tools search the public MIB; to retrieve a private object, put in the fully qualified object name or OID, beginning with a dot.

To turn *system.sysDescr.0* into an OID to put on the wire, *snmpget* searched the MIB files on the machine. One disadvantage to the UC Davis/CMU tools is that they read the MIB files in each time they are invoked. Other packages read in the MIB files and compile the MIB tree into memory so that you don't need to regenerate the MIB tree repeatedly.

---

* It can often be amusing to telnet to mail servers at major corporations and enter the HELO command.

Historically, the major flaw in the UC Davis/CMU SNMP utilities has been the difficulty of using them in a script. Some utilities do not return error codes when the commands fail, and error messages are not always directed to standard error. To make the output as readable as possible, the authors attempted to format the data returned by remote agents as cleanly as possible. Strange characters in ASCII strings or very short strings will occasionally cause the program to print strings as hexadecimal data. Correctly handling all the cases in a script can be overwhelming.

Several vendors have implemented command line tools similar to these, but with some minor refinements. By precompiling the MIB files, performance can be improved. Several minor changes can be made to improve the behavior of these utilities within a script as well.

SNMP Perl Module

True system administrators make extensive use of scripts, many of which are coded in Perl. An SNMP module for Perl 5 is available from CPAN* mirrors throughout the world, or from the ports collection on the open source BSD family of operating systems. The module allows you to easily access SNMP data from remote machines within a Perl script and use Perl's pattern matching and string processing to write complex results to any kind of file.

One of our favorite examples is the *Multi-Router Traffic Grapher* (MRTG), which uses SNMP to create network utilization graphs, although it can easily be adapted to monitor and graph any SNMP variable, including the number of pages printed. MRTG is freely available under the GNU GPL from *http://ee-staff.ethz.ch/~oetiker/webtools/mrtg/mrtg.html*.

MRTG defaults to displaying data in number of things (usually bits or bytes) per second. For printers, however, pages per minute is a more interesting measure. If MRTG is configured to plot the value of the page count OID, it will produce a graph of pages per second. Unless the printer in question is very fast, pages per second is not an especially useful measure of utilization, especially because MRTG drops fractional parts of numbers. Current versions of MRTG incorporate the *perminute* option in the configuration file to generate per-minute statistics. MRTG was designed to create graphs of multiple variables; due to this design flaw, monitoring only one variable requires plotting it twice.

The *MaxBytes* option is used to let MRTG know the print engine's maximum capacity. Utilization statistics printed out by MRTG use *MaxBytes* to determine the fraction of capacity that is used. For example, if the monitoring count determined

* The Comprehensive Perl Archive Network (CPAN) is where you can find all things Perl. Its URL is *http://www.cpan.org*.

that 12 pages per minute were being printed on a printer with a capacity of 24 pages per minute, then utilization would be calculated at 50%. Normally, MRTG throws out any value more than *MaxBytes*. If *AbsMax* is set as well, then any number greater than *AbsMax* is labeled as a bogus value and thrown out. *AbsMax* is set higher because we don't want slight timing details to cause a calculation thrown out in error. An MRTG configuration file is shown in Example 9-2.

Example 9-2. MRTG Configuration File

```
# OID for prtMarkerLifeCount is .1.3.6.1.2.1.43.10.2.1.4
# (That's .iso.org.dod.internet.mgmt.mib-2.printmib.prtMarker.prtMarkerTable.\
#  prtMarkerEntry.prtMarkerLifeCount, in case you care)

Target[treekiller]: 1.3.6.1.2.1.43.10.2.1.4&1.3.6.1.2.1.43.10.2.1.4:public@treekiller
Directory[treekiller]: /usr/local/mrtg/data/treekiller
Options[treekiller]: growright, perminute
YLegend[treekiller]: Pages/min
ShortLegend[treekiller]: ppm
MaxBytes[treekiller]: 24
AbsMax[treekiller]: 30
Legend1[treekiller]: ppm
Legend2[treekiller]: ppm
Legend3[treekiller]:
Legend4[treekiller]:
LegendI[treekiller]:
LegendO[treekiller]:
```

When using this configuration file, the output of MRTG looks like Figure 9-2. The In and Out lines shown below the graphs are identical because the same variable is plotted twice.

npadmin

npadmin grew out of Ben Woodard's desire to create a fast, scriptable network management tool designed specifically for managing printers. Because the C interface to the CMU SNMP library required extensive string handling, he created his own tool and implemented an SNMP library from scratch.

npadmin can be used within shell or Perl scripts, and it returns information in a way that can easily be parsed by the script language of your choice because the output is clearly delimited with key characters. To improve the ability for both humans and scripts to make sense of the output, items are grouped together logically rather than in the order they appear in the MIB. *npadmin* is available from *ftp://pasta.penguincomputing.com/pub/prtools*, or as part of the CEPS distribution.

Here are some examples using *npadmin*:

```
snmp-nms$ npadmin --model --vendor --netconfig k2-opsteam
vendor="HP";model="LaserJet5Si";ipaddr="171.68.205.25";hwaddr="08:00:09:c9:e4:
86";netmask="255.255.255.0";gateway="171.68.205.1";
```

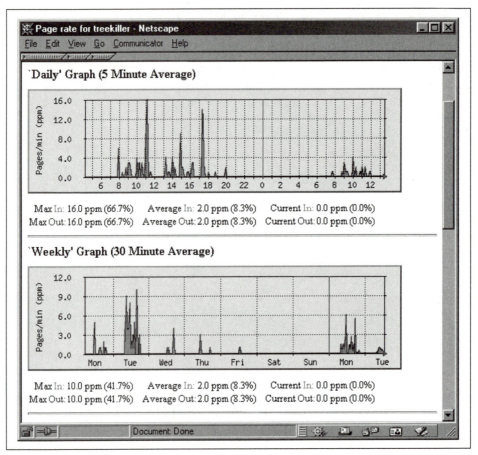

Figure 9-2. Page count data displayed by MRTG

```
snmp-nms$ npadmin --languages k2-opsteam
langFamily="Automatic";langLevel="Version1.
3";langVersion="19961220";description="Automatic Language
Switching";version="19961220";orientation="portrait";feedAddressability="600";xFee
dAddressability="600";twoWay="N";
langFamily="PJL";langLevel="Version 1.
3";langVersion="19961220";description="PJL";version="19961220";orientation="portra
it";feedAddressability="600";xFeedAddressability="600";twoWay="Y";
langFamily="PCL";langLevel="Version 5.
00E";langVersion="19961220";description="PCL";version="19961220";orientation="port
rait";feedAddressability="600";xFeedAddressability="600";twoWay="Y";
langFamily="PS";langLevel="Version 2014.
108";langVersion="19960724";description="PostScript";version="19960724";orientatio
n="portrait";feedAddressability="-1";xFeedAddressability="-1";twoWay="Y";
```

Like all open source software, *npadmin* is a work in progress. Current development efforts are focused on improving portability across operating systems and improving the number of printers supported by the program.

10

Using Boot Servers for Basic Printer Configuration

Modern network printers are sophisticated pieces of machinery. When a printer is connected to the network, end hosts can send jobs to printers orders of magnitude faster than serial- or parallel-port connections. Establishing and maintaining the network connection, though, is a non-trivial task.

At times, you may feel like taking your frustration out on the printer, and hear the song "Boot to the Head" in your mind. Basic network configuration consists of hostnames and network numbers, but depending on your print server architecture, you may need to consider support for other protocols (AppleTalk, IPX, or NetBEUI). Networked devices require some degree of access control to enforce policies on who (or what, in the case of print servers) may use a printer, and where and when access is allowed. You may also need to engage your network infrastructure team if you need to set up boot servers, log servers, or SNMP management stations.

Generally speaking, network printer configuration falls into two categories: pre-boot and post-boot configuration. To put these steps into perspective, consider the boot process. When a printer is first powered up, it needs to be configured to communicate with the network. For a printer speaking IP, this implies configuring an IP address, a subnet mask, and a default gateway. After configuring the network stack, additional configuration may be required, such as turning off unused protocols and locking the control panel.

Configuring the IP stack on a printer can usually be done with one of three main methods: using the front panel, telnet, or a boot protocol like BOOTP or DHCP. Each method has strengths and weaknesses, so we will take a look at all three.

Front Panel Configuration

Most printers can be configured with the control panel. This usually involves navigating some sort of cryptic menu system using the buttons on the printer. Front panel configuration may be suitable for a very small number of printers, but it isn't scalable because a human must go physically to the printer and touch it to reconfigure the network settings.

Just to convince you that front panel configuration is a bad idea, here is an example, using an HP JetDirect MIO card:

1. Take the printer offline by pressing the GO key. The printer's front panel will change from READY to OFFLINE, indicating the printer is ready to obey your command.

2. You want to configure the MIO card, so press the MENU key repeatedly until HP MIO MENU is displayed on the front panel.

3. Next, configure the network. Press the ITEM key, and CFG NETWORK=NO* appears. You want to configure the network, so press the VALUE key to change the display until it changes to CFG NETWORK=YES*.

4. Configure TCP/IP by using the ITEM key to scroll through each network protocol until CFG TCP/IP=NO* is displayed. To access the TCP/IP configuration menu, press VALUE and then press SELECT. The display will change to CFG TCP/IP=YES*.

5. To use BOOTP, press ITEM until you see BOOTP=YES*, and skip to step 11. If you're not using a boot protocol, press ITEM until BOOTP=NO* appears.

6. Because BOOTP=NO*, TCP/IP must be configured manually. Press ITEM to configure each TCP/IP parameter.

7. The first parameter is the first byte of the IP address. When IP BYTE 1=10* is displayed on the control panel, press VALUE until the desired value appears. (We hope you have low numbers in the IP addresses you're configuring!) To save the value, press SELECT.

8. You're not done with that IP address. Press ITEM to move on to the second, third, and fourth bytes.

9. Thank networking equipment vendors for squabbling over IPv6, which has kept it out of deployment. As a practical matter, this means that you only need to configure a short IPv4 address. Just imagine the pain of entering an IPv6 address with the panel.

10. After you configure the IP address, you need to configure the subnet mask (SM), syslog server IP address (LG), default gateway (GW), and timeout (TIMEOUT) in the same manner.

11. Activate the printer and save your changes by pressing GO.

Front panel configuration is too ponderous to be useful for more than one, or at most two, printers. We are sorry if the following note gives you nightmares, but we want to make sure that you do not use front panel configuration for anything other than emergencies.

 Imagine configuring 500 (yes, 500!) printers with only the front panel.

Now that you are with us, let's move on to more civilized configuration methods.

Telnet

Which came first, the IP address or the ARP entry? Using telnet to configure printers is inherently a chicken and egg problem. How do you telnet to something you're trying to give an IP address to?

One possibility is to manually add an ARP table entry for the printer's Ethernet address.* A second possibility is that some printers will come up with a well known IP address if they do not receive a reply to boot configuration requests. For example, HP printers will initialize the stack with an address of 192.0.0.1. Hosts on the same network can then manually add a route to enable telnet access.†

Here is an example telnet session. This example assumes that the printer is already on the network and that its hostname is *hp5*. We'll start from our local Unix host and launch the telnet session:

```
unixhost% telnet hp5
Trying 10.10.1.124...
Connected to hp5.
Escape character is '^]'.

Please type [Return] two times, to initialize telnet configuration
For HELP type "?"
>
```

---

* Use a command line like this:

host% **arp -s 10.10.10.10 00:08:20:00:00:00**

Refer to the man page for *arp(8)* for more details.

† Most hosts implement IP address conflict discovery and reporting mechanisms. If you boot multiple HP printers on the same network without a boot server handy, they will all configure their ports to be 192.0.0.1. Normally, address collisions result in interfaces being shut down. A design goal for HP's code was to allow multiple printers to boot with the same IP address; HP modified the printer TCP/IP code to ignore IP address conflicts. You may discover this when an HP printer and a workstation fight it out over a duplicate address on your network.

By default, no password is set. A password may be set up by using the password command (*passwd*). Once a password is set, password protection is enabled, and the password may be changed, but password protection may not be disabled unless a cold reset is performed.

We are given a > prompt. To see the available command list, enter ? for help:

```
> ?

        To Change/Configure Parameters Enter:
        Parameter-name: value <Carriage Return>

        Parameter-name   Type of value
        ip:              IP-address in dotted notation
        subnet-mask:     address in dotted notation
        default-gw:      address in dotted notation
        syslog-svr:      address in dotted notation
        idle-timeout:    seconds in integers
        set-cmnty-name:  alpha-numeric string (32 chars max)
        host-name:       alpha-numeric string (upper case only, 32 chars max)
        dhcp-config:     0 to disable, 1 to enable
        novell:          0 to disable, 1 to enable
        dlc-llc:         0 to disable, 1 to enable
        ethertalk:       0 to disable, 1 to enable
        banner:          0 to disable, 1 to enable

        Type passwd to change the password.

     Type "?" for HELP, "/" for current settings or "quit" to save-and-exit.
     Or type "exit" to exit without saving configuration parameter entries
```

Configure the IP address, subnet mask, default gateway, and *syslog* server. *syslog* is important for network printers because they do not have copious amounts of space to devote to displaying error messages:

```
> ip: 10.10.1.124
> subnet-mask: 255.255.255.0
> default-gw: 10.10.1.1
> syslog-svr: 10.10.1.199
```

The `idle-timeout` parameter specifies the number of seconds an idle print data connection is allowed to remain open. If this parameter is set to 0, the connection does not terminate, and no other host is able to make a connection:

```
> idle-timeout: 60
```

Next, set the SNMP community name to allow network management systems to write configuration variables in the MIB. The name can be from 1 to 32 alphanumeric characters and can include the minus (–) and underscore (_) signs:

```
> set-cmnty-name: MY_SNMP_NAME
```

Set the hostname. The hostname string must be alphanumeric, with no more than 32 characters. Also, all alpha characters must be upper case:

> **host-name: HP5**

If the **dhcp-config** variable is set to 1, no other variables need to be set because the DHCP provides data. If the DHCP configuration state is changed from disabled to enabled, the print server assumes it should acquire its configuration information from a DHCP server. This means that, when the telnet session is completed, the TCP/IP stack for the print server is re-initialized and all current configuration information is deleted. The print server then attempts to acquire new configuration information by broadcasting DHCP requests:

> **dhcp-config: 0**

The next three parameters turn off their respective networking protocols. Our printing architecture is based on directing all print jobs through a Unix server, so protocols other than IP are not needed:

> **novell: 0**
> **dlc-llc: 0**
> **ethertalk: 0**

Finally, turn off the banner page. The spooler on the print server will generate banners for you:

> **banner: 0**
> **quit**

Quit, saving changes (to quit without saving changes, type **exit**):

```
===JetDirect Parameters Configured===

     IP Address      : 10.10.1.124
     Subnet Mask     : 255.255.255.0
     Default Gateway : 10.10.1.1
     Syslog Server   : 10.10.1.199
     Idle Timeout    : 60 Seconds
     Set Cmnty Name  : MY_SNMP_NAME
     Host Name       : HP5

     DHCP Config     : Disabled
     Passwd          : Disabled
     Novell          : Disabled
     DLC/LLC         : Disabled
     Ethertalk       : Disabled
     Banner page     : Disabled
User Quitting
Connection closed by foreign host.
unixhost%
```

telnet configuration varies considerably, even between different printers made by the same vendor. To avoid problems, always check the documentation that accompanied the printer or the online help.

Using telnet to configure printers allows you to configure a printer without being physically present, which is a big plus over front panel configuration. For large environments with fluid networks, changes to individual devices are still required.

BOOTP

The bootstrap protocol, documented in RFC 951, allows a client machine to discover a complete set of configuration parameters, such as its own IP address, the address of a server host, and the name of a file to be loaded into memory and executed each time a device is started.

Boot Process Using BOOTP

BOOTP clients broadcast a BOOTP configuration request to the local network when they are powered on, and BOOTP servers respond with configuration information. In a bit more detail, here is an overview of how the BOOTP-assisted process works:

1. A BOOTP client is powered on and broadcasts a configuration request on the local network.

2. Any BOOTP server(s) receiving the query checks BOOTP configuration files for a matching hardware address. Unix servers running *bootpd* will look at the ha tags in */etc/bootptab*.

3. If the hardware address is a match, the server replies with configuration information. At the bare minimum, the configuration is an IP address.

4. The client configures its network interface with the IP address, and then loads a configuration file with the TFTP protocol. TFTP is often a companion to BOOTP; we discuss it in the next section.

Advantages to BOOTP

Compared to front panel button pushing and telnet, BOOTP is attractive because it centralizes configuration on the BOOTP servers. Renumbering devices is a matter of editing configuration files, and there are no worries about printers crashing and losing configuration information because they obtain it from the BOOTP server when they are powered up. The downside is that configuration files must be maintained.*

---

* Maintaining and distributing BOOTP configuration files manually for a large site can be problematic. Part of what the Cisco print management system does is to make distribution of configuration files easier.

Finding the Printer's Hardware Address

To successfully configure network boot services like BOOTP and DHCP, you must know the hardware address of the printer. In nearly all cases, the network hardware is Ethernet. Many people use the terms *hardware address*, *Ethernet address*, and *MAC address* interchangeably. (The last term refers to Ethernet's Media Access Control functions.)

The simplest way to get a printer to report its hardware address is to print a configuration page. Some printers will automatically spit out a configuration page when they boot, while others require front panel manipulation. See your vendor's documentation for details.

Using configuration pages is impractical when the printer is in a different location. In those cases, you may be able to get the hardware address from another host or router on the network by examining ARP tables, or by querying the *ifPhysicalAddress* object with SNMP.

In the past, network administrators needed to maintain one BOOTP server on each network because good network engineering practices did not allow broadcasts to be forwarded between networks. Modern routers, as well as the *bootpgw* program, transform BOOTP requests into unicast packets at network boundaries and forward them on to servers. By using BOOTP forwarding, network administrators can use only one BOOTP server for several networks.

Configuring Unix Servers Running bootpd

On Unix servers, the BOOTP protocol is implemented by the *bootpd* daemon, which stores its configuration database in the *bootptab* file. By now, its format should be comfortably familiar because it bears a strong resemblance to *printcap*. The general format of a *bootptab* file is:

```
hostname:\
    :tag=value:\
    :tag=value:\
    : ... :\
    :lasttag=value:
```

In the previous example, `hostname` is the name of the BOOTP client and `tag` is a two-character tag symbol. Table 10-1 shows the most commonly used tag symbols. Of course, many more options exist. To quench a burning desire to know more, see the *bootptab(5)* man page for details.

Table 10-1. Commonly Used bootptab Tags

Name	Description
ht	The type of network hardware used by this host. Except in rare cases, it is set to `ether`, which is the code for Ethernet.
ha	The hardware address for the host described in the entry, entered as a string of characters.
vm	vm stands for "vendor magic." Vendor magic numbers were originally devised as a way of extending BOOTP replies to include vendor-specific extension information. This is almost always set to `rfc1048`, after the RFC that defined vendor magic extensions.
tn (1 < n < 254)	BOOTP data fields are tagged with numbers for interpretation. The subnet mask field, for example, is given a tag number of 1. Tag numbers 128 through 254 are reserved for private use.
sm	Used to specify the subnet mask.
gw	Used to specify the default router.
ip	Used to specify the IP address.
tc	tc stands for "table continuation" and is used to include the contents of another entry into the entry it appears in. It works like the tc tag in LPRng and offers similar functionality to the C preprocessor.

A typically *bootptab* entry looks something like this:

```
printer1:\
        :ht=ether:\
        :ha=00005e123456:\
        :vm=rfc1048:\
        :sm=255.255.255.0:\
        :gw=10.10.10.1:\
        :ip=10.10.10.10
        :T144="hpnp/hp5.cfg":
```

What does this entry mean?

- This entry is for a device named *printer1*.

- *printer1* has an Ethernet MAC address of 00:00:5e:12:34:56.

- The BOOTP server will respond with RFC 1048 vendor extensions.

- The printer is 10.10.10.1 on the 10.10.10/24 network, and it uses 10.10.10.1 as a gateway.

- The most interesting part of the entry is the last tag, which specifies where *bootpd* finds the post-boot configuration file, using vendor tag number 144. Firmware on this printer recognizes that tag 144 is a post-boot configuration file.

hp5.cfg stores post-boot configuration. A simple example might set the community name and a few other options, like this:

```
# Printer: hp5

allow: 10.10.1.100
set-community-name: bookprnt
idle-timeout: 45
location: On the printed page
contact: George Spelvin
```

Using Printer Access Control to Enforce Centralized Queuing

In the post-boot configuration file shown, there is an option named *allow*. Only hosts named in the *allow* line are able to connect to the printer and send jobs. Other hosts may, of course, send their jobs to a host in the *allow* line.

This book makes a big deal about the advantages of using a centralized queuing model. (If you only remember one point from this whole book, it should be the centralized queuing model!) You can use printer access controls to mandate the use of the central print server.[a] HP's *allow* option is intuitively simple. Other vendors implementations of a similar access control feature vary widely.

---

a. It's fair to note that *allow* only gives you source IP based filtering, which could easily be defeated by a wide variety of attacks. The point is not that *allow* gives you ironclad control over who connects, but that it makes it easier to direct users towards the print server.

You may use the `tc` tag to specify a template record to be included in subsequent entries. This allows you to group repetitive information such as gateway address, subnet mask, and other details in a single record entry:

```
common:\
        :ht=ether:\
        :sm=255.255.255.0:\
        :gw=10.10.10.1
        :vm=rfc1048:\
        :hd=/tftpboot:\
        :T144="hpnp/hp5":
printer1:\
        :tc=common:\
        :ha=0060b123456:\
        :ip=10.10.10.10
printer2:\
        :tc=common:\
        :ha=0060b654321:\
        :ip=10.10.10.11
```

BOOTP's Partner in Crime: TFTP

BOOTP's partner in crime is TFTP, the Trivial File Transfer Protocol. After a BOOTP server supplies an IP address to a BOOTP client, the client frequently requests a boot image or post-boot configuration information. Rather than building file transfer capabilities into BOOTP, protocol designers specified the use of TFTP. As you might guess from the name, TFTP is simple. TFTP is implemented over a lightweight UDP protocol and omits user authentication entirely.

 Because TFTP does not perform any user authentication, you must configure your server carefully to avoid security problems.

Starting the TFTP Server

Depending on the operating system, TFTP service is provided by *tftpd* or *in.tftpd* on port 69. Offering TFTP service requires an entry in */etc/services* like this:

```
# Host specific functions
#
tftp           69/udp
```

Next, edit *inetd.conf* to start the TFTP server when connections are received on UDP port 69. In many operating systems, *inetd.conf* contains a commented out entry for *tftpd*, so all you need to do is remove the comment character, a hash sign (#), and send SIGHUP to *inetd*:

```
# Tftp service is provided primarily for booting.
# Most sites run this only on "boot servers."
#
tftp dgram udp  wait  root  /usr/sbin/in.tftpd \
    in.tftpd -s /tftpboot
```

Notice the *–s /tftpboot* option, which specifies that *tftpd* should run in *secure* mode. In secure mode, the daemon changes its root directory to */tftpboot* with the *chroot()* system call. Files can be written only if they already exist and are publicly writable, but TFTP considers the public to be all users on all hosts that have network connectivity! Obviously, this may not be desirable in many situations.

With appropriate entries in *inetd.conf* and the *services* files, send a SIGHUP signal to *inetd* to complete the installation:

```
host1# ps -ef | grep inetd
root    146    1  0   May 26 ?        0:01 /usr/sbin/inetd -s
root 12678 12221  0 15:44:57 pts/4    0:00 grep inetd
host1# kill -HUP 146
```

```
host1# tftp
tftp> connect
(to) host2
tftp> get testfile
Received 183 bytes in 0.1 seconds
tftp> quit
host1# ls -al
total 6
drwxr-xr-x   2 root    sysadmin     512 May 23 21:03 .
drwxr-xr-x  10 root    sysadmin     512 May 23 21:03 ..
-rw-r--r--   1 root    sysadmin     174 May 23 21:03 testfile
host1#
```

TFTP is set up and working correctly. Boot files can be placed in the */tftpboot* directory.

DHCP

DHCP, the Dynamic Host Configuration Protocol, serves a similar function to BOOTP. Indeed, at the protocol level, DHCP is quite similar to BOOTP, and the DHCP specification, RFC 1531, mandates that DHCP servers offer service to BOOTP clients.

Designers of DHCP made two major changes to BOOTP. First, DHCP operates on leases, which allow the use of an IP address only for fixed periods of time. After the lease on an IP address expires, it may be reassigned to a different client. Leases may be offered to previously unknown clients—with DHCP, the hardware address is not needed to configure service for a client. DHCP supplies everything needed by the client to configure an interface.

The most common DHCP server for Unix is written by the Internet Software Consortium and is freely available in source form from ISC's web site at *http://www.isc. org*. The ISC DHCP server, *dhcpd*, is configured with the *dhcpd.conf* file. When DHCP clients request leases, *dhcpd* uses the configuration information in *dhcpd. conf* to provide configuration information.

Configuring dhcpd

dhcpd needs to know the network numbers and masks of all subnets for which it will be providing service. On each subnet, *dhcpd* can be configured with ranges of available addresses for clients. A very simple configuration might look like this:

```
server-identifier dhcp.domain.com;
shared-network SOME-NETWORK-NAME {
    subnet 10.10.10.0 netmask 255.255.255.0 {
      range 10.10.10.10 10.10.10.200;
    }
}
```

In the previous example, *dhcpd* is configured to give out leases out of the pool from 10.10.10.10 to 10.10.10.200. In practice, this trivial configuration would not be useful, though. Hosts on the 10.10.10/24 subnet need to reach the rest of the world. Most hosts reach the world by sending traffic to a default gateway. To decide what IP address to send traffic to, hosts will usually consult a nearby domain name server to find out the IP address associated with a particular name. *dhcpd* can configure the gateway, domain name, and name server(s) by using the *routers* option, the *domain-name* option, and *domain-name-servers* option. A configuration file making use of these options might look something like this:

```
server-identifier dhcp.domain.com
shared-network DOMAIN-INTERNAL-NET {
    option  domain-name "domain.com";
    option  domain-name-servers ns1.domain.com, ns2.domain.com;

    subnet 10.10.10.0 netmask 255.255.255.0 {
        option routers 10.10.10.1;
        range 10.10.10.10 10.10.10.200;
    }
}
```

dhcpd allows you to specify DNS servers by hostname because it will look up the IP addresses for those hostnames and supply the IP addresses to the client. You now have the bare minimum for a functioning DHCP server, and it's enough to configure end user hosts on the network. Print servers, however, don't like printers with changing IP addresses. It is quite difficult to send a job to a location that may change. DHCP attempts to assign the same address to a host each time it comes up, but by default, the same address is not guaranteed.

dhcpd provides two useful configuration options for serving printer boot information. One is the ability to group printers to share configuration information. The second is that DHCP can assign a fixed IP address to an Ethernet address.

In the following example, printers from three different vendors are grouped together. As in the BOOTP section, printers will use TFTP to get post-boot configuration files. Printers obtain the post-boot file specified by `filename` from the server named by `next-server`:

```
group {
    filename "HP-bootfile";
    next-server hp-boot-server;
    host hp1 {
        hardware ethernet 08:00:09:00:00:01;
        fixed-address 10.10.10.201;
    }
    host hp2 {
        hardware ethernet 08:00:09:00:00:02;
        fixed-address 10.10.10.202;
    }
```

```
      host hp3 {
         hardware ethernet 08:00:09:00:00:03;
         fixed-address 10.10.10.203;
      }
   }
   group {
      filename "xerox-bootfile";
      next-server xerox-boot-server;
      host x1 {
         hardware ethernet 08:00:07:00:00:01;
         fixed-address 10.10.10.210;
      }
      host x2 {
         hardware ethernet 08:00:07:00:00:02;
         fixed-address 10.10.10.211;
      }
      host x3 {
         hardware ethernet 08:00:07:00:00:03;
         fixed-address 10.10.10.212;
      }
   }
   group {
      filename "Tek-bootfile";
      next-server tek-boot-server;
      host tek1 {
         hardware ethernet 08:00:11:00:00:01;
         fixed-address 10.10.10.220;
      }
      host tek2 {
         hardware ethernet 08:00:11:00:00:02;
         fixed-address 10.10.10.221;
      }
      host tek3 {
         hardware ethernet 08:00:11:00:00:03;
         fixed-address 10.10.10.222;
      }
   }
```

BOOTP or DHCP?

Although BOOTP and DHCP theoretically interoperate, in practice it is best to choose one or the other. If you already run DHCP for PC client configuration and only have a few printers, you may as well use DHCP for printer configuration. If you plan to use a BOOTP-based package, such as CEPS, then start off with BOOTP.

Configuring Printers for Dynamic Booting

Each vendor has a different way of enabling BOOTP or DHCP on its printers, so consult your vendor's documentation for details. Due to the large variety of methods by which DHCP or BOOTP is enabled, we cannot possibly review them all here. We can, however, show a representative sample using HP's JetAdmin software.

Using HP JetAdmin Software

HP's JetAdmin software provides ability to install, monitor, and troubleshoot HP printers over the network.

Before running HP's JetAdmin software, you should have the hardware address of the printer and you should be able to power cycle the printer. If the printer is located in another country, you'll need to make arrangements for someone remotely located to power cycle it for you. HP LaserJet printers boot by using BOOTP and then TFTP additional configuration information. Our example shows the configuration of a LaserJet 5, and we'll only set one option in the interest of brevity.

1. Log in to the BOOTP server and launch the HP JetAdmin software:

```
# jetadmin

            **************************************************
            *                    MAIN MENU                   *
            *    HP JetAdmin Utility for UNIX (Rev. D.06.15) *
            **************************************************

         1) Configuration (super-user only):
             - configure printer, add printer to spooler

         2) Diagnostics:
             - diagnose printing problems

         3) Administration (super-user only):
             - manage HP printer, JetDirect

         4) Administration (super-user only):
             - manage JetAdmin

         5) Printer Status:
             - show printer status, location, and contact

                 ?) Help          q) Quit

   Please enter a selection (q - quit): 1
```

2. Select `Configuration → Create printer configuration in BOOTP/TFTP database`. The software will guide you through adjusting the appropriate configuration parameters and will then edit the appropriate configuration files:

```
    ****************************************
    *             CONFIGURATION            *
    *      HP JetAdmin Utility for Unix    *
    ****************************************

    Printer Network Interface:
        1) Create printer configuration in BOOTP/TFTP database
        2) Remove printer configuration from BOOTP/TFTP

    Spooler:
        3) Add printer to local spooler
        4) Delete printer from local spooler
        5) Modify existing spooler queue(s)

            ?) Help              q) Quit

Please enter selection: 1

    You will be asked a series of questions. After all of the questions have
    been answered, the responses are used to create an /etc/bootptab entry, and
    an optional configuration file. This configuration file is retrieved by
    the network printer with TFTP after it receives the BOOTP response.

    These responses apply to all questions:
        "q"      - returns you to the next higher level menu
        "?"      - prints help text
        <return> - skips optional parameters or selects the default value


Enter the printer's LAN hardware address: 080009123456

Enter the network printer name (q - quit): hp5


    Following are optional parameters you may set for JetDirect. Select any
    non-zero numbers to make the changes. The settings are used to create
    a BOOTP/TFTP database when '0' is selected. To abort the operation, press
    'q'

Other optional parameters:
-----------------------
        1) Set printer location (uses tftp)
        2) Set printer contact  (uses tftp)
        3) Set subnetmask
        4) Set gateway
        5) Set syslog (uses tftp)
        6) Change idle timeout (uses tftp)
        7) Create access list (up to 10 names). (Default: all allowed). (uses tftp)
```

```
      8) Other SNMP parameters:  (uses tftp)
         (GET/SET community name, trap and community name, authentication trap)
      9) set HP JetDirect lpd banner page

  Select an item for change, or '0' to configure (q - quit): 1

  Enter the printer location (q - quit): San Jose Sales Office

      Following are optional parameters you may set for JetDirect. Select any
      non-zero numbers to make the changes. The settings are used to create
      a BOOTP/TFTP database when '0' is selected. To abort the operation, press
      'q'

  Other optional parameters:
  ------------------------
      1) Set printer location (uses tftp)
      2) Set printer contact  (uses tftp)
      3) Set subnetmask
      4) Set gateway
      5) Set syslog (uses tftp)
      6) Change idle timeout (uses tftp)
      7) Create access list (up to 10 names). (Default: all allowed). (uses tftp)
      8) Other SNMP parameters:  (uses tftp)
         (GET/SET community name, trap and community name, authentication trap)
      9) set HP JetDirect lpd banner page

  Select an item for change, or '0' to configure (q - quit): 0
  (configuring) ...
```

3. The JetAdmin software modifies the BOOTP and TFTP databases and then tests the configuration. You are prompted to power cycle the printer so that it receives its configuration from the BOOTP and TFTP server(s):

```
  Completed creating BOOTP/TFTP configuration database for hp5.
  Please wait...
  (testing, please wait) ...
  Testing BOOTP with 080009000000...:
   RESULT: Passed BOOTP test 1 with 080009000000.
  ......
  BOOTP/TFTP has been verified functional.

      Configuration data is now in place. The next test is to ping the
      printer for the IP name you just assigned it. To continue the test,
      you MUST do the following so that the printer can configure itself
      with the configuration data:

          Power cycle the printer.
          Wait until the printer finishes the self test.
             (Note: It may take 20 sec to 1 min for a token ring HP
             JetDirect interface to finish the configuration.)
          Press the return key to continue the test.
```

4. Power on the printer. The printer will receive its configuration from the network servers. The JetAdmin program will test the configuration by pinging the

printer, and it also offers you the option of sending a file to the printer, which is a more thorough test. If all went well, your printer should produce a test page:

```
If you are not ready for the next test (for example, the IP name
has not taken affect in your DNS server), press 'q' to return to
the configuration menu now.


Do you want to send test file(s) to this printer (y/n, default=n)? y

    This test is using test files to demonstrate that data bytes can be
    transmitted across the HP JetDirect interface setup. As long as a
    few characters print out, the test is successful.
    The printer must be ready, i.e. online and not printing anything.
    The following types of test files can be sent to the printer:

        1) text file       (if printer is in PCL or AUTO mode)
        2) PostScript file (if printer is in PS or AUTO mode)
        3) HP-GL/2 file    (if it is a HPGL/2 plotter)
        4) User supplied file

Which one should be transmitted? (1/2/3/4/q, default=1) 2

================================================================

    Sending a test file to hp5 ...


    Result: The file has been successfully sent to hp5. Check output!

================================================================

Press the return key to continue  ...

            ***************************************
            *           CONFIGURATION             *
            *      HP JetAdmin Utility for Unix    *
            ***************************************

    Printer Network Interface:
        1) Create printer configuration in BOOTP/TFTP database
        2) Remove printer configuration from BOOTP/TFTP

    Spooler:
        3) Add printer to local spooler
        4) Delete printer from local spooler
        5) Modify existing spooler queue(s)

            ?) Help            q) Quit

Please enter selection: q
```

Configuration created by JetAdmin

The JetAdmin software modifies two configuration files. They are */etc/bootptab* and */tftpboot/hpnp/hp5.cfg*. The former configures the BOOTP server to give the printer an IP address, and the latter contains the post-boot configuration:

```
# cat /etc/bootptab
hp5:\
        :ht=ether:\
        :ha=080009e53b9d:\
        :hn:\
        :ip=10.10.1.124:\
        :T144="hpnp/hp5.cfg":\
        :vm=rfc1048:
# cat /tftpboot/hpnp/hp5.cfg
idle-timeout: 120
location: San Jose Sales Office
```

If we add a few more entries to the *hp5.cfg* file, we will have a working printer-sconfiguration file like this:

```
allow: 10.10.1.100
idle-timeout: 120
set-community-name: PRT_COMM
name: hp5
contact: Admin x1234 admin@domain.com
location: San Jose Sales Office
```

11

Centralized Configuration with LDAP

What does LDAP have to do with printing?
—The most frequently asked question about this chapter when described to friends

By now, it should be obvious that the central theme of this book is the centralization of printer management. Implementing what was described in the previous chapters would result in central management, but with decentralized configuration files strewn about over all your print servers. Printer configuration is an application that is well suited to some sort of a database. A *directory* is a specialized database that is suited to the read-many, write-seldom model. Recent developments in directory technology have resulted in a standard method of accessing a directory—the Lightweight Directory Access Protocol.

By definition, centrally maintained configuration information can easily be distributed to all print servers. Whether print servers query the LDAP server whenever they receive a job, or whether a script on the print servers pulls down configuration information as part of a periodic update, only one data set must be maintained. Centralizing configuration information is one of the keys to administrative scalability because changes in the directory are sent to all your print servers. Directory based administration also helps to ensure that every print server has a standard configuration, which dramatically reduces concerns about synchronization of configuration information.

What Is a Directory?

Like a database, a directory stores information. Unlike databases, however, directory information is read and searched far more often than it is written. Directory information tends to be descriptive, such as a phone number or email address.

As a result of these differences, directory servers are optimized to respond quickly to queries and do not support complex transactional models or data structures. A modification to the data store either succeeds or fails; there's no logic for rolling back related operations if one operation fails.

Either a directory or a database could be used for storing centralized printer configuration information. High quality open source SQL servers exist and would provide more than adequate performance for the task. Simplicity offers one significant advantage for directories over databases. Basic directory administration can be put in a single chapter, but basic database administration would require a second volume.* As always, network services should be deployed with standards in mind. When building a directory service, there is one clear standard: the Lightweight Directory Access Protocol (LDAP), most recently standardized in RFC 2251.

A Short Introduction to LDAP

Directories as a computing concept are not new. LDAP's lineage begins with ISO's OSI networking. Directories in the OSI realm were constructed according to the X.500 specifications, which included a mechanism for extracting information from the directory—the X.500 Directory Access Protocol (DAP). DAP is very powerful, but at the cost of extreme complexity. Organizations that deployed X.500 directories found that most queries did not need DAP's full functionality and wrote front-ends that supported custom-coded simpler access methods. LDAP grew out of these simpler access methods. Eliminating some of the complexity of X.500 directories made LDAP directories faster, more efficient, and capable of being developed and deployed more quickly.

Data Storage

Like SNMP, LDAP organizes data into a tree. In this case, similarity is only skin deep. LDAP is radically different.† LDAP directories are usually built with a minimum of hierarchy, as in Figure 11-1.

The building blocks of LDAP directories are *entries*. An entry may serve as a *container* for additional entries, and it may have *attributes* to store information. Although not forbidden by standards, early experience with LDAP deployment suggests that an entry should either be a container or have attributes, but not both. We refer to an entry with attributes as a *leaf node* because it only stores information.

---

* This chapter is not a comprehensive introduction to directory management. Our intent is to provide a narrowly focused introduction to directory management suited to printer configuration management with LDAP. If it piques your interest, see *Understanding and Deploying LDAP Directory Services,* by Timothy A. Howes, Mark C. Smith, and Gordon S. Good (Macmillan, 1998).

† X.500 specifies the use of ASN.1 object identifiers for the contents of the directory. LDAP allows the use of OIDs, but does not require it.

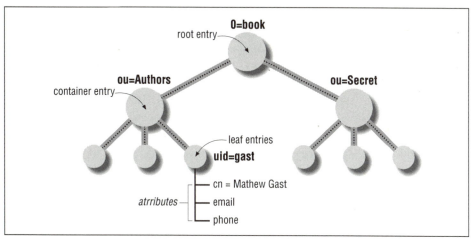

Figure 11-1. The LDAP hierarchy

What's in a name?

The Distinguished Name (DN) is a unique identifier for the entry throughout the directory. DNs are constructed by taking the common name (cn) of an entry and appending the names of each parent node back to the root of the directory. For example, the leaf entry *uid=gast* in Figure 11-1 has a DN of *uid=gast, ou=Authors, o=book*. Common names need only be unique within a directory subtree.

Object classes and schemas

Each item in a directory belongs to one or more *object classes*. An object class is just a way of defining what you expect to find with an object, and extra information that may be included. An object may belong to several classes, each of which has their own set of attributes. If a directory holds information about people, it must contain names, but may not have email addresses or web home pages. To illustrate the use of object classes, we will present a simple example: creating a sample schema for the pets in Matthew's household.

Matthew has two cats, but no dogs. However, he may have other pets in the future. To preserve future extensibility, allow objects to have several object classes and define unique things to that type of object in a class. For example, to build a pet directory, create a generic `pet` object class that has common attributes for any animal, such as a name, and then define a `cat` object class that contains objects specific to cats. After acquiring more pets, add object classes for them. For example, when Matthew acquires fish, the `fish` object class would have an attribute for whether the fish is a saltwater fish or a freshwater fish. Finally, each object belongs to the object class `top`, which defines attributes for anything put in the directory.

In carrying out his duty to his cats, Matthew came up with the following *schema*. Schemas are formalized representations of the limitations imposed by an object class. There is a generic object class of `pet`, which has an entry for the type of pet, as well as a cn entry for the pet's name. The `cat` object class includes whether or not the cat is declawed, but does not need to have a cn attribute because any entry that is in the `cat` object class will also be put in the `pet` object class, and will already have the cn attribute defined. The following schema prototype is the start of the `pet` and `cat` object classes, using the schema definition syntax from OpenLDAP:[*]

```
objectclass pet
        requires
                animalType
        allows
                cn,
                color,
                weight
objectclass cat
        allows
                breed,
                declawed,
                humanSlavePhone,
                humanSlaveAddress
```

The LDAP Data Interchange Format (LDIF)

Getting data into or out of an LDAP directory rquires the use of LDIF. LDIF is a standard method of taking data stored in a directory and boiling it down to simple ASCII text. Each entry has one attribute per line, single spaced. A blank line separates entries. Each attribute starts at the beginning of a line, followed by a colon, and then a value. When describing the pets in Matthew's household, an observer might use the following LDIF file (note that each object belongs to several classes, including the `top` class):

```
dn: cn=Chloe, o=book
objectclass: top
objectclass: pet
objectclass: cat
cn: Chloe
cn: Her Majesty the Empress Chloe
animalType: cat
color: grey
weight: 7 lb
breed: tabby
```

---

[*] A schema also needs to define the data types for each attribute and how that data will be searched. The name, for example, is a string; strings are compared as either case sensitive or case insensitive. However, for the purposes of this example, we have simplified the schema for readability. Don't worry—a schema in its full glory will be presented later.

```
declawed: no

dn: cn=Qwan-Yin, o=book
objectclass: top
objectclass: pet
objectclass: cat
cn: Qwan-Yin
cn: Piglet
animalType: cat
color: brown and white
weight: 14 lb
breed: Maine Coon
declawed: no
```

Organizing the Directory Namespace

Many larger organizations have deployed directories for simple phone book applications, and the advice from the earliest LDAP adopters is that a minimum of hierarchy should be used. There is little purpose in having an entry for a printer that has several sub-entries for additional attributes when the printer entry could belong to several object classes at once.

For the rest of the chapter, we will work with an organizational unit for printers (*ou=Printers*) underneath the root of our directory. All the printers are directly under the *Printers* organizational unit (see Figure 11-2). Each printer device has a location code to identify its geographic location. Geographic locations themselves are held in a separate unit under the *Printers* unit (*ou=Locations, ou=Printers*). Each location is assigned a location code and has one print server to handle job queuing before sending the job to the printer.

OpenLDAP

The University of Michigan wrote the initial versions of the open source LDAP code. Due to the liberal copyrights on the software, many vendors subsequently incorporated that code into a wide variety of commercial products. Development of the open source implementation has continued under the direction of the OpenLDAP Project (*http://www.openldap.org/*). OpenLDAP's origins in the University of Michigan code mean that, for the moment, most commercial tools have a strong resemblance to OpenLDAP's tools.

Installing OpenLDAP

OpenLDAP installation is almost identical to other open source software packages we have mentioned throughout the book.

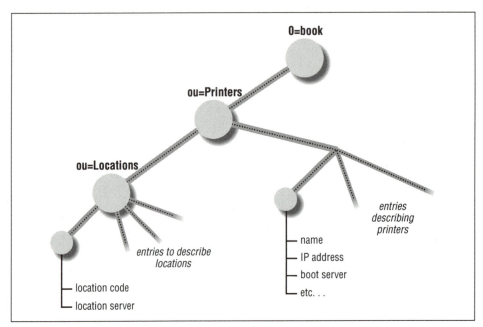

Figure 11-2. ou=Locations, ou=Printers LDAP subtree

Obtaining and compiling

The OpenLDAP software distribution can be downloaded from *http://www. openldap.org/software/download/*. Building OpenLDAP requires a DBM database library and a regular expression library. To use replication, install a thread package.

Like the other major open source software packages in this book, OpenLDAP uses the GNU *autoconf* system. Building the software is quite simple and follows similar lines to all other packages. One noteworthy exception is the inclusion of a test suite to validate basic LDAP server operation. Commands such as the following would be used to build and test the software:

```
dirsvr:~$ tar -xzf openldap-stable.tgz
dirsvr:~$ cd ldap
dirsvr:~/ldap$ ./configure
dirsvr:~/ldap$ make depend
dirsvr:~/ldap$ make
dirsvr:~/ldap$ cd tests
dirsvr:~/ldap/tests$ make
```

To complete the installation, run *make install* as *root*:

```
dirsvr:~/ldap$ su -
# make install
```

Configuration

The standalone LDAP server *slapd* will be installed in your local daemon directory. Depending on the operating system, the daemon path is */usr/local/sbin* or */usr/local/libexec*. The command line tools *ldapdelete*, *ldapadd*, and *ldapsearch* will be installed to */usr/local/bin*.

Configuration files are stored in */usr/local/etc/openldap*. *slapd*'s main configuration file is *slapd.conf*, which you edit to reflect the planned directory structure accurately. Most likely, the *suffix* entry must be modified to reflect your organization name, and the *directory* setting must be changed to a real directory that exists on the server's file system. In the interest of maintaining data integrity, turn schema checking on. An example *slapd.conf* is shown in Example 11-1. *slapd* is configured with the suffix *o=book*, with an administrator DN of *cn=root, o=book* and a password of *secret.** *slapd* will store its DBM files in */usr/local/ldap/data*.

Example 11-1. Sample slapd.conf

```
include          /usr/local/etc/openldap/slapd.at.conf
include          /usr/local/etc/openldap/slapd.oc.conf
schemacheck      on
referral         ldap://root.openldap.org/

pidfile          /usr/local/var/slapd.pid
argsfile         /usr/local/var/slapd.args

database         ldbm
suffix           "o=book"
rootdn           "cn=root, o=book"
rootpw           secret
directory        /usr/local/ldap/data
```

A word of warning about errors

OpenLDAP seldom offers helpful error messages. During testing of new services, we often run the server in debug mode to see detailed activity traces. Refer to the *ldap.h* source file in the distribution for details on what is printed at each debug level. For most problems, only debug level 1, a general trace, is necessary.

Putting Data Into a Directory

For a directory to be useful, it must contain data. Before entering data, install a schema to protect the integrity of the directory's future contents.

---

* Static reusable passwords for administrative access are a bad idea. See the documentation for OpenLDAP for alternatives.

Installing a new schema

No standard printer schema exists, so one must be created and installed. Of those two tasks, the latter is the easier. Put the new schema definition in a file, and then tell *slapd* to read that file for new schema as it starts up.

Defining the schema is the hard part. A schema implements your object class definitions by defining what attributes can be stored and which attributes must be present before saving a new entry. Each attribute is also given a type, which is either *cis, ces, tel,* or *bin.* The first three are strings. *cis* matches ignoring case, while *ces* requires an exact match. *tel* is a special mechanism for matching telephone numbers: dashes and blanks are ignored, and the remainder is matched like a *cis* string. *bin* specifies arbitrary binary data and is frequently used to hold files.* The following example shows the proposed *pet* schema with variable type definitions:

```
attribute animalType cis
attribute color cis
attribute weight cis
attribute picture bin

objectclass pet
        requires
                objectclass,
                animalType
        allows
                color,
                weight,
                picture

attribute breed ces
attribute declawed cis
attribute humanSlavePhone tel

objectclass cat
        requires
                objectclass
        allows
                breed,
                declawed,
                humanSlavePhone
```

To insert the *pet* and *cat* schemas into an LDAP directory, save the schema to *pet-schema.conf* in */usr/local/etc/openldap.* Modify *slapd.conf* to configure *slapd* to read *pet-schema.conf* on startup by adding an *include* line such as this to *slapd.conf:*

```
include          /usr/local/etc/openldap/pet-schema.conf
```

---

* An excellent experimental introduction to LDAP would be to use LDAP to store roaming profiles for Netscape. A September 1999 LinuxWorld article by Kartik Subbarao is a detailed step-by-step guide; it is on the Web at *http://www.linuxworld.com/linuxworld/lw-1999-09/f_lw-09-ldap-netscape.html.*

After restarting *slapd*, the new schema will be applied, and new data can be added to the directory after passing the schema check.

Inserting the contents of an LDIF file

The *ldapadd* adds LDIF-formatted data into a directory. Adding information into the directory is a privileged operation requiring the *–D* option to work as a privileged directory user. In the following example, the entries are added by using the directory administrator's identity and password:

```
bastet:~/book$ ldapadd -D "cn=root, o=book" -w secret < cats.ldif
adding new entry cn=Chloe, o=book
adding new entry cn=Qwan-Yin, o=book
```

Searching the Directory

The *ldapsearch* command, not surprisingly, searches the directory. When running *ldapsearch*, provide a search root node in the directory with the *–b* option. To search the entire directory, use a search root of *o=organization*, as in the following example. The LDAP search query is simple in this case—to print out all the objects with an object class of cat:

```
bastet:~/book$ ldapsearch -b "o=book" '(objectclass=cat)'
cn=Chloe, o=book
objectclass=top
objectclass=pet
objectclass=cat
cn=Chloe
cn=Her Majesty the Empress Chloe
animaltype=cat
color=grey
weight=7 lb
breed=tabby
declawed=no
creatorsname=cn=root, o=book
modifiersname=cn=root, o=book
createtimestamp=19991101023052Z
modifytimestamp=19991101023052Z

cn=Qwan-Yin, o=book
objectclass=top
objectclass=pet
objectclass=cat
cn=Qwan-Yin
cn=Piglet
animaltype=cat
color=brown and white
weight=14 lb
breed=Maine Coon
declawed=no
creatorsname=cn=root, o=book
```

```
modifiersname=cn=root, o=book
createtimestamp=19991101023053Z
modifytimestamp=19991101023053Z
```

Deleting Data

Deleting items from a directory is easy: just specify the DN of the entry to delete on the command line to *ldapdelete*. Deleting entries from the directory requires submitting the query with directory administrator privileges. Use the *–D* option to specify the administrator credentials:

```
bastet:~$ ldapdelete -D "cn=root, o=book" -w secret "cn=Chloe, o=book"
```

To delete the results of a search, store the results in a temporary file and pass the file as an argument to *ldapdelete* with *–f.* Deleting names obtained from *ldapsearch* can be tricky, though. *ldapsearch* prints out DNs prefixed with dn:_, so the first four characters must be removed. The following example uses the *cut* command to strip off the first four characters:

```
bastet:~$ ldapsearch -b "o=book" -L '(objectclass=cat)' | grep "dn:" \
   | cut -c5- > zap.names
bastet:~$ ldapdelete -D "cn=root, o=top" -w secret -f zap.names
```

Practical LDAP Printer Management

When we initially told friends that this book would have a chapter on LDAP, reactions ranged from strange looks to snorting and chuckling, until we explained that LDAP is well suited to building a back-end configuration database. The final section of the chapter is devoted to using LDAP to make printer-administration easier.

Building a Printer Schema

Before creating the schema, figure out what information the directory will be storing. Naturally, we have a few suggestions.

Administriva

LDAP is widely used for phone book applications. Usually, the phone books are for people, but each printer may be associated with several pieces of contact information. Users need to know how to contact a local help desk for support. Difficult problems may need to be escalated within your organization to printer experts. Escalation support engineers will need to contact vendors. When working with vendor support organizations, it always speeds the process if support agreement details are handy.

Creating a schema for contact information is straightforward. Internal support desks are usually reached via phone or email, so those fields are required. System designers and architects are escalation resources for many problems, but contact methods vary, so the escalation contact information is optional. In our schema, the "whack-it" contact is stored as *vicinityPhone* to avoid offending anybody listed in that field. Problems requiring remote hand support are frequently urgent, so only a telephone number is stored:

```
# General support contact information

attribute supportPhone tel
attribute supportEMail cis
attribute escalationPhone tel
attribute escalationEMail cis
attribute escalationPager tel
attribute vicinityPhone tel

objectclass printerSupport
        requires
                objectclass,
                supportPhone,
                supportEMail
        allows
                escalationPhone,
                escalationEmail,
                escalationPager,
                vicinityPhone
```

Some problems must be escalated to the vendor for additional support. Some support agreements may only offer limited contact methods. For that reason, all the attributes are left optional for vendor support contact information. For vendors that offer several support options, it may also be worth maintaining a contract description field to summarize response times:

```
# Vendor support information

attribute vendorSupportPhone tel
attribute vendorSupportEMail cis
attribute vendorSupportFax tel
attribute vendorSupportURL cis
attribute vendorContractNumber cis
attribute vendorContractExpires cis

objectclass printerVendorSupport
        requires
                objectclass
        allows
                vendorSupportPhone,
                vendorSupportEMail,
                vendorSupportFax,
                vendorSupportURL,
                vendorContractNumber,
                vendorContractExpires
```

Printer capabilities

Printer capabilities are the most important items stored in the directory. There are many different distinctions between printers that could be made: color/black and white, networked/connected to server port. Each distinction comes with its own set of features. Rather than cram all features into a single object class, each type of printer gets its own object class. The `printer` object class serves only to tag entries as printers for easy searching:

```
# Printer object class to make it easy to identify printer devices

objectclass printer
        requires
                objectclass
```

Building *printcap* files from a directory requires two critical pieces of information: the name and location of the printer. Everything else may depend on the type of printer, so everything else in the schema is optional.

If print servers run filter scripts, building a *printcap* file will require the name of the print filter script. Installing a standard print server software package means that filter scripts are installed to an identical location on each print server. Selecting a filter script for use with a particular printer may depend on the printer vendor and model, so the schema allows storage of that information.

Printers should be identified as PostScript capable or non-Postscript capable. For non-PostScript printers, the Ghostscript driver is required. Color printers should be identified as color capable, both for user benefit and the potential to route color jobs to color printers. If there is frequently used information, such as whether or not printers have duplexer units installed, that information may be stored in the directory:

```
# Information used to build printcap files

attribute cn cis
attribute locationCode cis
attribute filter cis
attribute GSdriver cis
attribute PScapable cis
attribute color cis
attribute vendorName cis
attribute vendorModel cis
attribute pagesPrinted cis
attribute duplexer cis

objectclass printerCapabilities
        requires
                objectclass,
                cn,
                locationCode
```

```
allows
        filter,
        GSdriver,
        PScapable,
        color,
        vendorName,
        vendorModel,
        pagesPrinted,
        duplexer
```

Network printers must boot correctly before print servers can access them. Booting parameters for network printers can be stored in the directory for later distribution as BOOTP or DHCP configuration information. Configuration of the network interface requires at least three parameters: the IP address, network mask, and default router. Three other optional parameters are stored in the directory to keep information about how jobs are submitted to network printers. For printers that implement *lpd*-compatible servers, the DNS name and remote queue name can be used to submit jobs. For printers that accept print files on a TCP socket, the DNS name and TCP port can be used:

```
# printcap information for networked printers

attribute ipAddress cis
attribute subnetMask cis
attribute defaultRouter cis
attribute dnsName cis
attribute hardwareQueueName cis
attribute queuePort cis

objectclass networkPrinterInfo
        requires
                objectclass
                ipAddress,
                subnetMask,
                defaultRouter,

        allows
                dnsName,
                hardwareQueueName,
                queuePort
```

printcap generators must know about printers attached to server communication ports so that the device name appears correctly in the *printcap* file. Serial devices may require additional flags in *printcap*, so that is an optional field:

```
# printcap information for printers attached to ports on the server

attribute deviceName cis
attribute deviceFlags cis

objectclass portPrinterInfo
        requires
```

```
            objectclass,
            deviceName
allows
            deviceFlags
```

SNMP information

If there is SNMP information that is used extensively, put it in the directory so that you can work with the data without sending large amounts of SNMP over the network. For example, scripts to generate boot server configurations depend on the hardware address of the network interface. Hardware addresses can be easily obtained with SNMP and then stored in the directory for use by BOOTP/DHCP configuration distributors.

Catalog of web front-ends

The past five years have seen a tremendous push to web-based tools. Scripts run on print servers can provide valuable information about the state of the server. By including a URL to the print server's web front-end, any information that might be useful to support staff can be made available without creating logins on each print server. For example, a simple CGI script could be used to get the contents of a print-queue, while another CGI script could be used to provide limited administrative access to queues for the front line support personnel.

Many printers provide web interfaces. After determining that a queue is working, a web front-end to the printer can be used to check the status of the hardware. If a problem can be diagnosed remotely, it saves a trip to the physical location of the printer.

Importing SNMP data into LDAP leads to one potential problem: there is no guarantee that the data is correct. One possible solution is to write a script to compare the LDAP data to the SNMP data and make it part of the web front-end to the printing system, along with a server script to regenerate configuration files based on SNMP if the SNMP-derived data was refreshed.

The basic URLs that might be associated with a printer are end user problem report forms, a web interface to the print-queue, a URL that points to the print server to show what printers it serves, a web interface for print server administration, and perhaps a *telnet://* URL to the print server:

```
# URL catalog

attribute endUserProblemReportURL cis
attribute queueViewURL cis
attribute printServerURL cis
attribute printServerAdminURL cis
attribute printServerTelnetURL cis
```

```
objectclass printerURLs
        requires
                objectclass
        allows
                endUserProblemReportURL,
                queueViewURL,
                printServerURL,
                printServerAdminURL,
                printServerTelnetURL
```

DNS information

If printer managers assign printer DNS names, the directory can be used to push information to the DNS administrators. Alternatively, DNS servers could use LDAP clients to pull information out of the directory and propagate DNS changes for the *printers* subdomain of your institution's top level domain.

Booting requirements

The main requirements for the boot server are to have the Ethernet address of the printer and the IP address to assign. Each printer probably will also need a default route. Some printers also require an additional boot file, which may be fetched from a second server. All these requirements make up the following object class for booting information:

```
# Information used for booting files

attribute ethernetAddress cis
attribute groupCode cis
attribute bootServer cis
attribute bootFile cis
attribute bootFileServer cis

objectclass printerBootInfo
        requires
                objectclass,
                ethernetAddress,
                groupCode,
                bootServer
        allows
                bootFile,
                bootFileServer
```

printcap distribution

A print server has queue entries for two types of printers: those it manages the queue for and those it does not. Jobs for remote printers can be processed locally and passed on to the remote print server or they can be sent directly to the second print server without processing. By consulting the directory, a server can create the appropriate entry for a printer to either pass on to a remote print server or to process locally. Each location has an associated print server and must be assigned a location code:

```
# Location information

attribute locationCode cis
attribute locationServer cis

objectclass printServerLocation
        requires
                objectclass,
                locationCode,
                locationServer
```

Directory Enabled Spooling Architecture

The key to creating configuration scripts is to break up the user population into areas by a location code, which can be matched as a text string by the LDAP server. One print server is responsible for one location code. Physical location codes might be based on the city the print server is in, or further subdivided by building name or floor number.

Keeping it simple

Wherever possible, use variables like %p to stand for printer names so that configuration files are completely generic and must only be *rdist*ed on to an existing Unix installation. Recall from Chapter 6, *Connecting Windows to Unix Servers: Let's Samba*, that the only parameter altered by the installation was the */var/spool/ciscolp/conf/smbconf.d/servernames* file, which could easily be built by LDAP if we added Samba configuration data to the directory.

Future possibilities

LDAP puts flexibility into the print system, and much more is possible. Here are some ideas:

- Email was one of the first applications to be directory-enabled. Why not have scripts that use an LDAP directory to report failures by email?

- LPRng allows the routing of print jobs with a script. While it's certainly possible to write a script that calls the directory, the routing function could be built into LPRng itself based on information it has received from the directory. With luck, a programmer much better than either of us can write that code.

- A directory probably doesn't supply the right back-end for printer accounting, but a SQL database with a sufficiently high transaction rate could.

- As we'll see in the section "Distributing printcap" later in this chapter, LDAP can be used to supply printcap information to the LPRng programs, or to supply DHCP with its configuration database by building *dhcpd.conf.*

- None of the application configuration is stored in the database, although it would be possible to use LDAP to distribute Samba configuration information.

A Sample Schema

Example 11-2 is a synthesis of the various ideas presented in the previous sections.

Example 11-2. Our Printer Schema

```
# Sample printer schema for Printing Book

# Location information

attribute locationCode cis
attribute locationServer cis

objectclass printServerLocation
        requires
                objectclass,
                locationCode,
                locationServer

# Printer object class to make it easy to identify printer devices

objectclass printer
        requires
                objectclass

# Information used to build printcap files

attribute cn cis
attribute locationCode cis
attribute filter cis
attribute GSdriver cis
attribute PScapable cis
attribute color cis
attribute vendorName cis
attribute vendorModel cis
attribute pagesPrinted cis
attribute duplexer cis

objectclass printerCapabilities
        requires
                objectclass,
                cn,
                locationCode
        allows
                filter,
                GSdriver,
```

Example 11-2. Our Printer Schema (continued)

```
                    PScapable,
                    color,
              .     vendorName,
                    vendorModel,
                    pagesPrinted,
                    duplexer

# printcap information for networked printers

attribute ipAddress cis
attribute subnetMask cis
attribute defaultRouter cis
attribute dnsName cis
attribute hardwareQueueName cis
attribute queuePort cis

objectclass networkPrinterInfo
        requires
                    objectclass,
                    ipAddress,
                    subnetMask,
                    defaultRouter,

        allows
                    dnsName,
                    hardwareQueueName,
                    queuePort

# printcap information for printers attached to ports on the server

attribute deviceName cis
attribute deviceFlags cis

objectclass portPrinterInfo
        requires
                    objectclass,
                    deviceName
        allows
                    deviceFlags

# Information used for booting files

attribute ethernetAddress cis
attribute groupCode cis
attribute bootServer cis
attribute bootFile cis
attribute bootFileServer cis

objectclass printerBootInfo
        requires
                    objectclass,
                    ethernetAddress,
```

Example 11-2. Our Printer Schema (continued)

```
                groupCode,
                bootServer
        allows
                bootFile,
                bootFileServer

# General support contact information

attribute supportPhone tel
attribute supportEMail cis
attribute escalationPhone tel
attribute escalationEMail cis
attribute escalationPager tel
attribute vicinityPhone tel

objectclass printerSupport
        requires
                objectclass,
                supportPhone,
                supportEMail
        allows
                escalationPhone,
                escalationEmail,
                escalationPager,
                vicinityPhone

# URL catalog

attribute endUserProblemReportURL cis
attribute queueViewURL cis
attribute printServerURL cis
attribute printServerAdminURL cis
attribute printServerTelnetURL cis

objectclass printerURLs
        requires
                objectclass
        allows
                endUserProblemReportURL,
                queueViewURL,
                printServerURL,
                printServerAdminURL,
                printServerTelnetURL

# Vendor support information

attribute vendorSupportPhone tel
attribute vendorSupportEMail cis
attribute vendorSupportFax tel
attribute vendorSupportURL cis
attribute vendorContractNumber cis
attribute vendorContractExpires cis
```

Example 11-2. Our Printer Schema (continued)

```
objectclass printerVendorSupport
        requires
                objectclass
        allows
                vendorSupportPhone,
                vendorSupportEMail,
                vendorSupportFax,
                vendorSupportURL,
                vendorContractNumber,
                vendorContractExpires
```

LDAP and Perl

Because LDAP is used to build configuration files, the LDAP data must eventually be turned into text files. We have chosen Perl for our examples. Perl bindings for LDAP are mature and stable.

The Net::LDAP module

Using the *Net::LDAP* Perl module, you can access information in a directory from a Perl script. *Net::LDAP* is written in Perl so it is available on all Perl platforms. Perl's excellent text processing facilities make it ideal for writing configuration files from directory information. To install *Net::LDAP*, first install *MIME::Base64*, *URI::ldap*, *Digest::MD5*, and *Convert::BER*. Installation of a Perl module from CPAN is standard and simple. Unpack the module, use Perl to create a *Makefile*, and then build the software:

```
$ tar -xzf module.tgz
$ cd module
$ perl Makefile.PL
$ make
$ make test
$ su -
# make install
```

Net::LDAP is available from *http://www.pobox.com/~gbarr/perl-ldap* and from the CPAN archives at *http://www.cpan.org*.

Distributing printcap

A Perl script can be used to generate *printcap*. Example 11-2 is one possible implementation. LPRng could use that script to generate *printcap* information on the fly, or that script could be run as a *cron* job every day. The specific architecture you choose depends on the complexity that you are willing to accept and the available network bandwidth. At smaller institutions, a centralized LDAP server could handle all *printcap* requests from the entire network. When there are multiple busy print servers, it is obviously undesirable to have each print job create network traffic. One solution would be to run a master LDAP server and have each print server maintain a slave LDAP server and enable replication at periodic intervals.

LPRng's *lpd* can be configured to use an external command in *lpd.conf*. The script is given one argument, either the name of the printer to get the *printcap* entry for, or *all* for the entire *printcap*. Assuming you put the script in */usr/local/etc*, then you'd just add the following line to *lpd.conf*:

```
printcap_path=|/usr/local/etc/printcapgen
```

Distributing DHCP and BOOTP Information

The sample schema presented previously contains attributes for boot server information. DHCP and BOOTP configuration files are not very complex.

Using LDAP and Perl

To illustrate generating configuration files from an LDAP directory, we'll take the following simplified scenario. A small company has two offices: one in Berkeley, California and one in Minneapolis, Minnesota, with printers in each. Assigning location codes is simple: we'll use "Berkeley" and "Minneapolis."

An LDIF description of the printers

The following LDIF file describes the two geographic locations plus the three printers owned by this organization. After importing it into a directory, we can then use the directory information to generate *printcap* information:

```
dn: o=book, c=US
objectclass: top

dn: ou=Printers, o=book, c=US
objectclass: top
objectclass: organizationalUnit
ou: Printers

dn: ou=Location, ou=Printers, o=book, c=US
objectclass: top
objectclass: organizationalUnit
ou: Location, ou=Printers

dn: cn=Berkeley, ou=Location, ou=Printers, o=book, c=US
objectclass: top
objectclass: printerLocation
locationCode: Berkeley
locationServer: print-bk.corp.com

dn: cn=Minneapolis, ou=Location, ou=Printers, o=book, c=US
objectclass: top
```

```
objectclass: printerLocation
locationCode: Minneapolis
locationServer: print-mn.corp.com


dn: cn=noir, ou=Printers, o=book, c=US
objectclass: top
objectclass: printer
objectclass: printerCapabilities
objectclass: networkPrinterInfo
objectclass: printerBootInfo
cn: noir
locationCode: Berkeley
groupCode: hp
color: no
GSdriver: ljet4
PScapable: no
filter: /var/spool/spool-system/filters/apsfilter
vendorName: Hewlett-Packard
vendorModel: LaserJet 8000 Series
dnsName: noir.corp.com
hardwareQueueName: raw
queuePort: 9100
ipAddress: 10.10.10.201
ethernetAddress: 00:00:5e:12:34:56
bootServer: bs.bk.corp.com
bootFile: hp-bf
bootFileServer: bs.bk.corp.com


dn: cn=blanc, ou=Printers, o=book, c=US
objectclass: top
objectclass: printer
objectclass: printerCapabilities
objectclass: networkPrinterInfo
objectclass: printerBootInfo
cn: blanc
locationCode: Berkeley
groupCode: hp
color: no
GSdriver: ljet4
PScapable: no
filter: /var/spool/spool-system/filters/apsfilter
vendorName: Hewlett-Packard
vendorModel: LaserJet 4000 Series
dnsName: blanc.corp.com
hardwareQueueName: raw
queuePort: 9100
ipAddress: 10.10.10.202
ethernetAddress: 00:00:5e:65:43:21
bootServer: bs.bk.corp.com
bootFile: hp-bf
bootFileServer: bs.bk.corp.com


dn: cn=psychedelic, ou=Printers, o=book, c=US
objectclass: top
```

```
objectclass: printer
objectclass: printerCapabilities
objectclass: networkPrinterInfo
objectclass: printerBootInfo
cn: psychedelic
locationCode: Berkeley
groupCode: tek
color: yes
PScapable: yes
vendorName: Tektronix
vendorModel: Phaser 850
dnsName: look-at-the-colors.corp.com
hardwareQueueName: raw
queuePort: 9100
filter: /var/spool/spool-system/filters/apsfilter
ipAddress: 10.10.10.203
ethernetAddress: 00:00:5e:45:67:89
bootServer: bs.bk.corp.com
bootFile: tek-bf
bootFileServer: bs.bk.corp.com

dn: cn=paisley, ou=Printers, o=book, c=US
objectclass: top
objectclass: printer
objectclass: printerCapabilities
objectclass: networkPrinterInfo
objectclass: printerBootInfo
cn: paisley
locationCode: Berkeley
groupCode: tek
color: yes
PScapable: yes
vendorName: Tektronix
vendorModel: Phaser 300
dnsName: paisley.corp.com
hardwareQueueName: raw
queuePort: 9100
filter: /var/spool/spool-system/filters/apsfilter
ipAddress: 10.10.10.204
ethernetAddress: 00:00:5e:98:76:54
bootServer: bs.bk.corp.com
bootFile: tek-bf
bootFileServer: bs.bk.corp.com

dn: cn=plaid ou=Printers, o=book, c=US
objectclass: top
objectclass: printer
objectclass: printerCapabilities
objectclass: networkPrinterInfo
objectclass: printerBootInfo
cn: plaid
locationCode: Minneapolis
groupCode: tek
color: yes
```

```
PScapable: yes
vendorName: Tektronix
vendorModel: Phaser 450
dnsName: plaid.corp.com
hardwareQueueName: raw
queuePort: 9100
filter: /var/spool/spool-system/filters/apsfilter
ipAddress: 10.20.20.105
ethernetAddress: 00:00:5e:c0:ff:ee
bootServer: bs.mn.corp.com
bootFile: tek-bf
bootFileServer: bs.mn.corp.com

dn: cn=icebox, ou=Printers, o=book, c=US
objectclass: top
objectclass: printer
objectclass: printerCapabilities
objectclass: portPrinterInfo
cn: icebox
locationCode: Minneapolis
filter: /var/spool/spool-system/filters/apsfilter
color: no
GSdriver: ljet4
PScapable: no
devicename: /dev/lp0
```

printcap Generation Using LDAP and Perl

Distributing *printcap* files with Perl is a conceptually simple task. Each printer has two associated queues. A front-end queue is exposed to the world and exists only to change the queue name to a name with meaning to APS Filter. Back-end queues run filters and are responsible for forwarding the job to its final destination.

For flexiblity, command line options specify parameters that change from print server to print server. Generating *printcap* files for different locations should be accomplished with only a single command line flag. The script should also gracefully deal with a change of LDAP server or directory root. (If your organization is acquired by a much larger company, you may need to quickly change the directory root from *o=Small Startup* to *ou=Rich People at Small Unit, o=Big Company with Money.*)

LPRng can obtain *printcap* information from an external program defined in *lpd. conf.* The program takes one argument, which is either the name of the printer to generate a *printcap* entry for, or the word *all* to generate *printcap* entries for every printer. The script must support both of these query types. It must also cope with the back-end queuing system by generating back-end queues on demand, as well as when they are required by the *all* command.

To support the desired flexibility, our *printcapgen.pl* script will support the command line flags in Table 11-1.

Table 11-1. Flags to printcapgen.pl

Argument	Description
−*d*	Directory server to use for the search
−*s*	Suffix to add on to the end of *ou=Printers*, typically *o=Your Organization*
−*l*	Location code to generate *printcap* entries for
printername or *all*	The printer name to generate a *printcap* entry for, or the word *all* to generate a *printcap* for the entire organization

The first part of the script is simple. It contains variable declarations to be used by the *Getopt* module for interpreting command line arguments and variables to hold the results of directory searches:

```
#!/usr/bin/perl
use strict;
use Net::LDAP;
use Getopt::Std;
use vars qw ($opt_l $opt_s $opt_d);

my $printerlist;  # List of printers in the directory
my $codesearch;   # List of locations in the directory
```

Step 1. Parse the command line to see what options were specified. If options were not specified, they should be assigned default values:

```
##
## STEP 1: Read in command line arguments and set default values
##

# Default values for important constants
# (These may be site specific - modify them if you want.)
my $LDAPServer = "localhost";
my $myLocationCode = "Berkeley";
my $suffix = "o=book, c=US";
```

Perl supplies the *getopt* function, which takes letters as arguments and places the value of those arguments into *opt_letter*. The following *getopt* function takes the arguments supplied with −*l*, −*s*, and −*d*, and places the values in *opt_l*, *opt_s*, and *opt_d*. The *shift* function takes the first remaining part of the command line, which should be either a printer name or the word *all*, and saves its value as *$query*:

```
&getopt('lsd');
my $query = shift;
```

Automatically generated *printcap* files may have comments. When automatically generating files, it is always a good practice to timestamp the data for later trouble-shooting purposes:

```
print "#\n";
my $now = localtime;
print "# Printcap file generated automatically at ",$now,"\n";
print "#\n";
```

Look at the command line options supplied. If they are defined, save the values used on the command line. Otherwise, use the default values defined previously:

```
if ($opt_d) {
  $LDAPServer=$opt_d;
  print "# Using specifed ";
}
else {
  print "# Using default ";
}
print "LDAP server \"$LDAPServer\"\n";

if ($opt_s) {
  $suffix=$opt_s;
  print "# Using specifed ";
}
else {
  print "# Using default ";
}
print "suffix of \"$suffix\"\n";

if ($opt_l) {
  $myLocationCode=$opt_l;
  print "# Using specifed ";
}
else {
  print "# Using default ";
}
print "location code of \"$myLocationCode\"\n";

if ($query) {
  print "# Running specified ";
}
else {
  $query="all";
  print "# Running default ";
}
print "query of \"$query\"\n";
print "#\n#\n";
```

Step 2. Getting the data from the LDAP server is straightforward, thanks to Perl's *Net::LDAP* module. We run two searches. The first is for all objects with an object class of *printer* in the *ou=Printers* subtree of the search base that we specified.

The second search is for all objects with an object class of `printerLocation` in the *ou=Location, ou=Printers* subtree:

```
my $ldap = Net::LDAP->new ($LDAPServer);

# Look in ou=Printers + org suffix for printer objects
my $searchbase = join("","ou=Printers, ",$suffix);
$printerlist = $ldap -> search ( base    => $searchbase,
                                 filter => "objectclass=printer"
                               );

# Look in ou=Location, ou=Printers + org suffix for location info
$searchbase = join("","ou=Location, ou=Printers, ",$suffix);
$codesearch = $ldap -> search (base    => $searchbase,
                               filter => "objectclass=printerLocation"
                              );

# That's all we need for now; disconnect to preserve server resources
$ldap->unbind;
```

Step 3. By this point, we have all the data needed, and all that is left is to format it appropriately.

Perl uses a double hash to store the results of LDAP searches. A small utility function, *getAttrib*, takes an LDAP entry and returns a specified attribute of that entry:

```
sub getAttrib {
# We will frequently need to dereference the double hashes returned by
# LDAP searches; this routine makes it simpler to look at
        my $object = @_[0];
        my $attrib = @_[1];
        return $object->{$attrib}->[0];
}
```

Rather than use a *.common* entry in *printcap*, the script can define its own common *printcap* tags with a subroutine named *commonStuff*:

```
sub commonStuff {
# Common entries in each printcap; customize to your requirements
  print "\t:shi:\\\n";
  print "\t:mx#0:\\\n";
  print "\t:sd=/var/spool/lpd/%P:\\\n";
}
```

The heavy lifting in printing out a *printcap* entry is confined to a subroutine for readability. The *printPrinterEntry* function takes one argument, a Perl reference to the LDAP entry for the printer, and generates the *printcap* entry for it, based on its location and the location of the server running the script:

```
sub printPrinterEntry {

my $Printer = @_[0];
my $qname;
my $LocDN;
```

```
my $Location;

# Print out the printcap entry for a printer

# Get some information about the geographic location.  Doing
# this lets us pull up information about other zones when dealing with
# non-local printers

# Where are printer locations stored in the directory?
my $locationsuffix=join("",",", ou=Location, ou=Printers, ",$suffix);

# Get a handy Perl reference to the directory entry of the location
$LocDN=join("","cn=",getAttrib($Printer,"locationcode"),$locationsuffix);
$Location=$codesearch->as_struct->{$LocDN};

# This is the printer we're presenting information on
print getAttrib($Printer,"cn"),":\\\n";

# Local printer case: printer location code matches our location code
if (getAttrib($Printer,"locationcode") eq $myLocationCode) {
   &commonStuff;
   print "\t:lp=",getAttrib($Printer,"cn"),"-backend\@localhost:\\\n";
   print "\t:qq:\\\n";

   # We force the queuename to make APS Filter do its magic
   # Step 1: Is it a PS capable printer?
   if (getAttrib($Printer,"pscapable") eq "yes") {
      $qname=join("-","aps","ps","letter","auto");
   }
   else {
      $qname=join("-","aps",getAttrib($Printer,"gsdriver"),"letter","auto");
   }
   # Step 2: Is it a color printer?
   if (getAttrib($Printer,"color") eq "yes") {
      $qname=join("-",$qname,"color");
   }
   else {
      $qname=join("-",$qname,"mono");
   }
   print "\t:force_queuename=",$qname,"\n";
}
else {
   # Remote printer case: just spool to the server for that location code
   &commonStuff;
   print "\t:lp=",getAttrib($Printer,"cn"),"\@";
   # lookup server for remote location code
   print getAttrib($Location,"locationserver"),"\n";
}
}
```

Our *printcap* generator script must also print out back-end entries used by the front-end entries. A back-end entry uses *lpr_bounce* to apply the input filter before sending the job, and it must know the location of the filter on the local hard disk.

To use a script such as this with LPRng, make sure that a filter package is installed
in the same location on all the print servers you plan to use:

```
sub printBackendEntry {

my $Printer = @_[0];

# Queues only have back-ends when they are local; remote queues
# should only be referred to the remote server.

if (getAttrib($Printer,"locationcode") eq $myLocationCode) {
    print getAttrib($Printer,"cn"),"-backend:\\\n";
    print "\t:server:\\\n";
    &commonStuff;
    print "\t:lpr_bounce:\\\n";
    print "\t:if=",getAttrib($Printer,"filter"),":\\\n";

    # If we have a device name, it's a locally attached printer;
    # otherwise, it's a networked printer and we should go over the network
    if (getAttrib($Printer,"devicename")) {
        print "\t:lp=",getAttrib($Printer,"devicename"),"\n";
    }
    else {
        print "\t:lp=",getAttrib($Printer,"hardwarequeuename");
        print "\@",getAttrib($Printer,"dnsname");
        if (getAttrib($Printer,"queueport")) {
            print "%",getAttrib($Printer,"queueport");
        }
        print "\n";
    }
}
}
```

The main loop of the script is quite simple. It runs through the results of the
search, printing out *printcap* entries if they are required by the *$query* argument to
the script. The only pitfall is that the script must be aware of the back-end queues
and generate entries for them if required:

```
# Generate entries for each printer in the directory
my $i;
my $Printer;
my $result;

for ($i=0; $i<$printerlist->count; $i++) {
    # These two variables get information about the current printer
    $result=$printerlist->entry($i);
    $Printer=$printerlist->as_struct->{$result->dn};

    if ($query ne "all") {
        # Not everything is being printed

        # If the query name matches the printer name, print it
        my $printerName = getAttrib($Printer,"cn");
        if ($query eq $printerName) {
```

```
            &printPrinterEntry ($Printer);
        }
        else {
            # printer-backend queues do not exist in LDAP, but can
            # can be built from LDAP information
            my $backendQueue=join("-",$printerName,"backend");
            if ($query eq $backendQueue) {
                &printBackendEntry($Printer);
            }
        }
    }
    else {
        # If everything is being printed, print both the entry and its
        # back-end queue
        &printPrinterEntry ($Printer);
        &printBackendEntry ($Printer);
    }
}
```

When the fragments are assembled into an entire script, you get the script in
Example 11-3.

Example 11-3. Perl printcap Generation Script

```perl
#!/usr/bin/perl
use strict;
use Net::LDAP;
use Getopt::Std;
use vars qw ($opt_l $opt_s $opt_d);

my $printerlist;   # List of printers in the directory
my $codesearch;    # List of locations in the directory

##
## STEP 1: Read in command-line arguments and set default values
##

# Default values for important constants
# (These may be site specific - modify them if you want.)
my $LDAPServer = "localhost";
my $myLocationCode = "Berkeley";
my $suffix = "o=book, c=US";

&getopt('lsd');
my $query = shift;

print "#\n";
my $now = localtime;
print "# Printcap file generated automatically at ",$now,"\n";
print "#\n";

if ($opt_d) {
  $LDAPServer=$opt_d;
  print "# Using specifed ";
```

Example 11-3. Perl printcap Generation Script (continued)

```perl
}
else {
  print "# Using default ";
}
print "LDAP server \"$LDAPServer\"\n";

if ($opt_s) {
  $suffix=$opt_s;
  print "# Using specifed ";
}
else {
  print "# Using default ";
}
print "suffix of \"$suffix\"\n";

if ($opt_l) {
  $myLocationCode=$opt_l;
  print "# Using specifed ";
}
else {
  print "# Using default ";
}
print "location code of \"$myLocationCode\"\n";

if ($query) {
  print "# Running specified ";
}
else {
  $query="all";
  print "# Running default ";
}
print "query of \"$query\"\n";
print "#\n#\n";

##
## STEP 2: Get data from LDAP server
##

my $ldap = Net::LDAP->new ($LDAPServer);

# Look in ou=Printers + org suffix for printer objects
my $searchbase = join("","ou=Printers, ",$suffix);
$printerlist = $ldap -> search ( base   => $searchbase,
                                 filter => "objectclass=printer"
                               );

# Look in ou=Location, ou=Printers + org suffix for location info
$searchbase = join("","ou=Location, ou=Printers, ",$suffix);
$codesearch = $ldap -> search (base    => $searchbase,
                               filter => "objectclass=printerLocation"
                              );
```

Example 11-3. Perl printcap Generation Script (continued)

```perl
# That's all we need for now; disconnect to preserve server resources
$ldap->unbind;


##
## STEP 3: Print out the stuff
##

sub getAttrib {
# We will frequently need to dereference the double hashes returned by
# LDAP searches; this routine makes it simpler to look at
        my $object = @_[0];
        my $attrib = @_[1];
        return $object->{$attrib}->[0];
}

sub commonStuff {
# Common entries in each printcap; customize to your requirements
  print "\t:sh:\\\n";
  print "\t:mx#0:\\\n";
  print "\t:sd=/var/spool/lpd/%P:\\\n";
}

sub printPrinterEntry {

my $Printer = @_[0];
my $qname;
my $LocDN;
my $Location;

# Print out the printcap entry for a printer

# Now, get some information about the geographic location. Doing
# this lets us pull up information about other zones when dealing with
# non-local printers

my $locationsuffix=join("",", ou=Location, ou=Printers, ",$suffix);
$LocDN=join("","cn=",getAttrib($Printer,"locationcode"),$locationsuffix);
$Location=$codesearch->as_struct->{$LocDN};

print getAttrib($Printer,"cn"),":\\\n";

# Local printer case: printer location code matches our location code
if (getAttrib($Printer,"locationcode") eq $myLocationCode) {
  &commonStuff;
  print "\t:lp=",getAttrib($Printer,"cn"),"-backend\@localhost:\\\n";
  print "\t:qq:\\\n";

  # We force the queuename to make APS Filter do its magic
  # Step 1: Is it a PS capable printer?
  if (getAttrib($Printer,"pscapable") eq "yes") {
     $qname=join("-","aps","ps","letter","auto");
  }
```

Example 11-3. Perl printcap Generation Script (continued)

```perl
    else {
        $qname=join("-","aps",getAttrib($Printer,"gsdriver"),"letter","auto");
    }
    # Step 2: Is it a color printer?
    if (getAttrib($Printer,"color") eq "yes") {
        $qname=join("-",$qname,"color");
    }
    else {
        $qname=join("-",$qname,"mono");
    }
    print "\t:force_queuename=",$qname,":\n";
}
else {
    # Remote printer case: just spool to the server for that location code
    &commonStuff;
    print "\t:lp=",getAttrib($Printer,"cn"),"\@";
    # lookup server for remote location code
    print getAttrib($Location,"locationserver"),":\n";
}

}

sub printBackendEntry {

my $Printer = @_[0];

# Queues only have back-ends when they are local; remote queues
# should only be referred to the remote server.

if (getAttrib($Printer,"locationcode") eq $myLocationCode) {
    print getAttrib($Printer,"cn"),"-backend:\\\n";
    print "\t:server:\\\n";
    &commonStuff;
    print "\t:lpr_bounce:\\\n";
    print "\t:if=",getAttrib($Printer,"filter"),":\\\n";

    # If we have a device name, it's a locally attached printer;
    # otherwise, it's a networked printer and we should go over the network
    if (getAttrib($Printer,"devicename")) {
        print "\t:lp=",getAttrib($Printer,"devicename"),":\n";
    }
    else {
        print "\t:lp=",getAttrib($Printer,"hardwarequeuename");
        print "\@",getAttrib($Printer,"dnsname");
        if (getAttrib($Printer,"queueport")) {
            print "%",getAttrib($Printer,"queueport");
        }
        print ":\n";
    }
}
}
```

Example 11-3. Perl printcap Generation Script (continued)

```perl
# Generate entries for each printer in the directory
my $i;
my $Printer;
my $result;

for ($i=0; $i<$printerlist->count; $i++) {
    # These two variables get information about the current printer
    $result=$printerlist->entry($i);
    $Printer=$printerlist->as_struct->{$result->dn};

    if ($query ne "all") {
        # Not everything is being printed

        # If the query name matches the printer name, print it
        my $printerName = getAttrib($Printer,"cn");
        if ($query eq $printerName) {
            &printPrinterEntry ($Printer);
        }
        else {
            # printer-backend queues do not exist in LDAP, but can
            # can be built from LDAP information
            my $backendQueue=join("-",$printerName,"backend");
            if ($query eq $backendQueue) {
                &printBackendEntry($Printer);
            }
        }
    }
    else {
        # If everything is being printed, print both the entry and its
        # back-end queue
        &printPrinterEntry ($Printer);
        &printBackendEntry ($Printer);
    }
}
```

Running printcapgen.pl

For illustrative purposes, we will show two runs of the *printcapgen.pl* script. The first example shows the output of the script when run in Berkeley. The script creates local and back-end queues for *noir, blanc, paisley,* and *psychedelic,* but jobs for *plaid* and *icebox* are referred to *print-mn.corp.com*:

```
dirsvr# ./printcapgen.pl
#
#
# Printcap file generated automatically at Sat Jul  8 22:54:32 2000
#
# Using default LDAP server "localhost"
# Using default suffix of "o=book, c=US"
# Using default location code of "Berkeley"
# Running default query of "all"
#
#
```

```
noir:\
        :sh:\
        :mx#0:\
        :sd=/var/spool/lpd/%P:\
        :lp=noir-backend@localhost:\
        :qq:\
        :force_queuename=aps-ljet4-letter-auto-mono:
noir-backend:\
        :server:\
        :sh:\
        :mx#0:\
        :sd=/var/spool/lpd/%P:\
        :lpr_bounce:\
        :if=/var/spool/spool-system/filters/apsfilter:\
        :lp=raw@noir.corp.com%9100:
blanc:\
        :sh:\
        :mx#0:\
        :sd=/var/spool/lpd/%P:\
        :lp=blanc-backend@localhost:\
        :qq:\
        :force_queuename=aps-ljet4-letter-auto-mono:
blanc-backend:\
        :server:\
        :sh:\
        :mx#0:\
        :sd=/var/spool/lpd/%P:\
        :lpr_bounce:\
        :if=/var/spool/spool-system/filters/apsfilter:\
        :lp=raw@blanc.corp.com%9100:
psychedelic:\
        :sh:\
        :mx#0:\
        :sd=/var/spool/lpd/%P:\
        :lp=psychedelic-backend@localhost:\
        :qq:\
        :force_queuename=aps-ps-letter-auto-color:
psychedelic-backend:\
        :server:\
        :sh:\
        :mx#0:\
        :sd=/var/spool/lpd/%P:\
        :lpr_bounce:\
        :if=/var/spool/spool-system/filters/apsfilter:\
        :lp=raw@look-at-the-colors.corp.com%9100:
paisley:\
        :sh:\
        :mx#0:\
        :sd=/var/spool/lpd/%P:\
        :lp=paisley-backend@localhost:\
        :qq:\
        :force_queuename=aps-ps-letter-auto-color:
paisley-backend:\
        :server:\
```

```
        :sh:\
        :mx#0:\
        :sd=/var/spool/lpd/%P:\
        :lpr_bounce:\
        :if=/var/spool/spool-system/filters/apsfilter:\
        :lp=raw@paisley.corp.com%9100:
plaid:\
        :sh:\
        :mx#0:\
        :sd=/var/spool/lpd/%P:\
        :lp=plaid@print-mn.corp.com:
icebox:\
        :sh:\
        :mx#0:\
        :sd=/var/spool/lpd/%P:\
        :lp=icebox@print-mn.corp.com:
```

When *printcapgen.pl* is run with the *–l* flag to generate a *printcap* file for the Minneapolis server, *plaid* and *icebox* printers are given a back-end queue, and jobs for the Berkeley printers are forwarded to *print-bk.corp.com*:

```
dirsvr# ./printcapgen.pl -l Minneapolis
#
# Printcap file generated automatically at Sun Jul  9 11:25:30 2000
#
# Using default LDAP server "localhost"
# Using default suffix of "o=book, c=US"
# Using specifed location code of "Minneapolis"
# Running default query of "all"
#
#
noir:\
        :sh:\
        :mx#0:\
        :sd=/var/spool/lpd/%P:\
        :lp=noir@print-bk.corp.com:
blanc:\
        :sh:\
        :mx#0:\
        :sd=/var/spool/lpd/%P:\
        :lp=blanc@print-bk.corp.com:
psychadelic:\
        :sh:\
        :mx#0:\
        :sd=/var/spool/lpd/%P:\
        :lp=psychadelic@print-bk.corp.com:
paisley:\
        :sh:\
        :mx#0:\
        :sd=/var/spool/lpd/%P:\
        :lp=paisley@print-bk.corp.com:
plaid:\
        :sh:\
        :mx#0:\
```

```
            :sd=/var/spool/lpd/%P:\
            :lp=plaid-backend@localhost:\
            :qq:\
            :force_queuename=aps-ps-letter-auto-color:
plaid-backend:\
            :server:\
            :sh:\
            :mx#0:\
            :sd=/var/spool/lpd/%P:\
            :lpr_bounce:\
            :if=/var/spool/spool-system/filters/apsfilter:\
            :lp=raw@plaid.corp.com%9100:
icebox:\
            :sh:\
            :mx#0:\
            :sd=/var/spool/lpd/%P:\
            :lp=icebox-backend@localhost:\
            :qq:\
            :force_queuename=aps-ljet4-letter-auto-mono:
icebox-backend:\
            :server:\
            :sh:\
            :mx#0:\
            :sd=/var/spool/lpd/%P:\
            :lpr_bounce:\
            :if=/var/spool/spool-system/filters/apsfilter:\
            :lp=/dev/lp0:
```

DHCP Configuration with LDAP and Perl

With *printcap* distributed automatically, queues are configured once the printers boot. Getting printers into a usable state after powering on requires configuring boot management.

Much of the structure of the *dhcpd.conf* generation script is similar to the *printcap* generation script from the previous section.

Getting data from the script is exactly the same as the *printcap* information, and *Net::LDAP* makes it easy. For ease of use, the *getAttrib* function will be held over from the previous script:

```
$ldap = Net::LDAP->new ($LDAPServer);
$printerlist = $ldap -> search ( base   => 'ou=Printers, o=book, c=US',
                                 filter => "objectclass=printer"
                                 );

$codesearch = $ldap -> search (base   => 'ou=Location, ou=Printers, o=book, c=US',
                               filter => "objectclass=printerLocation"
                               );
# That's all we need for now; disconnect to preserve server resources
$ldap->unbind;
```

After searching the directory and storing the results, we'll loop through the results
and create an array of printers:

```
# Get info for each printer in the directory!
for ($i=0; $i<$printerlist->count; $i++) {
    # These two variables get information about the current printer
    $result=$printerlist->entry($i);
    $Printer=$printerlist->as_struct->{$result->dn};

    # Make an array of printers.
    push(@ptrs, $Printer);
}

$now = localtime;  # When used like this, localtime generates a readable string
print "#\n";
print "# dhcpd.conf file generated automatically at ",$now,"\n";
print "#\n\n";
```

Then we'll print out some information about when the file was created and the
global parameters and subnet information. For simplicity we have hard-coded the
subnet data:

```
# Print the global header stuff.
print "option  domain-name \"book.com\"\;\n";
print "option  domain-name-servers 10.10.10.1, 192.168.0.1\;\n\n";

# Print subnet stuff.
print "subnet 10.10.10.0 netmask 255.255.255.0 {\n";
print "\trange 10.10.10.32 10.10.10.99\;\n";
print "\toption routers 10.10.10.1\;\n";
print "}\n\n";

print "subnet 10.20.20.64 netmask 255.255.255.192 {\n";
print "\trange 10.20.20.32 10.20.20.99\;\n";
print "\toption routers 10.20.20.65\;\n";
print "}\n\n";
```

Now we will step through the array of printers and generate a host entry for each
one. Each printer is given a fixed IP address, default route, post-boot server, and
post-boot configuration file:

```
# Now generate "host" entries for each host that is
# going to have a fixed IP address.
foreach $ptr(@ptrs){
    $name = getAttrib($ptr, "cn");
    $ip = &getAttrib($ptr,"ipaddress");
    $mac = getAttrib($ptr,"ethernetaddress");
    $bf = getAttrib($ptr,"bootfile");
    $ns = getAttrib($ptr,"bootfileserver");
    $router = getAttrib($ptr, "defaultrouter");
    if ($ip){
        print "host $name {\n";
        print "\thardware ethernet $mac\;\n";
        print "\tfixed-address $ip\;\n";
```

```
            print "\tfilename \"$bf\"\;\n";
            print "\tnext-server $ns\;\n";
            print "\toption routers $router\;\n";
            print "}\n";
    }
```

Example 11-4 shows the DHCP generator script in its entirety.

Example 11-4. dhcp_gen.pl

```perl
#!/usr/bin/perl

use strict;
use Net::LDAP;

# Global constants to be redefined for each server
my $LDAPServer = "localhost";

my ($ldap, $printerlist, $codesearch, $now, $result, $Printer);
my ($i, $name, $ns, $bf, $ptr, $ip, $mac, @ptrs, $router);


# Get data from LDAP server
$ldap = Net::LDAP->new ($LDAPServer);
$printerlist = $ldap -> search ( base   => 'ou=Printers, o=book, c=US',
                                 filter => "objectclass=printer"
                               );
$codesearch = $ldap -> search (base   => 'ou=Location, ou=Printers, o=book, c=US',
                               filter => "objectclass=printerLocation"
                              );
# That's all we need for now; disconnect to preserve server resources
$ldap->unbind;

sub getAttrib {
# We will frequently need to dereference the double hashes returned by
# LDAP searches; this routine makes it simpler to look at
    my $object = @_[0];
    my $attrib = @_[1];
    return $object->{$attrib}->[0];
}


# Get info for each printer in the directory!
for ($i=0; $i<$printerlist->count; $i++) {
    # These two variables get information about the current printer
    $result=$printerlist->entry($i);
    $Printer=$printerlist->as_struct->{$result->dn};

    # Make an array of printers.
    push(@ptrs, $Printer);
}

$now = localtime;  # When used like this, localtime generates a readable string
print "#\n";
print "#  dhcpd.conf file generated automatically at ",$now,"\n";
```

Example 11-4. dhcp_gen.pl (continued)

```
print "#\n\n";

# Print the global header stuff.
print "option  domain-name \"book.com\"\;\n";
print "option  domain-name-servers 10.10.10.1, 192.168.0.1\;\n\n";

# Print subnet stuff.
print "subnet 10.10.10.0 netmask 255.255.255.0 {\n";
print "\trange 10.10.10.32 10.10.10.99\;\n";
print "\toption routers 10.10.10.1\;\n";
print "}\n\n";

print "subnet 10.20.20.64 netmask 255.255.255.192 {\n";
print "\trange 10.20.20.32 10.20.20.99\;\n";
print "\toption routers 10.20.20.65\;\n";
print "}\n\n";

# Now generate "host" entries for each host that is
# going to have a fixed ip address.
foreach $ptr(@ptrs){
    $name = getAttrib($ptr, "cn");
    $ip = &getAttrib($ptr,"ipaddress");
    $mac = getAttrib($ptr,"ethernetaddress");
    $bf = getAttrib($ptr,"bootfile");
    $ns = getAttrib($ptr,"bootfileserver");
    $router = getAttrib($ptr, "defaultrouter");
    if ($ip){
        print "host $name {\n";
        print "\thardware ethernet $mac\;\n";
        print "\tfixed-address $ip\;\n";
        print "\tfilename \"$bf\"\;\n";
        print "\tnext-server $ns\;\n";
        print "\toption routers $router\;\n";
        print "}\n";
    }
}
```

Running the script is straightforward; Example 11-5 shows the results. No arguments are required because location is not as important to boot servers as it is to print servers. No problems will arise if boot servers have entries for faraway clients because they will not be used.

Example 11-5. Running dhcp_gen.pl

```
dirsvr# ./dhcp_gen.pl

#
# dhcpd.conf file generated automatically at Thu Jul 20 18:20:09 2000
#

option  domain-name "book.com";
option  domain-name-servers 10.10.10.1, 192.168.0.1;
```

Example 11-5. Running dhcp_gen.pl (continued)

```
subnet 10.10.10.0 netmask 255.255.255.0 {
        range 10.10.10.32 10.10.10.99;
        option routers 10.10.10.1;
}

subnet 10.20.20.64 netmask 255.255.255.192 {
        range 10.20.20.32 10.20.20.99;
        option routers 10.20.20.65;
}

host noir {
        hardware ethernet 00:00:5e:12:34:56;
        fixed-address 10.10.10.201;
        filename "hp-bf";
        next-server bs.bk.corp.com;
        option routers 10.10.10.1;
}
host blanc {
        hardware ethernet 00:00:5e:65:43:21;
        fixed-address 10.10.10.202;
        filename "hp-bf";
        next-server bs.bk.corp.com;
        option routers 10.10.10.1;
}
host psychedelic {
        hardware ethernet 00:00:5e:45:67:89;
        fixed-address 10.10.10.203;
        filename "tek-bf";
        next-server bs.bk.corp.com;
        option routers 10.10.10.1;
}
host paisley {
        hardware ethernet 00:00:5e:98:76:54;
        fixed-address 10.10.10.204;
        filename "tek-bf";
        next-server bs.bk.corp.com;
        option routers 10.10.10.1;
}
host plaid {
        hardware ethernet 00:00:5e:c0:ff:ee;
        fixed-address 10.20.20.105;
        filename "tek-bf";
        next-server bs.mn.corp.com;
        option routers 10.20.20.65;
}
```

12

In this chapter:
- *Accounting*
- *Security*
- *Performance Monitoring and Tuning*

Accounting, Security, and Performance

This chapter examines the intersection of general system administration and printer administration: accounting, security, and performance tuning. Keeping a record of who printed how many of what, and to which printer, is valuable. It may assist in justifying budgets and new job requisitions, as well planning future infrastructure upgrades. With the explosion of Internet connectivity, security is a critical component of any network service you offer. Finally, squeezing performance out of a print server preserves investment and makes financial types happy.

Accounting

System accounting is a topic broad enough to warrant its own book. In this section we are going to focus only on printer accounting. Printer accounting may be turned on even if you do not plan on charging for printer use. Accounting data provides valuable information on what, when, for whom, and from where jobs were printed. This information is for planning when to add new printers. It is also useful to have this data for performance tuning.

There are two methods for printer accounting: periodic and real-time. Of the two, periodic accounting is the most commonly used method. With periodic accounting, when a user submits a print request, the spooler processes it and print filters logs the user, host, and number of pages printed to an accounting file. Reports are generated periodically from the data in the accounting files. Report generation may be manual or with an automated method such as *cron*.

Real-time accounting is less common because it is much more difficult. Real-time accounting has the filters charge users for printouts as soon as they are produced. Users are prevented from printing when their account goes above a certain level.

This is more complex, and it requires some database code to track users and the users' quotas.

Activating Accounting

lpd records printer accounting information when there is an **af** entry in the *printcap* file for the associated printer. Standard practice is to name these files *acct*. If the accounting file is not named with a fully qualified path, it will be placed in the spool directory for the associated printer. Naturally, the file named by **af** must exist and be writeable by *lpd*.

For this example, we will place our accounting files in spool directories and name them *acct*. By this convention, the accounting file for a printer named *epson* with a spool directory at */var/spool/lpd/epson* would have an accounting file at */var/spool/lpd/epson/acct*. To create this file, go to the desired directory and *touch acct*:

```
mandelbrot# cd /var/spool/lpd/epson
mandelbrot# touch acct
mandelbrot# chown daemon.daemon acct
```

Accounting for Text Jobs

With basic accounting turned on, the task is half complete. We must now build the second half by using a filter to generate the accounting data. Filters are desig-nated by the **if** tag in the printcap file. Most free versions of Unix come with *lpf*, a simple text filter that will handle printing and accounting for basic text files. Sim-ple text accounting requires that the **if** tag uses *lpf*:

```
lp|generic text printer:\
        :lp=/dev/lpt0:\
        :sd=/var/spool/lpd/epson:\
        :lf=/var/spool/lpd/epson/log:\
        :af=/var/spool/lpd/epson/acct:\
        :if=/usr/libexec/lpr/lpf:\
        :mx#0:\
        :sh:
```

When recording accounting data, the spooler uses the **pw** (page width) and **pl** (page length) tags to calculate number of pages. By default, the page width is 132 characters, with a page length of 66 lines.

When pages are printed, *lpf* records the number of pages printed, along with the username and host. Hostnames of remote Windows clients are in upper case let-ters, and, for some odd reason, page usage is recorded to the hundredth of a page:

```
2.00 mandelbrot:todd
2.00 LAGRANGE:todd
3.00 EULER:todd
3.00 CAUCHY:todd
```

Building a PDL Accounting Filter

Calculating page usage for PDL based print jobs (PostScript, PCL, etc.) is a more complex task. Because a PDL is a specialized programming language, a multi-megabyte PostScript file may generate only one graphically rich page of output. Counting lines as with *lpf* is totally inadequate for PDL based jobs. PostScript has a function that returns the printer's page count; page counts are also available using SNMP.*

Getting the page count of a PostScript printer

In PostScript, the following command can be used over a bidirectional I/O channel to request page count information:

```
statusdict begin pagecount == end flush
```

We can use Perl's `IO::Socket` module to establish a connection to port 9100 on the remote printer, send the PostScript code, and collect the page count. One implementation of the page count script is shown in Example 12-1.

Example 12-1. Perl Script to Get Page Count of Remote Printer

```
#!/usr/bin/perl
#
# getpc - get the page count of a remote printer.

use strict;
use IO::Socket;

# Hard-coded defaults; could easily make these command-line arguments

my $server = "hp1";
my $port = 9100;
my $remote;
my $pc;

$remote = IO::Socket::INET->new(
   Proto=>"tcp",
   PeerAddr=>$server,
   PeerPort=>$port,
   Reuse=>1
) or die "Can't connect to $server\n";

print $remote "statusdict begin pagecount == end flush\n";
$pc = <$remote>;
close $remote;
chop($pc); chop($pc);
```

---

* Filter scripts are not run for remote printers with the classic Berkeley spooler, so use the double queue strategy discussed in Chapter 4, *Extending the Berkeley Spooler with Print Filters*. With LPRng, a bounce queue will locally filter a job bound for a remote printer.

Example 12-1. Perl Script to Get Page Count of Remote Printer (continued)

```
print "Page count of $server is: $pc\n";

exit;
```

Running the script simply prints out the page count of the printer:

```
mandelbrot# ./getpc
Page count of hp1 is: 490
```

Print filter environment

When *lpd* runs a filter script, certain arguments will be passed to it. By using a simple filter script that prints out the *@ARGV* array, we can determine what arguments *lpd* is passing to the filter script. For example:

```
-w132 -l66 -i0 -n todd -h mandelbrot /var/spool/lpd/hp1/acct
```

These arguments (and their order) may vary between operating systems, but the essential elements are in place:

* *-n todd* tells us that the user *todd* submitted the job.

* *-h mandelbrot* tells us that the job was submitted from *mandelbrot*.

* Finally, */var/spool/lpd/hp1/acct* is the accounting file to be used.

An accounting script for PDL jobs

For a complete accounting solution for use with PDLs, SNMP and the printer MIB provide the best solution. SNMP is printer-language independent and can be used with both PostScript and PCL. If the printer MIB is unavailable, page count information may be available in a private MIB. At a high level, the script looks like this:

1. Get the arguments to the script.

2. Record the page count of the remote printer before beginning the job.

3. Filter the job and wait for the filter to finish processing.

4. Send the job to the remote queue.

5. Record the page count of the remote printer after finishing the job.

6. Record the number of pages printed, hostname, and username to the accounting file.

Example 12-2 is one possible implementation of the script, written in Perl. If it seems a bit intimidating off the bat, don't worry because we will break it down step by step.

Example 12-2. PostScript Job Accounting Script for the Berkeley Spooler

```perl
#!/usr/bin/perl
use strict;
use Net::SNMP;
use Getopt::Std;
use vars qw($opt_n $opt_h);

my $stat_oid = ' 1.3.6.1.2.1.43.16.5.1.2.1';
my $pc_oid = ' 1.3.6.1.2.1.43.10.2.1.4.1';
my $community = "BOOK_PUB";
my $snmp_port = 161;
my $server = "hp1"
my $rq = "hp1-remote";
my $lpr = "/usr/bin/lpr";
my ($startpage, $endpage, $total, $status, $printer_busy);
my ($snmpkey, $session, $error, $response, $val);

sub snmp_query {
    ($session, $error) = Net::SNMP->session(
        -hostname  => $server,
        -community => $community,
        -port      => $snmp_port
    );
    $response = $session->get_table($_[0]);
    foreach $snmpkey (keys %{$response}) {
        $val = "$response->{$snmpkey}";
    }
    $session->close;
return $val;
}

sub log{
    open(ACCT, ">>$acctfile") or die "Can't open $acctfile: $!\n";
        print ACCT "$total $opt_h:$opt_n\n";
    close(ACCT);
}

&getopt('nh');
my $acctfile = shift;
$startpage = &snmp_query($pc_oid);

open(LPR, "|$lpr -P$rq") or die "Can't open $rq: $!\n";
while (<STDIN>){
    print LPR;
}
close(LPR);

$printer_busy = 0;
while(!$printer_busy){
    $status = &snmp_query($stat_oid);
    $printer_busy = 1 if $status !~ /READY/;
    sleep(1);
}
```

Example 12-2. PostScript Job Accounting Script for the Berkeley Spooler (continued)

```
while($printer_busy){
    $status = &snmp_query($stat_oid);
    $printer_busy = 0 if $status =~ /READY/;
    sleep(1);
}
$endpage = &snmp_query($pc_oid);
$total = $endpage - $startpage;
&log;
exit;
```

The weirdest part of this script is the printer must be ready when we ask for the page count, and it must have completed the job the second time. In the future, the Job Monitoring MIB[*] from the Printer Working Group will fill this void by sending SNMP traps with the information we want. Until then, we will need to develop another mechanism.

For our example, we will consider an HP printer with a JetDirect card. Because the JetDirect card supports the printer MIB, SNMP can be used to retrieve information in the script. Using Perl's `Net::SNMP` module, it is easy to query the page count.

The first part of the script defines the modules to be used:

```
#!/usr/bin/perl
use strict;
use Net::SNMP;
use Getopt::Std;
use vars qw($opt_n $opt_h);
```

Now we declare some variables. For SNMP, we need the OIDs that report printer status and page count, along with the SNMP community name and the port number. To report status, SNMP can be used to read the display by querying the printer console display buffer table. Page count is reported by *prtMarkerLifeCount*. To send queries to the right location, the hostname must be defined. Finally, a filter script for the classic Berkeley spooler must re-queue the job to a second queue so the job is passed to the remote machine; thus, the script must know the location of the *lpr* binary. If a script is moved to another queue, only these variables must be changed:[†]

```
my $stat_oid = ' 1.3.6.1.2.1.43.16.5.1.2.1';
my $pc_oid = ' 1.3.6.1.2.1.43.10.2.1.4.1';
my $community = "FOFZ_PUB";
my $snmp_port = 161;
my $server = "hp1"
my $rq = "hp1-remote";
my $lpr = "/usr/bin/lpr";
```

---

[*] See *http://www.pwg.org/jmp/index.html* for more information on the Job Monitoring MIB.

[†] Of course, if the script were really sophisticated, it would bind to an LDAP directory and pull all of the local variables out of the directory.

We end the variable declaration section with a few more variables. The first set is used in the main loop and is straightforward. The second set is for variables used in the SNMP subroutine:

```
my ($startpage, $endpage, $total, $status, $printer_busy);
my ($snmpkey, $session, $error, $response, $val);
```

We have two subroutines. One performs SNMP queries, and the second puts accumulated data at the end of the log file.

snmp_query establishes an SNMP session with the remote printer and queries the OID passed as an argument. It returns the value stored in that OID. The queried host is named by the *$server* variable:

```
sub snmp_query {
    ($session, $error) = Net::SNMP->session(
        -hostname  => $server,
        -community => $community,
        -port      => $snmp_port
    );
    $response = $session->get_table($_[0]);
    foreach $snmpkey (keys %{$response}) {
        $val = "$response->{$snmpkey}";
    }
    $session->close;
    return $val;
}
```

The *log* routine is called at the end of the script to append the accounting data to *$acctfile*. The `Getopt` module returns the parameter declared with *–n* in *$opt_n* and the parameter declared with *–h* in *$opt_h*. Naturally, after writing the data to the file, it is closed:

```
sub log{
    open(ACCT, ">>$acctfile") or die "Can't open $acctfile: $!\n";
        print ACCT "$total $opt_h:$opt_n\n";
    close(ACCT);
}
```

As mentioned previously, `Getopt` is used to retrieve the values of the *–n* and *–h* options. `Getopt` processes arguments to the script until none begin with a dash. At this point, the only argument remaining in *@ARGV* is the accounting filename, which we assign to *$acctfile* with the *shift* function:

```
&getopt('nh');
my $acctfile = shift;
```

Before beginning job processing, we call *snmp_query* to save the page count before starting as *$startpage*:

```
$startpage = &snmp_query($pc_oid);
```

Because this script is written for the Berkeley spooler, the filter script must re-queue the job into a remote queue. To re-queue the job, use *lpr*. First open a Perl pipe with *lpr* to the queue defined as *$rq*. The print job on standard input is passed to standard output until end of file is reached, and the *lpr* pipe is closed:

```
open(LPR, "|$lpr -P$rq") or die "Can't open $rq: $!\n";
while (<STDIN>){
    print LPR;
}
close(LPR);
```

Re-queuing the job sends it to a queue defined in *printcap* with the rm and rp flags, which sends the job to the remote printer. At this point, the filter script must wait until the printer processes the job before recording the new page count.

Two loops are used. In the first loop, the filter script waits for the script to begin processing. Every second, the filter script checks the status of the printer until it doesn't contain the word READY, meaning the job has begun processing:

```
$printer_busy = 0;
while(!$printer_busy){
    $status = &snmp_query($stat_oid);
    $printer_busy = 1 if $status !~ /READY/;
    sleep(1);
}
```

In the second loop, the filter script tests for the opposite condition. The script repeatedly tests the status until it does contain the word READY, which means that the job has finished:

```
while($printer_busy){
    $status = &snmp_query($stat_oid);
    $printer_busy = 0 if $status =~ /READY/;
    sleep(1);
}
```

When the job has finished, the script can query for the new page count and store it in *$endpage*. With the values of *$startpage* and *$endpage*, the filter script can easily calculate the number of pages used and store that in *$total*:

```
$endpage = &snmp_query($pc_oid);
$total = $endpage - $startpage;
```

Recording the accounting data is simple—the script just needs to call the *log* function before exiting:

```
&log;
exit;
```

Extracting Information from the Accounting System

Once you have accounting properly set up and are collecting data, you may use the printer accounting program *pac* to print reports on usage. The *–P* option to *pac* defines the print-queue to report on, and *–p* defines the price per page:

```
mandelbrot# pac -Pepson -p0.10
   Login                  pages/feet   runs    price
CAUCHY:todd                    3.00     1   $  0.30
EULER:todd                    22.00     8   $  2.20
LAGRANGE:todd                  2.00     1   $  0.20
mandelbrot.fofz.com:todd       6.00     3   $  0.60
muleshkov:root                 2.00     1   $  0.20

total                         35.00    14   $  3.50
```

When *pac* is run with the *–s* option, it summarizes the output and records it in a summary accounting file. Typically, the summary accounting file has the same name as the accounting file, but with *_sum* appended. In our example, the summary accounting file would be named */var/spool/lpd/epson/acct_sum*. When accounting summarization is performed, the raw accounting file is emptied.

Security

There are several ways for controlling access to your print server. This section describes controlling access and restricting usage of print services.

Restricting Access

Print services can be restricted on a host basis by IP address and hostname, as previously discussed. Print services can also be restricted on a user or group basis.

/etc/hosts.lpd and /etc/hosts.equiv

Remote host access to *lpd* can be restricted with */etc/hosts.lpd* or */etc/hosts.equiv*. *lpd* will check to be sure incoming requests arrive from a host listed in one of these files. If not, *lpd* will refuse the request.

The file */etc/hosts.equiv* affects programs like *rsh* and *rcp*, so be careful. Trusted host security is a good idea only on a network where you trust all the hosts, and you are confident that your other security mechanisms will prevent intruders from accessing your network.

The format of these files is simple. Each line can contain one hostname or IP address. The plus sign (+) can be used to allow access to all hosts.

This is probably obvious, but we feel the need to say it anyway: do not use + in */etc/hosts.equiv*!

For example, say that */etc/hosts.lpd* on *mandelbrot* had three lines such as these:

```
euler
muleshkov
lagrange
```

mandelbrot would accept requests from *euler*, *muleshkov*, and *lagrange*, but would refuse other requests.

Access restrictions based on Unix groups

The rg tag in the *printcap* file restricts access to users in the Unix group named by rg. In the following example, only members of the *printers* group are allowed to access print services (the rg tag must also be specified on all remote hosts):

```
lp|epson|generic text printer:\
        :lp=/dev/lpt0:\
        :sd=/var/spool/lpd/epson:\
        :lf=/var/spool/lpd/epson/log:\
        :af=/var/spool/lpd/epson/acct:\
        :if=/usr/libexec/lpr/lpf:\
        :mx#0:\
        :sh:\
        :rg=printers:
```

lpr returns error messages when users not in the restricted group attempt to access restricted print-queues:

```
mandelbrot% lpr -Pepson words.txt
lpr: Not a member of the restricted group
```

Suppressing multiple copies

The Berkeley spooler allows users to print multiple copies of a file using the –# option to *lpr*:

```
host% lpr -#3 resume.ps
```

Using the sc option in *printcap* limits users to one copy; when multiple copies are submitted, *lpr* will print an error message:

```
host% lpr -Php1 -#3 resume.ps
lpr: multiple copies are not allowed
```

Like rg, sc is required on all remote hosts as well. sc does not prevent users from running *lpr* multiple times or submitting the same file in one job. None of the following jobs will be prevented by the sc tag:

```
host% lpr resume.ps
host% lpr resume.ps
host% lpr resume.ps resume.ps resume.ps
```

User account requirements

Further user checks can be implemented with the rs tag in *printcap*. When rs is present for a locally attached printer, *lpd* will print jobs only if the user submitting the job has the same account name on the local host.

When remote users try to send print jobs, normally they will be sent an email message stating the print request couldn't be completed. Because the rs tag is present in the following *printcap*, remote users without a local account are denied access:

```
txt|generic text printer:\
        :lp=/dev/lpt0:\
        :sd=/var/spool/lpd/epson:\
        :lf=/var/spool/lpd/epson/log:\
        :af=/var/spool/lpd/epson/acct:\
        :if=/usr/libexec/lpr/lpf:\
        :rg=printers:\
        :mx#0:\
        :sc:\
        :rs:\
        :sh:
```

When remote users without local accounts attempt to print jobs, they receive error messages in email, such as the following:

```
Message 201:
From daemon@mandelbrot.fofz.com Sun Sep 12 17:26:10 1999
From: Owner of many system processes <daemon@mandelbrot.fofz.com>
To: gast@muleshkov.fofz.com
Subject: txt printer job "<unknown>"
Reply-To: root@mandelbrot.fofz.com

Your printer job could not be printed without an account on mandelbrot.fofz.com
```

Additionally, problems are noted in */var/log/lpd-errs* on the system where the queue resides:

```
Sep 12 17:12:02 mandelbrot lpd[8946]: mail sent to user gast about job <unknown>
on printer txt (NOACCT)
Sep 12 17:12:02 mandelbrot lpd[8946]: txt: job could not be printed
(cfA021muleshkov)
```

Restricting the size of print requests

Disk space on spooling hosts is finite, so *lpd* supports a cap on the file size that can be submitted to the queue with the mx tag. Each file in a print job may be up to the number of blocks defined by the mx tag. The block size is *BUFSIZ*, a system defined constant in *stdio.h* usually defined as 1024 bytes. When mx is not used, a default limit of 1000 blocks is enforced.

The limit the mx tag enforces applies to files in a job, not the total size of a job.

When a file larger than the value of mx is queued, *lpd* will print up to the mx limit and throw the remainder away. Also, the mx tag must be specified on remote hosts.

Controlling free disk space

To prevent disk-filling attacks, the Berkeley spooler supports setting a lower limit on the free disk space for jobs to be accepted. If the *minfree* file is present in the spooling directory for a local printer, *lpd* will not accept new jobs unless *minfree* blocks of free space are present.

To add this capability, look at the *printcap* file to find the spool directory. For the following *printcap* entry, the spool directory is */var/spool/lpd/hp1*:

```
laser|hp1|HP LaserJet 5M:\
        :sh:\
        :sc:\
        :lp=/dev/lpt1:\
        :sd=/var/spool/lpd/hp1:\
        :lf=/var/spool/lpd/hp1/log:\
        :af=/var/spool/lpd/hp1/acct:\
        :mx#0:
```

Each disk block is 512 bytes. To ensure that 50 megabytes of disk space are free, 102400 disk blocks must be free. Therefore, the file */var/spool/lpd/hp1/minfree* must contain the number 102400:

```
# echo 102400 > /var/spool/lpd/hp1/minfree
```

Security Outside the Spooler

Spooler based access controls are only part of the story. A good general security policy is necessary.* Depending on where jobs are originating, you may wish to have users tunnel print jobs through some sort of Virtual Private Network (VPN).

---

* For Unix host security, consult *Practical Unix and Internet Security,* by Simson Garfinkel and Eugene Spafford (O'Reilly).

Depending on the sensitivity of the printed information, you may wish to deploy a commercial package to make sure that print jobs will not sit in the output tray for the whole world to see. We have seen employee reviews, offer letters, confidential engineering documents, and even classified documents (!) waiting for owner pick-up. Commercial packages can address this problem by placing a terminal physically close to the printer and requiring user authentication before sending the job to the printer hardware.

In the future, printers may build in this functionality. Jobs would be held in printer memory and users would trigger processing with employee badges or smart cards.

Performance Monitoring and Tuning

Performance tuning of Unix systems is a very broad topic. As this book was written, competent system administrators were far more expensive than hardware upgrades, and Moore's law appears to keep expanding the gap. Therefore, we will show you how to determine what is holding back performance and guide you to an appropriate system upgrade.

uptime

When users complain about poor performance, start the investigation with *uptime*. When run, *uptime* reports the time and system load:

```
mandelbrot{104}% uptime
11:54PM  up 54 days, 14:09, 1 user, load averages: 0.00, 0.00, 0.00
```

uptime reports the current time and the length of time the system has been booted. For performance assessment purposes, the interesting part of *uptime*'s report is the remainder of its output, which consists of the number of users on the system and *load averages* for the last minute, five minutes, and fifteen minutes. Different operating systems compute load average in different ways; refer to your system's documentation or source code for details. As you can see, *mandelbrot* was not very busy when this output was collected.

vmstat

vmstat reports kernel statistics about process, virtual memory, disk, and CPU activity. *vmstat* is commonly used to detect *thrashing* (high paging activity) or large numbers of waiting processes, both of which can grind performance into the ground. The following example shows the output of *vmstat* run with the *−w 5* option, which will display one line for every five seconds:

```
mandelbrot{107}% vmstat -w 5
 procs     memory      page                    disks       faults      cpu
```

```
 r b w     avm   fre  flt  re  pi  po  fr  sr da0 da1 cd0   in  sy  cs us sy  id
 0 0 0    4300 10136    1   0   0   0   1   0   0   0   0  229  12   3  0  0 100
 0 0 0    3684  6416    1   0   0   0   0   0   1   0   0  230   5   2  0  0 100
 0 0 0    4020  6416    1   0   0   0   0   0   0   0   0  229   4   3  0  0 100
 0 0 0    4008  6416    2   0   0   0   1   0   0   0   0  229   6   3  0  0 100
 0 0 0    3828 10136    3   0   0   0   0   0   0   0   0  233  13   4  0  2  98
```

For the purposes of running a print server, the interesting columns are the b, w, and po columns. If the print server is responsible for running Ghostscript as well, then the id column at the far right end is also of interest. A quick guide to print server interpretation of *vmstat* output is shown in Table 12-1.

Table 12-1. vmstat Interpretation for a Print Server

Column Header	Interpretation and Diagnosis
b	Shows the number of processes blocked but waiting for resources (I/O, paging, etc.). This column is consistently high when processes are waiting on the disk system. To alleviate the problem, consider spreading out disks over multiple controllers.
w	Processes in runnable state but swapped out due to lack of resources. If this is not zero, invest in more memory promptly.
po	The number of memory pages paged out, and an indication of the system's paging activity. When this column is greater than zero for several cycles, it indicates that the system is coping with the load, but more memory will be required shortly.
id	CPU idle time. If you are using Ghostscript to render computationally intensive jobs, keep an eye on this.

Other

The most important performance parameter on a print server is disk throughput. SCSI disks will wring extra performance out of the disk subsystem and improve response time. Placing */var/spool/lpd* on a separate disk slice on the fastest disk in the system will prevent problems due to lack of disk space on other partitions.

Many other tools, such as *ps*, *top*, *iostat* and others, can provide insight into the performance of your system. If you need more detailed performance tuning advice, consult other sources of information, including *System Performance Tuning* by Mike Loukides (O'Reilly, 1990).

Epilogue

*printing discussion (n., Xerox PARC) A protracted,
low-level, time-consuming, generally pointless
discussion of something only peripherally
interesting to all.*
—The Jargon File, Version 4.2.0

It is hard to resist putting a postscript in a book about printing.

The central theme of this book is your importance and the value of your time. Never forget that, even if your management does.

IV

Appendixes

A

printcap Reference

Table A-1 lists standard *printcap* capabilities, and Table A-2 lists LPRng *printcap* capablilites.

Table A-1. printcap Capability Definitions

Short Name	Long Name	Type	Default Value	Description
af	acct.file	String	Null	Accounting file
br	tty.rate	Number	None	Baud rate
cf	filt.cifplot	String	Null	*cifplot* data filter
ct	remote.timeout	Number	120	TCP connection timeout
df	filt.dvi	String	Null	TeX data filter
ff	job.formfeed	String	\f	String to send for a form feed
fo	job.topofform	Boolean	False	Print a form feed when device is opened
gf	filt.plot	String	Null	Graph data filter
hl	banner.last	Boolean	False	Print the burst header page last
ic		Boolean	False	Driver supports *ioctl* to *ident* printout
if	filt.input	String	Null	Name of input filter
lf	spool.log	String	*/dev/console*	Name of log file
lo	spool.lock	String	Lock	Name of lock file
lp	tty.device	String	*/dev/lp*	Device name to open for output
ms	tty.mode	String	Null	List describing the *tty* modes
mx	max.blocks	Number	1000	Maximum file size
nd		String	Null	Next directory (unimplemented)

Table A-1. printcap Capability Definitions (continued)

Short Name	Long Name	Type	Default Value	Description
nf	filt.ditroff	String	Null	*ditroff* data filter
of	filt.output	String	Null	Name of output filter
pc	acct.price	Number	200	Price per foot/page
pl	page.length	Number	66	Page length (lines)
pw	page.width	Number	132	Page width (characters)
px	page.pwidth	Number	0	Page width in pixels
py	page.plength	Number	0	Page length in pixels
rf	filt.fortran	String	Null	FORTRAN filter
rg	daemon.restrictgrp	String	Null	Restricted group
rm	remote.host	String	Null	Machine name of remote host
rp	remote.queue	String	*lp*	Remote printer name
rs	daemon.restricted	Boolean	False	Restrict remote users to those with local accounts
rw	tty.rw	Boolean	False	Open printer device for reading and writing
sb	banner.short	Boolean	False	Short banner
sc	job.no_copies	Boolean	False	Suppress multiple copies
sd	spool.dir	String	*/var/spool/lpd*	Spool directory
sf	job.no_formfeed	Boolean	False	Suppress form feeds
sh	banner.disable	Boolean	False	Suppress printing of header
st	spool.status	String	Status	Status file name
tf		String	Null	troff data filter
tr	job.trailer	String	Null	Trailer string to print when queue empties
vf	filt.raster	String	Null	Raster image filter

Table A-2. LPRng printcap Capabilities

Name	Use	Type	Default	Description
Xf	D	String	Null	Output filter for format X (used by *lpd*); `filter` sets default filter.
ab	D	Boolean	False	Always print banner, ignore *lpr –b* option.
achk	D	Boolean	False	If True, LPD will check for an 'ACCEPT' reply to the initial accounting information written to a filter at the start of a job.
ae	D	String	Accounting	Format for end of job (see also af, la, and ar).

Table A-2. LPRng printcap Capabilities (continued)

Name	Use	Type	Default	Description
af	D	String	Null	Name of accounting file or server (see also la and ar). If the af field has the format |*program*, a filter will be started and used for recording accounting information; if the format is *host%port*, a TCP socket connection will be made to the port on the host. The as and ae strings will be printed to the specified destination. This connection will be passed to filters as file descriptor 3. The accounting file will not be created; it must exist for LPD to append data to it.
ah	D	Boolean	False	Autohold: job held until explicitly released.
all	A	String	Null	A list of all printers.
allow_ duplicate_ flags	A	Boolean	False	Allow duplicate command line flags; last overwrites earlier.
allow_getenv	A	Boolean	(Compile time)	Allows LPRng software to use the LPD_CONF environment variable to specify the location of a configuration file. This is for testing only.
allow_user_ logging	A	Boolean	False	If mail is requested using *lpr-m host%port,protocol* operations, and the allow_user_logging flag is true, then job logging information will be sent to *host%port,protocol*. See also lpr_bsd
ar	D	Boolean	True	Write remote transfer accounting (if af, and as/ae set).
architecture	A	String	(Compile time)	Architecture the software was compiled for (obsolete).
as	D	String	Accounting	Format for start of job (see also af, la, and ar).
auth	R	String	Null	Client to server authentication type.
auth_client_ filter	A	String-String	Null	Program used by client to do authentication to server.
auth_forward	A	String	Null	Server to server authentication type.
auth_forward_ id	A	String	Null	Remote server ID used when doing server-to-server authentication.
auth_forward_ filter	A	String	Null	Program used by originating server to do server-to-server authentication.
auth_receive_ filter	A	String	Null	Program used by receiving server to do authentication.

Table A-2. LPRng printcap Capabilities (continued)

Name	Use	Type	Default	Description
auth_server_id	A	String	Null	Server ID used when doing client-to-server or server-to-server authentication.
be	D	String	Banner	Printing program for end (overrides bp and hl).
bk	R	Boolean	False	Berkeley-compatible. Be strictly RFC-compliant or more exactly, BSD LPR compatible when sending jobs.
bkf	R	Boolean	False	Use bk_filter_options and bk_of_filter_options when invoking print filter.
bk_filter_options	D	String	(See source code)	When bk flag is set, options for non of print filters
bk_of_filter_options	D	String	(See source code)	When bk flag is set, options for of print filters.
bl	D	String	Banner	Line sent to banner printer program; default $-'C $-'n Job.
bp	D	String	Banner	Printing program (see hl) (default configuration variable is default_banner_printer)
bq	D	String	Null	Specifies the next destination for jobs sent to this queue. Job data files are first sent through any filters listed in printcap entry before transfer.
bq_format	D	String	l	Format of output from bounce queue filters.
br	D	Num	None	If *lp* is a tty, set the baud rate (see tty).
break_classname_priority_link	A	flag	False	Do not set priority to first letter of class name.
bs	D	String	Banner	Printing program for start (overrides bp and hl).
cf	D	String	Null	*cifplot* data filter.
check_for_nonprintable	R	Boolean	True	*lpr* checks f and p formats for printable files.
check_idle	D	String	Null	Program used to check for idle printer conditions before processing jobs.
class_in_status	A	Boolean	True	Show class name in *lpq* status rather than priority.
cm	A	String	Null	Comment identifying printer (lpq).
config_file	A	String	/etc/lpd.conf:/usr/etc/lpd.conf	Location of LPRng configuration information. Compile time option only (see allow_getenv).

Table A-2. LPRng printcap Capabilities (continued)

Name	Use	Type	Default	Description
connect_grace	A	Number	0	Time between jobs to allow printer recovery.
connect_interval	A	Number	10	Time between open or connection attempts.
connect_timeout	A	Number	10	Timeout value for connection or open.
control_filter	D	String	Null	Filter for control file. Used when sending job to remote spool queue.
db	A	String	Null	LPD debug options when serving this queue. See 1f (log file) entry as well.
default_format	R	String	*f*	Default format for printing jobs.
default_permission	D	String	*A*	Default permission for operation.
default_printer	A	String	*lp*	Default printer for printing jobs.
default_priority	R	String	*A*	Default priority for printing jobs.
default_remote_host	A	String	*localhost*	Default remote host for printing operations.
default_tmp_dir	A	String	*/tmp*	Default temporary directory.
destinations	D	String	Null	Names of printers that *lpq*/*lprm* should talk to find a job that has been processed by a router script.
df	D	String	Null	Tex data filter (DVI format).
fd	D	Boolean	False	If true, no forwarded jobs accepted.
ff	D	String	\f	String to send for a form feed.
filter	D	String	Null	Default filter to use for printing file.
filter_ld_path	D	String	(See source code)	The LD_LIBARY_PATH environment variable value for filters.
filter_options	D	String	(See source code)	When bk flag is clear, options for non of print filters.
filter_path	D	String	(See source code)	The PATH environment variable value for filters.
filter_poll_interval	D	Number	30	Interval to poll of filter.
fo	D	Boolean	False	Print a form feed when device is opened.
force_fqdn_hostname	A	Boolean	False	Force a fully qualified hostname in control file.

Table A-2. LPRng printcap Capabilities (continued)

Name	Use	Type	Default	Description
force_localhost	A	Boolean	False	Forces the clients programs (*lpr, lpc,* etc.) to send all print jobs and requests to the server running on the localhost entry for action. This flag effectively forces BSD LPR behaviour.
force_lpq_status	D	String	Null	Specifies a list of LPQ formats and hosts that get status returned in this format. force_lpq_status=s=pc*;l=mac* will cause hosts whose FQDN matches pc* to get short status and those that match mac* to get long format.
force_queuename	A	String	Null	When qq flag or use_queuename configuration is enabled, specifies the queuename to be used for control file Q information.
fq	D	Boolean	False	Print a form feed when device is closed.
full_time	D	Boolean	Detailed	Time format specification in log messages.
fx	A	String	Null	Valid output filter formats, i.e., flp would allow f, l, and p (default is to allow all formats).
gf	D	String	Null	Graph data filter. See *plot (3X).*
group	D	String	Daemon	LPD server group ID for execution.
hl	D	Boolean	False	Print banner after job instead of before.
if	D	String	Null	Filter command, run on a per-file basis.
ignore_requested_user_priority	D	Boolean	False	Ignore the requested user priority when ordering jobs. Prevents students... um... users from queue jumping.
ipv6	A	Boolean	False	Use IPV6.
kerberos_keytab	D	String	/etc/lpd.keytab	Kerberos *lpd* server keytab file.
kerberos_life	D	String	Null	Kerberos *lpd* server key lifetime.
kerberos_renew	D	String	Null	Kerberos *lpd* server key renewal time.
kerberos_server_principle	D	String	Null	Kerberos remote *lpd* server principal.
kerberos_service	D	String	*lpr*	Kerberos service used in principal requests.
la	D	Boolean	True	Write local printer accounting if af is set.
ld	D	String	Null	Leader string printed on printer open.
lf	D	String	Log	Error and debugging log file (LPD).
lk	D	Boolean	False	Lock the *lp* device to force arbitration.

Table A-2. LPRng printcap Capabilities (continued)

Name	Use	Type	Default	Description
lockfile	D	String	*/var/spool/ lpd/lpd*	*lpd* lock file (used only in *lpd.conf*). The lpd_port value is appended to the lockfile value to provide a unique lockfile even when different versions of LPRng are running on the same system.
logger_ destination	D	String	Null	Destination for logging information. Format is *host%port*.
logger_max_ size	D	Number	1024	Logger file maximum size in Kbytes.
logger_path	D	String	Null	Logger file pathname.
logger_timeout	D	Number	0	Logger connection timeout. 0 is no timeout.
longnumber	D	Boolean	False	Use 6-digit job numbers.
lp	D	String	Null	Device name or pipe to send output to.
lpd_bounce	A	Boolean	False	Forces *lpd* to filter jobs and then forward them.
lpd_force_poll	A	Boolean	False	Forces *lpd* to periodically poll *lpd* queues.
lpd_poll_time	A	Number	600	After this amount of idle time, *lpd* will poll queues.
lpd_port	D	String	Printer	Integer or port from */etc/services* for *lpd* server to accept connections.
lpd_printcap_ path	D	String	(See source code)	*printcap* path for *lpd*, in addition to normal one (configuration value only).
lpr_bounce	R	Boolean	True	Forces *lpr* to filter jobs and then send them.
lpr_bsd	R	Boolean	False	When set, LPR $-m$ will not take argument, but will use $USER value for return mail address.
mail_from	D	String	Null	Specifies the user part of email From address.
mail_operator_ on_error	D	String	Null	Send mail to this user when *lpd* encounters printing error.
max_connect_ interval	A	Number	60	Maximum time between connection attempts.
max_log_file_ size	D	Number	0	Maximum log file size in Kbytes (0 is unlimited). Spool queue log file truncated to min_log_file_size when value is nonzero and limited exceeded.
max_servers_ active	D	Number	0	Maximum servers that LPD will allow to be active at one time. 0 selects the system default, which is usually pretty small, perhaps 10 (configuration value only).

Table A-2. LPRng printcap Capabilities (continued)

Name	Use	Type	Default	Description
max_status_ line	D	Number	79	Maximum number of characters on an LPQ status line.
max_status_ size	D	Number	10	Maximum size (Kbytes) of status file.
mc	R	Number	1	Maximum copies allowed.
min_log_file_ size	D	Number	0	Minimum size (Kbytes) of log file.
min_status_ size	D	Number	2	Minimum size (Kbytes) of status file.
minfree	D	String	0	Minimum space (in K) for spool directory.
ml	R	Number	32	Minimum printable characters for printable check.
ms_time_ resolution	D	Boolean	False	Log time in milliseconds.
mx	R	Number	0	Maximum job size in K, 0=unlimited.
nb	D	Number	0	If non-zero, do a nonblocking open on *lp* device.
nf	D	String	Null	DITROFF data filter.
network_ connect_grace	A	Number	0	Time between attempts to send jobs to spooler. Useful when dealing with network printer using LPD interface to allow a bit of time between jobs.
of	D	String	Null	Output filter, run once for all output (used for banner printing, form feeds between files).
of_filter_ options	D	String	(See source code)	When bk flag is clear, options for OF print filters.
originate_port	A	String	512	1023 when originating a connection, use ports in this range.
oh	A	String	Null	Specific *printcap* entry for host; *printcap* entry ignored unless IP address of host and entry value match. Entry is used first to do glob style match against the host's fully qualified domain name, and then interpreted as a general IP address.
pass_env	A	String	PGPPASS, PGPPATH	If not the LPD server, sanitize and put these variables in a filter environment variable list.
perms_path	A	String	*/etc/lpd. perms*	*/usr/etc/lpd.perms* location of perms file (used in *lpd.conf*).
pl	D	Number	66	Page length (in lines).
pr	D	String	*/bin/pr*	*pr* program for *p* format.

Table A-2. LPRng printcap Capabilities (continued)

Name	Use	Type	Default	Description
printcap_path	A	String	/etc/print-cap:/usr/etc/printcap	Location of printcap file (used in *lpd.conf*).
ps	A	String	Status	Printer status filename.
pw	D	Number	132	Page width (in characters).
px	D	Number	0	page width in pixels (horizontal).
py	D	Number	0	page length in pixels (vertical).
qq	A	Boolean	False	*lpr*: puts in the queue name (Q entry) in the job control file when spooled or transferred. *lpd*: when receiving or transferring a job, if the queue name (Q entry) in the job control file is not present, puts in the queue name.
remote_support	A	String	Null	If non-null, specifies allowed operations to remote queue. Operations are specified by the letters R=lpr, M=lprm, Q=lpq, V=lpq -v, C=lpc. For example, remote_support=RM would only allow *lpr* and *lprm* operations.
report_server_as	A	String	Null	Use the string value as the name of the server when reporting *lpq* or *lpc* status.
retry_econnrefused	A	Boolean	True	If set, retry a connection to a remote system when an ECONNREFUSED error is returned.
retry_nolink	D	Boolean	True	If *lpd* is sending a job or opening a device for printing and the value is true, then the connection or device open is repeated indefinately.
return_short_status	D	String	Null	Some legacy (non-LPRng) *lpq* programs expect 'short' status to be returned. This option allows you to specify which hosts will get it. The value is a list of hosts and/or IP addresses and masks to which the *lpd* server will provide short status. E.g., return_short_status=192.8.0.0/16 will make LPD return short status to all requests from hosts in subnet 192.8.0.0. (See short_status_length).
reuse_addr	A	Boolean	False	If set, use SO_REUSEADDR on outgoing connection ports. This reduces the problems with exhausting port numbers. (usually only in *lpd.conf*).

Table A-2. LPRng printcap Capabilities (continued)

Name	Use	Type	Default	Description
reverse_lpq_ status	D	String	Null	When a *lpq* status request arrives from one of the specified hosts or IP addresses, then the LPQ status format is inverted. For example, if `reverse_lpq_` `status=host*,127.0.0.0/8`, then when a long status request arrives from host1 or from IP address 127.0.0.1, the short status will be returned.
rf	D	String	Null	Filter for printing FORTRAN style text files.
rm	A	String	Null	Remote queue machine (hostname) (with `rp`).
router	D	String	Null	Script that dynamically re-routes a job (see *README.routing* in the LPRng documentation).
rp	A	String	Null	Remote queue printer name (with `rm`).
rw	D	Boolean	False	Open the printer for reading and writing.
safe_chars	D	String	Null	Additional safe characters for control file contents.
save_on_error	D	Boolean	False	Save job when an error occurs to allow post-mortem diagnostics or reprinting. This should only be set on print queues. It is also a diagnostic aid.
save_when_done	D	Boolean	False	Save job when done (printed, transferred) to allow retry at a later time. This should only be set on print-queues. It is also a diagnostic aid.
sb	D	Boolean	False	Short banner (one line only).
sd	A	String	Null	Spool directory (only ONE printer per directory!).
send_block_ format	A	Boolean	False	Use the LPRng extended 'block job' job transmission method to send a job to a remote site.
send_data_ first	A	Boolean	False	Send data files then control files when sending a job to a remote host.
send_failure_ action	D	String	Abort	Action on print or transmission failure after *send_try* attempts. Use the following codes: *success* (JSUCC), treat as successful; *abort* (JABORT), abort printer; *retry* (JRETRY), retry job; *remove* (JREMOVE), remove job; *hold* (JHOLD), hold job. If the value is |/*filter*, the filter will be run and the number of attempts can be read from standard input. The filter should exit with one of the error codes listed above to cause the appropriate action.

Table A-2. LPRng printcap Capabilities (continued)

Name	Use	Type	Default	Description
send_job_rw_timeout	A	Number	6000	Timeout on read/write operations when sending job to printer or remote host (0 value is no timeout).
send_query_rw_timeout	A	Number	6000	Timeout on read/write operations when performing a status operation (0 value is no timeout.)
send_try	A	Number	3	Number of times to try sending or printing a job. 0 is infinite.
sendmail	D	String	*/usr/sbin/ sendmail −oi −t*	*sendmail* command to send mail to user. Flags must be set so that the address and other information are taken from standard input.
server	A	Boolean	False	*printcap* entry for server only.
server_auth_command	A	String	Null	Authentication command for server program.
server_tmp_dir	D	String	*/tmp*	Temporary directory for server to create files when there is no spool directory.
server_user	D	String	*daemon*	Server user name used in authentication operations.
sf	D	Boolean	False	Suppress form feeds separating jobs
sh	D	Boolean	False	Suppress headers and/or banner page.
shell	D	String	*/bin/sh*	SHELL enviornment variable value for filters.
short_status_length	D	Number	1	If the return_short_status value is used and has a match against a requesting address, this amount of status is set by the short_status_length option. For most legacy systems a 1 is suitable (1 line of status).
socket_linger	A	Number	10	If nonzero, forces a *SO_LINGER* operation to be done on all TCP/IP connections. This usually corrects a problem with missing last data transmissions to remote hosts.
spool_dir_perms	D	Number	042700	Permissions for spool directory.
spool_file_perms	D	Number	0600	Permissions for spool file.
spread_jobs	D	Number	0	Spread job numbers to avoid collisions.
ss	D	String	Null	Name of queue that server serves (with **sv**).
stalled_time	D	Number	120	Time after which to report an active job as stalled.

Table A-2. LPRng printcap Capabilities (continued)

Name	Use	Type	Default	Description
stop_on_abort	D	Boolean	True	Stop processing queue when print filter aborts.
stty	D	String	Null	*stty* settings for serial connected printer.
sv	D	String	Null	Names of servers for queue (with **ss**).
syslog_device	D	String	*/dev/console*	Name of syslog device to use if no syslog facility.
tc	A	String	Null	Reference to a *printcap* entry to include as part of the current entry.
tf	D	String	Null	troff data filter (C/A/T phototypesetter).
tr	D	String	Null	Trailer string to print when queue empties.
translate_format	D	String	Null	Translate job format (similar to *tr(1)* utility) only valid when transferring to remote spool queue. For example, with `translate_format=pfml`, p format is changed to f, m format to l.
use_auth	A	String	Null	Authentication to use.
use_date	A	Boolean	True	Add date line ('D') to control file.
use_identifier	R	Boolean	True	Add job identifier lines ('A') in the control file.
use_info_cache	D	Boolean	True	Cache *printcap* information.
use_shorthost	R	Boolean	False	Use only the hostname for job control and data filenames. Host information in job file will still be fully qualified domain name.
user	D	String	daemon	LPD effective user (EUID) for SUID operations.
user_auth_command	A	String	Null	Authentication command for user (client program).
vf	D	String	Null	(Versatek) raster image filter.

B

SNMP MIB Objects for Managing Printers

RFC 1213: MIB-II

RFC 1213 defines the most general piece of the MIB tree, called *MIB-II*, which is supported by every implementation of SNMP. MIB-II is located at *mgmt.mib-2.*[*] Here are the MIB-II objects relevant to printer mangement:

system.sysDescr (string, max length 255)

This object is a string that describes a managed device. The standard specifies that the string should include a description of both the hardware and software and that both the operating system and the networking software should be described. Of course, in many cases, the networking software is bundled with the operating system, and therefore the version of the OS is sufficient.

This object is a useful starting point when dealing with a printer in a script or program. Different vendors will put information in different places in the MIB, and this string can be used to determine where to look for further information. Ben Woodard's *npadmin* program checks this object more than any other object in the MIB for exactly this reason. Although most of the strings stored in this object are straightforward, at least one vendor stores an unreadable string in this object, claiming that the string is meaningful to its management software.

system.sysUpTime (TimeTicks)

Taken on its own, this object is only of limited interest. It keeps track of the uptime of the SNMP agent, not the system itself. For printers, however, it can

---

[*] From this point on in the appendix, we will leave off the *iso.dod.org.internet* prefix to objects in the MIB.

be used in conjunction with the alert table of the printer MIB to estimate the time of an alert. By subtracting the time of the alert from the system uptime, you can get a reasonable idea of when the alert occurred.

system.sysContact (string, max length 255)

This object stores a string with contact information for the human responsible for the device, for example, `Sir Galahad`. If no information is available, the contact will be the null string.

It's not a good idea to put your name in this field. Users know who to contact when printers are not working, and desktop support people certainly know how to get in touch with the printer management group. However, failed printers sometimes need to be power cycled, or just given a good whack, and it is often a problem to find somebody in the vicinity of the printer. Storing a local contact in this object helps the printer management group find a pair of remote hands near the printer.

HP 5 Series printers don't allow this object to be set.

system.sysName (string, max length 255)

This string is usually set to the device's DNS name, such as `printer.anthrax.com`. Like the contact string, an unknown node's name is set to the null string.

system.sysLocation (string, max length 255)

A string that holds the physical location of this node, such as `Castle Anthrax, Room 70`. The default value is the null string.

Like the contact information, this field is frequently out of date. The best way to keep it correct is by erasing the field when the printer is moved to a different subnet. The HP 5 Series does not allow this object to be set, either.

interfaces.ifTable.ifEntry.ifPhysAddress (PhysAddress, an octet string)

The data-link address of an interface. Although this will usually be an Ethernet MAC address, it may very well be a FDDI or ATM MAC address.

By using SNMP to an established printer, the Ethernet MAC address can be obtained and placed in the *bootptab*.

ip.ipAddrTable.ipAddrEntry.ipAdEntNetMask.<ipaddr> (IpAddress)

The interface's subnet mask. For example, if there were an interface with the IP address of 171.68.205.25, the object *ip.ipAddrTable.ipAddrEntry.ipAdEntNetMask.171.68.205.25* would have the subnet mask for that interface.

ip.ipRoutingTable.ipRouteEntry.ipRouteNextHop.ipaddr (IpAddress)

The IP address of the next hop to *ipaddr*. We aren't aware of any printer that runs a dynamic routing protocol, so the only entry is for an *ipaddr* of 0.0.0.0, in which case the IP address in the object would be the default route. However, some printers do not correctly set this object.

*tcp.tcpConnTable.tcpConnEntry.tcpConnRemAddress.**ipaddr** (IpAddress)*

If implemented properly, this could be one of the most useful troubleshooting objects in the MIB. When a connection is opened to a device, it should appear in the TCP connection table (consider the utility of the *netstat* command on Unix, for example). Viewing the TCP connection table remotely would give network administrators the ability to see which hosts were sending jobs to the printer based on TCP connections. Unfortunately, this table is unusable for reasons that differ from vendor to vendor.

RFC 1514: Host MIB

The host MIB was standardized in 1993, more than three years after SNMP was first standardized. This MIB was designed for hosts, and the authors defined a host as a computer that "...is directly used by one or more human beings." Here are the objects defined in the host MIB that are relevant to printer administration.

hrMemorySize (Integer32)

The number of kilobytes of RAM in the host. Since this object can store memory sizes up to almost 2 TB, it should be sufficient for any printer you might purchase.[*]

Printers use memory to prepare page images before printing, and some print jobs may not be printed properly if the printer does not have enough memory. If Windows print drivers are configured with the default memory setting and the printer has more memory, the printer client will not take full advantage of the printer hardware. Support personnel must determine the amount of memory in a printer before configuring the driver. Without SNMP, this requires either an educated guess or printing a test page. Printing a test page typically requires access to the console of the printer, which may be impossible if the printer and the support technician are in two different states (or countries!).

host.hrDevice.hrDeviceTable.hrDeviceEntry.hrDeviceDescr (string, max length 64)

A description of the device, including its manufacturer and revision. The string may also include the serial number. Usually, the model number is in this string as well, although some vendors put the model number in other places in the MIB.

host.hrDevice.hrDeviceEntry.hrDeviceStatus (integer enumeration)

This object reports the status of the device (1=unknown, 2=running, 3=warning, 4=testing, 5=down). *warning* is used to report that an unusual error has been detected, but that the device is still operational.

---

[*] Unless you have purchased printers that have a 64-bit memory address space, you should be safe.

host.hrDevice.hrPrinterTable.hrPrinterEntry.hrPrinterStatus (integer enumeration)
> This object reports the status of a printer (1=other, 2=unknown, 3=idle, 4=printing, 5=warmup).

host.hrDevice.hrPrinterTable.hrPrinterEntry.hrPrinterDetectedErrorState (binary string)
> This object reports error conditions detected by the printer, and it is a good "quick and dirty" check on the status of a printer. Far more comprehensive status information is available in the printer MIB. This entry is also present on devices that pre-date the printer MIB. Eight bits are used as Boolean flags to indicate error conditions, with 1 corresponding to true; the settings for the seven bits are shown in Table B-1. If no errors are detected, then no bits will be set and the value of this object will be zero. When multiple error conditions exist, then *hrDeviceStatus* will be set to the worst condition.

Table B-1. Settings of hrDetectedErrorState and hrDeviceStatus

Bit Number	Setting of hrDetectedErrorState	Setting of hrDeviceStatus
0	Low paper	Warning
1	No paper	Down
2	Low toner	Warning
3	No toner	Down
4	Door open	Down
5	Jammed	Down
6	Offline	Down
7	Service requested	Warning

Storage Table

The storage table reports on the logical, not physical, storage in a host. It is useful because you can often troubleshoot problems with printer memory by using this table. It will also tell you about a printer's hard disk if it has one. All the items in the storage table begin with the prefix *host.hrStorage.hrStorageTable.hrStorageEntry* (unfortunately, Tektronix printers do not implement the storage table).

hrStorageDescr (string, max length 255)
> A description of the type of storage, such as "Random Access Memory" or "Dynamic RAM Disk using system memory." Before deciphering the rest of the storage table, look at this entry to find out what is described in each row of the storage table.

hrStorageAllocationUnits (integer from 0 to $2^{31}-1$)
> Some storage devices, such as disks, require that space be allocated in blocks. This object is the number of bytes in an allocation block. Memory can be allocated byte by byte, so for memory, this number is typically 1.

hrStorageSize (integer from 1 to 2³¹–1)

The size of the storage device, in terms of storage allocation units.

hrStorageUsed (integer from 1 to 2³¹–1)

The number of storage allocation units in use on the device.

hrStorageAllocationFailures (Counter)

The number of storage requests that have failed because of insufficient available space on the device. One possible use for this object is to determine if a print job is failing due to inadequate memory. Check its value before sending a job and after the job has failed to see if the counter has been incremented.

RFC 1759: Printer MIB

Because of the obvious differences between general-purpose hosts and printers, the host MIB cannot provide the level of detail about the status of printers required by network managers. To address this shortcoming, the Printer Working Group of the IETF (*http://www.pwg.org*) was formed and published the Printer MIB in early 1995 as RFC 1759. This MIB makes remote printer management much easier than it would otherwise be, leading many institutions to make it a requirement for any printer they purchase.

Unfortunately, due to the incredible variety of printing technology and features, the printer MIB is very large and complex, which has held back implementation. At the time this book was written, the printer MIB was supported only by the newer HP 5 Series printers (excluding the Color LaserJet 5), the HP EIO 1000 Series printers, and the newer Lexmark, Tektronix, and Xerox DocuCenter printers. The complexity of the MIB has also led to subtle implementation differences between different vendors, but the slight incompatibilities are being ironed out.

One technique used by the MIB designers to achieve internationalization is to have configurable units of measure. Suppose there is a quantity called *foo* that printer managers might be interested in. The printer MIB would then have an object called *fooMeasureUnit*, which would have a value of metric or English. The *fooValue* object would have the value of *foo* in terms of *fooMeasureUnit*s.

In some places, the clarity of the printer MIB suffers from use of Bureaucratese. For example, the MIB uses the term *input sub-unit* for an input device on a printer, such as a paper tray. An input sub-unit on a laser printer would be a paper tray, and the remaining capacity would be measured in sheets. An input sub-unit on a continuous-feed printer would be the box of fanfold paper, and the remaining capacity may be measured in feet. To help improve clarity, for the most part, we will write about the MIB in terms of a laser printer with paper trays, and ignore other media types.

The General Table

The first table in the printer MIB is the general table. Every item in the general table begins with the prefix *printmib.prtGeneral.prtGeneralTable.prtGeneralEntry*:

prtGeneralReset (type 3 enumeration)

This object will always have the value *notResetting* when read. An operator can force a reset by setting this object to *powerCycleReset* or *resetToNVRAM* or *resetToFactoryDefaults*. As with many other products, rebooting a printer can often fix mysterious problems. This object can also be used to reboot a printer after reconfiguration.

prtInputDefaultIndex (Integer32)

This object can be used to specify the default paper tray. Although this object seems useful, most common PC printer drivers will set their own default paper tray using printer command language statements at the head of the job. Language statements in a print job will override any defaults set in the MIB, so the value of this object will not affect most PC print jobs.

prtMediaPathDefaultIndex (Integer32)

This object can be used to set the default media path, which usually controls whether jobs will be printed duplex. This particular object is useful for making the default print style duplex. Unfortunately, the language interpreter takes precedence over this object's value. Like the previous object, jobs from print clients will override this object.

prtConsoleDisable (integer)

This object can be used to disable the console. If enough people print enough pages, sooner or later an end user may get the bright idea of passing time by altering settings on the front-panel while waiting for a job to come out of the printer. To solve this problem, use this object to disable the console.

The input table

This table stores information about the input trays. Although one might think that the most useful piece of information in this table would be the amount of paper in each tray, accurate measurements of paper trays are not yet possible. You will have to settle for knowing the capacity of each tray and whether or not it is empty. All the objects in the printer table begin with the prefix *printmib.prtInput. prtInputTable.prtInputEntry*:

prtInputType (type 2 enumeration)

This object describes the mechanism that feeds paper into the printer. Its main use is to differentiate between manual and automatic paper feeds. Like many other objects in the MIB, different vendors may interpret this object different ways. Lexmark and Tektronix label manual feed trays as *sheetFeedManual,* while HP labels manual feed trays as *sheetFeedAutoNonRemovableTray.*

prtInputDimUnit (MediaUnit, a type defined in the RFC)

This object is the unit of measurement used by the input tray. It is either in units of ten thousandths of an inch or micrometers.

prtInputMediaDimFeedDirDeclared (Integer32)

This object tells how long the paper in the input tray measures in the feed direction, in units of *prtInputDimUnit.* Depending on how paper is fed into the print engine, the value of this object may have either the length or width of the paper.

In the long edge feed case shown in Figure B-1, the paper length along the paper feed direction would be 11 inches, and the cross feed length would be 8.5 inches. For the short-edge case, the dimensions would be reversed: the paper length along the feed direction would be 8.5 inches, and 11 inches in the cross feed direction.

prtInputMediaDimXFeedDirDeclared (Integer32)

This object tells how long the paper in the input tray measures along the cross feed direction, as in Figure B-1.

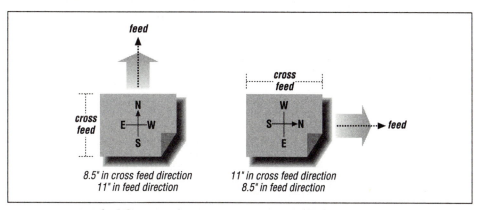

Figure B-1. Paper feed direction changes measurements and compass points

prtInputCapacityUnit (CapacityUnit)

This is a selection from an enumeration to report the capacity of an input tray or feed. It includes units such as *sheets* for paper trays as well as *feet* and *meters* for continuous fanfold paper.

prtInputMaxCapacity (Integer32)

The maximum capacity of the paper tray. *−1* indicates *other* and shows that there are no restrictions on this parameter, and *−2* is *unknown.*

prtInputCurrentLevel (Integer32)

> The current capacity of the paper tray. *−2* is *unknown,* and *−3* means at least one unit remains.

> The previous three objects tell you the maximum capacity of a tray and how much paper remains. Unfortunately, *prtInputCurrentLevel* is not well implemented by any vendor. If you were expecting to find out that a printer had 137 pages remaining in its input tray, you will be disappointed. Many printers simply report that the tray is not empty, and that another page can be printed. Other printers will report values such as "50 pages," which really should be interpreted as "some paper, but the tray is not full."

> Even if these values were measured accurately, the values in the MIB are not updated frequently. Some printers only update the MIB after printing a page. After an empty tray is filled, the tray will still be reported as empty until a page is printed. Other printers do not even react to the paper tray being removed. The bottom line: do not trust this object.

prtInputStatus (SubUnitStatus)

> Seven flags are used to report the status of the paper tray. The seven flags are a defined data type used to report on the status of any component of a printer, but the interpretation varies depending on what component that is. The *SubUnitStatus* structure is illustrated in Figure B-2.

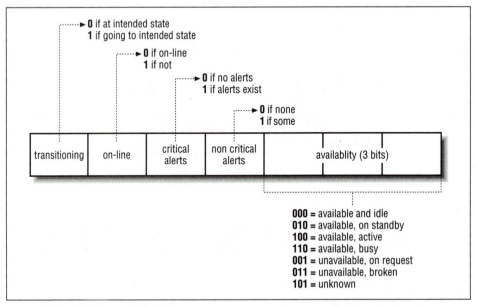

Figure B-2. SubUnitStatus flags

Like the previous set of objects, *prtInputStatus* is not as useful as it might first appear. For example, the situation of the remaining capacity of the input tray is reported as zero because there is only a small amount of paper remaining. In some printers, the "empty" paper tray will cause an alert to be posted on the input tray even though there is no problem.

This object is also subject to some interpretation problems. Lexmark printers return the status *available and active* on all input units, while other vendors set the status to *available and idle.* Lexmark printers will also label an empty paper tray as a *Critical Alerts Unavailable and OnRequest* although other vendors will return *Non-Critical Alerts Unavailable and OnRequest* for the same problem.

prtInputMediaName (string, max length 64)

A text label for the printer administrator of the type of media in the tray. It could be *letterhead, transparencies,* or even *plain.*

Marker table

In the context of the printer MIB, a *marker* is something that produces output, such as a laser print engine. The designers of the MIB recognized most printers have only one marker, so this table usually has one row. Because a printer's job is producing output, thie table tells you a lot about the printer. The table contains information about how much printing is done, the paper sizes that can be accepted by the print engine, and how fast the printer can produce output. All the items in the marker table have a prefix of *printmib.prtMarker.prtMarkerTable.prtMarkerEntry*:

prtMarkerMarkTech (type 2 enumeration)

The MIB defines 25 different technologies in the standard enumeration, from the mundane 9 pin dot matrix printer to ion deposition printers. This object is useful because some vendors, such as Tektronix, produce a number of models that use varying technologies.

prtMarkerCounterUnit (type 1 enumeration)

The unit of measure for the print engine's life (see the next object). It may be measured in linear distance, pages, or impressions. The difference between pages and impressions is that a duplexed sheet of paper is one page, but it has one impression on each side for a total of two impressions.

prtMarkerLifeCount (Counter32)

The amount of work done by the printer in its life, as measured in the units of the previous object.

prtMarkerCounterUnit and *prtMarkerLifeCount* report how much a printer is being used. Polling this object every month assesses monthly printer usage and thus allows estimation of variable costs. Another use for this value is to size printers to the task at hand. Most printers have a maximum recommended monthly page count, and it is a good idea not to exceed this value. With printer usage data, selecting a printer with a capacity large enough for the job at hand is made easier. Finally, the page count is like an odometer. Just as you should get an oil change every 3,000 miles, periodic maintenance on printers at certain page counts is essential to smooth operation and long lifetimes.

prtMarkerAddressabilityUnit (type 1 enumeration)

Determines whether the next two objects will be measured in metric or English units.

prtMarkerAddressabilityFeedDir (Integer32)

If measured in English units, the number of dots per inch the print engine can print vertically.

prtMarkerAddressabilityXFeedDir (Integer32)

If measured in English units, the number of dots per inch the printer can print horizontally.

The previous three objects return the physical resolution of print engine. All modern printers use resolution enhancing technology, which has the undesirable side effect of causing "enhanced" numbers to be quoted by sales representatives and brochures. These objects generally return the actual resolution, which could be a neat party trick for a system administration meeting.

prtMarkerNorthMargin (Integer32)

The minimum margin that the print engine must leave at the first edge that flows through the print engine. In many cases, the first edge is the top edge, but not always. Figure B-1 also incorporates compass points to illustrate how to label the edges with two different feed directions.

prtMarkerSouthMargin (Integer32)

The minimum margin on the south edge of the page.

prtMarkerWestMargin (Integer32)

The minimum margin on the west edge of the page.

prtMarkerEastMargin (Integer32)

The minimum margin on the east edge of the page. Although a printer may print on standard letter-size paper, in some circumstances you may be more interested in the part of the paper you can put ink on. Finding the MIB value can allow you to find out what the physical constraints of the printer are. Artists designing brochures for your organization may be interested in how close to the edge they can go.* To print a full 11"×17" page, look through each printer's MIB to find a printer capable of printing that large an area.

---

* There are other reasons for wanting to print as close to the edge as possible: the dreaded page limit on college writing assignments. Rather than depending on the word processing application to know the printer, instead query the printer MIB directly to find out the physical limits of the printer to squeeze as much print area as possible onto a single page.

prtMarkerStatus (SubUnitStatus)

The status of the print engine. It returns a *SubUnitStatus*, so see the *prtInputStatus* entry and Figure B-2 for details.

The marker supplies table

Many printers do not completely implement this table, in part because of the difficulty in doing so. (Have you ever tried to figure out how much toner was left in your printer by looking at the toner cartridge?) Only Tektronix printers implement this table with useful information. All of the objects in the marker supplies table have the prefix *printmib.prtMarkerSupplies.prtMarkerSuppliesTable.prtMarkerSuppliesEntry*:

prtMarkerSuppliesClass (type 1 enumeration)

The printer MIB defines two classes of marker supplies. One type is a *supply that is consumed* (3), such as a toner cartridge. The other class is a *receptacle that is filled* (4), such as an ink cartridge.

prtMarkerSuppliesType (type 3 enumeration)

This object describes the type of ink that is used by the print engine. The most common type is `toner`. Some vendors will put updated types into the printer MIB rather than specifying `other`.

prtMarkerSuppliesDescription (string, max length 255)

This object describes the supply used by the print engine. For example, `Toner Cartridge HP C3909A`.

prtMarkerSuppliesSupplyUnit (type 1 enumeration)

An enumerated type that defines how the capacity of the supply container is measured. Values are available for length, weight, and fluid amount; naturally, both English and metric types of each measure are available.

prtMarkerSuppliesMaxCapacity (Integer32)

The maximum capacity of the supply container expressed in *prtMarkerSuppliesSupplyUnit*. The value −2 means *unknown* and is common.

prtMarkerSuppliesLevel (Integer32)

The current supply of toner. −3 is for *some supply remains* and is very common. With the current state of the technology, it is not possible to have a printer management application automatically ordering toner when it runs low.

Media path table

A *media path* is how paper moves from the input tray through the print engine and to the output tray. It is a virtual path used by the printer as opposed to a physical paper path.

All the objects in the media path begin with the prefix *printmib.prtMediaPath.*
prtMediaPathTable.prtMediaPathEntry:

prtMediaPathMaxSpeedPrintUnit (type 1 enumerated integer)

The unit of measure used in specifying the speed of all media paths in the printer. For a laser printer, it will be *pages per hour.*

prtMediaPathMediaSizeUnit (MediaUnit enumeration)

Determines whether metric or English units are used in calculating the values in the media path table.

prtMediaPathMaxSpeed (Integer32)

The maximum speed of the media path, expressed in the chosen units. For a laser printer rated at 10 pages per minute, this number would be 600. There are two major caveats. First, print engines do not run continuously at top speed because each page must be rendered before the print engine transfers the image to paper. Second, laser print engines print different sizes of paper at different speeds. Most of the advertised numbers seem to be based on U.S. standard letter paper (8.5"×11").

The next set of objects describes both the minimum and maximum size of the paper that can be fed through a given media path. Just like with both *prtInputMediaDimFeedDirDeclared* and *prtInputMediaDimXFeedDirDeclared*, values will depend on the feed direction, as shown in Figure B-1.

prtMediaPathMaxMediaFeedDir (Integer32)

The maximum length paper possible to feed through along the feed direction.

prtMediaPathMaxMediaXFeedDir (Integer32)

The maximum width paper that can be fed through this path.

prtMediaPathMinMediaFeedDir (Integer32)

The minimum length paper that can be fed through this path.

prtMediaPathMinMediaXFeedDir (Integer32)

The minimum width paper that can be fed through this path.

prtMediaPathType (type 2 enumerated integer)

Whether or not the media path is duplex. There are two types of duplexing units, based on whether the pages are duplexed like a newspaper (along the long edge of the paper) or like a notepad (along the short edge of the paper). Figure B-3 shows the difference between newspaper and notepad duplexing by putting an arrow pointing to the top of the page on a duplexed sheet in each style.

prtMediaPathDescription (string, max length 255)

A string provided by the manufacturer to describe the media path, such as `Simplex` or `Long-Edge Duplex`.

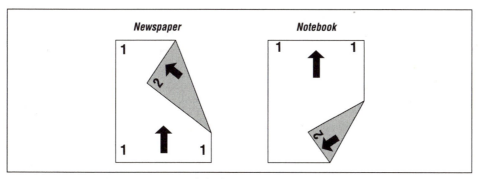

Figure B-3. Newspaper versus notepad duplexing

prtMediaPathStatus (SubUnitStatus)

The status of the path. It returns a *SubUnitStatus*, so see *prtInputStatus* and Figure B-2 for details.

Two versions of the firmware on the Xerox DocuCenter do not correctly implement this table. One version of the firmware did not list any duplex paths, and the next version did not properly implement the path.

The interpreter table

The interpreter table is a list of all the printer language interpreters supported by the printer. When a job prints from one printer and not from an identical printer, the culprit is often a slightly different version of the language interpreter. Some printers have been known to have problems with the implementation of this table.[*]

All the objects in the interpreter table begin with the prefix *printmib.prtInterpreter. prtInterpreterTable.prtInterpreterEntry*:

prtInterpreterLangFamily (type 2 enumeration)

The family name of a language the printer can interpret directly or emulate. The most common values are `langPS` (6) for PostScript and `langPCL` (3) for HP PCL.

prtInterpreterLangLevel (string, max length 31)

The level of the language that the interpreter can understand. A printer that interprets HP PCL 5E might set this string to `5.00E`.

---

[*] See Ben Woodard's post to the BUGTRAQ mailing list on September 5, 1998. (BUGTRAQ archives are available from *http://www.geek-girl.com/*). He notes that HP 5M and 5N printers will crash if parts of this table are accessed in a strange way. It can be reproduced with the UC Davis SNMP tools:

```
snmp-nms$ snmpgetnext scv-sirloin public 43.15.1.1.2.1.5 43.15.1.1.3.1.5 \
43.15.1.1.4.1.5 43.15.1.1.5.1.5 43.15.1.1.6.1.5 43.15.1.1.7.1.5 \
43.15.1.1.8.1.5 43.15.1.1.9.1.5 43.15.1.1.12.1.5
```

By the way, we highly recommend the BUGTRAQ mailing list as a source of full-disclosure security information as it breaks.

prtInterpreterLangVersion (string, max length 31)

A date code or version of the language. This is much like the patch level, since many times interpreters with the same language level will have a slightly different version. This is frequently the date code of the formatter or raster image processing engine of the printer.

prtInterpreterDefaultOrientation (type 1 enumeration)

Whether the default page orientation is `portrait` (3) or `landscape` (4).

prtInterpreterTwoWay (type 1 enumeration)

Whether or not this interpreter returns information back to the host. Some interpreters are capable of communicating errors directly back to the client software.

The channel table

A *channel* is a way of submitting jobs to a printer. It can be as simple as an RS-232 serial interface or as complicated as network protocols. Channels will listen on the network for print jobs and then pass them to the language interpreter. All the objects in the channel table start with the prefix *printmib.prtChannel. prtChannelTable.prtChannelEntry*:

prtChannelType (type 2 enumeration)

The type of the channel. Channel types range from `chSerialPort` (3) for a serial-port to full-blown protocol implementations. Common protocols are `chAppleTalkPAP` (7), `chLPDServer` (8), and `chServerMessageBlock` (27).

prtChannelProtocolVersion (string, max length 63)

The version of the protocol used on this channel. The numbering will depend on the channel type.

prtChannelCurrentJobCntlLangIndex (Integer32)

The index in the interpreter table for the job-control language used on this channel. HP printers, for example, will use PJL even if the page-description language is PostScript.

prtChannelDefaultPageDescLangIndex (Integer32)

The index in the interpreter table for the page-description language on the channel. Many printers will have an "automatic selection" language family in the interpreter table. In earlier versions of the Tektronix firmware, the value of *prtInterpreterLangFamily* was placed in this field instead of the index of the row in the printer interpreter table.

prtChannelState (type 1 enumeration)

The state of this print data channel. The value determines whether control information and print data is allowed through this channel or not.

prtChannelStatus (SubUnitStatus)

The current status of the channel.

The console table

This table allows administrators to read and set what is on the printer's display. If a printer were running low on toner, software reading the display and seeing a "toner low" error message could then report the problem.[*]

prtConsoleDisplayBufferText (string, max length 255)

> Writing a string to this object will cause that object to be displayed. A zero length string clears the display.

The alert table

For besieged support personnel, the alert table can be a lifesaver. Periodic polling and storing of the alert table can build a profile of malfunctions for each printer and help form judgements on printer reliability. Unfortunately, the alert table is erased on boot, so some information may be lost, especially because the "reboot mentality" may cause users to power-cycle a printer before calling for help. All the objects in this table begin with *printmib.prtAlert.prtAlertTable.prtAlertEntry*:

prtAlertSeverityLevel (type 1 enumeration)

> An alert can be either a **warning** (4) or **critical** (3).

prtAlertTrainingLevel (type 2 enumeration)

> The level of training needed to remedy the alert.

prtAlertGroup (type 1 enumeration)

> Specifies the subsystem where the alert originated, such as **input** (8), **output** (9), or **marker** (10).

prtAlertGroupIndex (Integer32)

> The index in the appropriate table pertaining to the alert. If the alert is an input alert, then the index will identify the input tray that caused the alert.

prtAlertLocation (Integer32)

> An index of the row within the principal table in the group identified by *prtAlertGroup*. This index represents the sub-unit of the printer that caused this alert. The combination of the *prtAlertGroup* and the *prtAlertGroupIndex* defines exactly which printer sub-unit caused the alert; for example, Input #3, Output #2, and Marker #1. Every object in this MIB is indexed with *hrDeviceIndex* and, optionally, another index variable. If this other index variable is present in the table that generated the alert, it will be used as the value for this object. Otherwise, this value will be –1.

---

[*] Unfortunately, no text can be sent to fancy bitmapped console displays.

prtAlertCode (type 2 enumeration)

Codes are used to describe different types of alerts. Some common examples include `coverOpen` (3), `inputMediaSupplyEmpty` (808), and `markerTonerEmpty` (1101).

prtAlertDescription (string, max length 255)

A text description used to elaborate on alerts whose *prtAlertCodes* are classified as `other` (1) or `unknown` (2).

Index

Symbols

::= (assignment) operator in ASN.1, 157
% (percent sign), in lp capability, 80
+ (plus sign), allowing print server access, 232
# (pound sign), removing from printcap entries, 85
--, beginning MIB comment lines, 156

A

a2ps utility, 71
AARP (AppleTalk Address Resolution Protocol), 121
Abstract Syntax Notation (ASN.1), 154
    assignment operator in, 157
access control, print servers, 232–235
    enforcing centralized queuing, 173
    limiting free disk space, 235
    restricting multiple copies, 233
    restricting size of print requests, 234
    restrictions based on Unix groups, 233
    restrictions on host basis, 232
    user account requirements, 234
accessing printers, methods, 4
accounting, 88–90, 224–232
    extracting information from, 232
    PDL filter, building for, 226–231
    PostScript job script, 228–231
    using accounting scripts, 89

addresses
    ARP (Address Resolution Protocol), 167
    DDP
        AppleTalk networks, 121
        caching, atalkd.conf and, 128
        reporting on Linux, 126
    IP
        assigning to printers, 167
        dhcpd server, configuring with, 176
    printer hardware address, 171
    translating network layer to link layer, 121
administration, using server names to scale (CEPS), 115
administrators, network
    challenges of modern networks, 4
    scalability, 6
Adobe PostScript, 20, 23–27
    PPD files, available from, 130
    web site information on, 23
    (see also PostScript)
aecho, 125
AFP (AppleTalk Filing Protocol), 125
afpd daemon, 125
agents, SNMP, 153
Aladdin Ghostscript, 71
Apache web server, 7
AppleShare IP, 126
AppleTalk
    control panel, 132
        choosing zone on network, 131

About the Authors

Todd Radermacher has been working with computer and network technology for the past 15 years, starting with Systems Programmer and Technologist positions at EG & G, and working with the Sandia, Livermore, and Los Alamos Laboratories. Todd moved into the commercial sector in 1994, and since then has held various technical and managerial positions with Silicon Valley start-up companies, primarily focusing on data security.

Matthew Gast was born on the Great Plains of the Midwest, near Chicago. Living on the Great Plains, he could almost see all the way to Iowa, where he later attended Grinnell College. In college, he started two significant long-term relationships. The first is with the fiercely independent Alison Burek, a musician, painter, and Renaissance woman. To the great joy of their two cats, they were married shortly after graduation.

The second "relationship" is with Unix, initially one of Matthew's prime methods of procrastination and later the gateway to network literacy. He uses his home network to experiment with new technologies, and scares away intruders by discussing its architecture. Currently, Matthew is interested in routing, security, cryptography, and mobile communications. He now works at Nokia as a travelling technical wizard and is the resident frequent travel reward program expert. In respites between business trips, Matthew lives in the San Francisco Bay Area with Ali, who is trying to make sure he doesn't grow up before his time, an event she hopes to postpone indefinitely.

Colophon

Our look is the result of reader comments, our own experimentation, and feedback from distribution channels. Distinctive covers complement our distinctive approach to technical topics, breathing personality and life into potentially dry subjects.

The animal on the cover of *Network Printing* is a steer. The steer is a gelded male cow, a domesticated farm animal of the bovine species that is an important part of the agricultural industry. The term "steer" refers to the young male cow; after it is a few years old, it is called an ox, which is frequently used as a draft animal.

The steer plays a central role in rodeos, which are an exhibition of riding and roping contests. Steer wrestling, also known as "bulldogging," involves a mounted cowboy chasing down a steer, then diving from the horse's back and wrestling the steer to the ground. In a steer roping contest, the cowboy lassos the steer by the horns, bringing it to the ground. Then the cowboy dismounts and ties the steer's feet as quickly as possible. The contests are judged by speed, and the fastest cowboy is the winner.

Colleen Gorman was the production editor and proofreader, and Catherine Morris was the copyeditor for *Network Printing*. Mary Sheehan and Nancy Kotary provided quality control. Rachel Wheeler provided production support. Ellen Troutman-Zaig wrote the index.

Edie Freedman designed the cover of this book. The cover image is a 19th-century engraving from the Dover Pictorial Archive. Emma Colby produced the cover layout with QuarkXPress 4.1 using Adobe's ITC Garamond font.

Alicia Cech and David Futato designed the interior layout based on a series design by Nancy Priest. Mike Sierra implemented the design in FrameMaker 5.5.6. The text and heading fonts are ITC Garamond Light and Garamond Book; the code font is Constant Willison. The illustrations that appear in the book were produced by Robert Romano using Macromedia FreeHand 8 and Adobe Photoshop 5. This colophon was written by Colleen Gorman.

Whenever possible, our books use a durable and flexible lay-flat binding. If the page count exceeds this binding's limit, perfect binding is used.

How This Book Was Printed

The O'Reilly Production Department produces PostScript files that are FTP'd to the printer's FTP site. The vendor's Preflight Department retrieves the files from the FTP site, prepares them for production and places them onto a server. The Prep Department retrieves the files from the server and runs it through a RIP (Raster Image Processor). After the files are ripped, plates are created using the Krause LaserStar 140C platesetter. The text is printed on 50# Glatfelter Thor on a 39" Timson T-32Q Web press. Covers are printed on Sedona 10 pt. C1S either on a Heidelberg Speedmaster (5/C) or Heidelberg SORMZ (2/C). After printing, the covers are film laminated on GBC Systems BillHoffer laminator. Covers are prepared for RepKover binding on RepKover Model RKM-612 Stripping and Auto-feeder machine. Signatures and covers are collated and bound on a Mueller-Martini Binder and Alpine Trimmer. Books are carton packed into 275# Test cartons and palletized for motor freight shipping per stringent warehouse specifications. This section of the colophon was written by Beth Drake of Malloy Lithographing.

O'REILLY®

O'Reilly & Associates, Inc.
101 Morris Street
Sebastopol, CA 95472-9902
1-800-998-9938

Visit us online at:
www.oreilly.com
order@oreilly.com

O'REILLY WOULD LIKE TO HEAR FROM YOU

Which book did this card come from?

_____

Where did you buy this book?
❏ Bookstore   ❏ Computer Store
❏ Direct from O'Reilly   ❏ Class/seminar
❏ Bundled with hardware/software
❏ Other _____

What operating system do you use?
❏ UNIX   ❏ Macintosh
❏ Windows NT   ❏ PC(Windows/DOS)
❏ Other _____

What is your job description?
❏ System Administrator   ❏ Programmer
❏ Network Administrator   ❏ Educator/Teacher
❏ Web Developer
❏ Other _____

❏ Please send me O'Reilly's catalog, containing
a complete listing of O'Reilly books and
software.

Name _____ Company/Organization _____

Address _____

City _____ State _____ Zip/Postal Code _____ Country _____

Telephone _____ Internet or other email address (specify network) _____

Nineteenth century wood engraving
of a bear from the O'Reilly &
Associates Nutshell Handbook®
Using & Managing UUCP.

· POST CARD ·

BUSINESS REPLY MAIL
FIRST CLASS MAIL   PERMIT NO. 80   SEBASTOPOL, CA

Postage will be paid by addressee

O'Reilly & Associates, Inc.
101 Morris Street
Sebastopol, CA 95472-9902

Network Printing